T0285766

"Clear, wise, and inspiring. Oren offers a raft of beautiful teachings and practices to awaken the heart, uplift the spirit, positively direct our lives, and embody our best selves."
—Jack Kornfield, author of *A Path with Heart*

"Oren is a brilliant teacher. The teachings and practices in this book will lead to true inner fulfillment and a more compassionate and just society. A must-read for those seeking to cultivate authentic change from the inside out. *Your Heart Was Made for This* is exactly what our world needs at this moment in time."
—Kaira Jewel Lingo, author of *We Were Made for These Times: Ten Lessons for Moving through Change, Loss, and Disruption*

"The falling apart of our known world can bring forward our spiritual strengths. *Your Heart Was Made for This* guides us in responding to our societal confusion and suffering with skillful, wise, and caring hearts."
—Tara Brach, author of *Radical Acceptance* and *Radical Compassion*

"Oren Jay Sofer's book was made for this moment. Everyone I know is justifiably anxious (to put it mildly) about the state of our politics and our planet. And often this anxiety leads us to turn away or to act in ways that don't change anything. *Your Heart Was Made for This* offers transformative, non-pollyannish practices of resilience so that we can remain engaged, balanced, and able to actually help."
—Jay Michaelson, author of *The Gate of Tears: Sadness and the Spiritual Path*

"In *Your Heart Was Made for This,* Oren Jay Sofer demonstrates the transformative potential inherent in Buddhist contemplative practices. Readers no longer have to choose between spiritual growth and social change. Through a lyrical blend of personal narrative, inspiring quotes, and concrete invitations to action, Sofer guides all readers, regardless of experience, on a journey that will reveal their capacity to respond powerfully and choicefully to the many crises facing our world today."

—Roxy Manning, author of *How to Have
Antiracist Conversations: Embracing Our Full
Humanity to Challenge White Supremacy*

"I can't think of a contemporary book that creates such a beautiful interweaving of Buddhist teachings, healing practices, and social, racial, and environmental justice concerns. Sofer offers concrete guidance for flourishing in a way that connects the major issues of our time, all while being extraordinarily attuned to the needs of those with trauma, diverse socio-economic situations, and historically oppressed or marginalized backgrounds. I'll be handing this book to young adults and students—spiritual seekers, beginners, Buddhists, and activists—for comprehensive answers to their many pressing questions."

—Sumi Loundon Kim, Buddhist chaplain, Yale University

"Sofer calls us back to love as the focus of our contemplative practice. We are reminded that in stillness and silence, with each breath, we are reaching into our hearts and moving past a strong desire for individual improvement. Fortunately, Sofer guides us on a path in which we can discover our deepest humanity."

—Zenju Earthlyn Manuel, author of *Opening to Darkness*
and *The Shamanic Bones of Zen*

"*Your Heart Was Made for This* is a captivating and transformative read that delves into the depths of human connection and social transformation. Sofer's profound insights and practical guidance illuminate the path to cultivating authentic relationships and fostering true understanding. With heartfelt wisdom and a gentle yet empowering approach, this book serves as an invaluable resource for anyone seeking to navigate the intricacies of the human heart and embrace the transformative power of contemplative practice to heal our world."

—David A. Treleaven, author of
*Trauma-Sensitive Mindfulness: Practices for
Safe and Transformative Healing*

"We all have the great good fortune to receive and practice with Oren's vast experience, mind, heart, and ability to explain complex dynamics with clarity. Often there are important ideas and concepts delivered to a reader and yet the question remains, 'Well, what should I do with this?' Oren delivers just that—not only the *what* but also the *how*—through practices and possibilities, in a world that is on fire."

—JoAnna Hardy, meditation teacher,
mother, and dog lover

"Oren Jay Sofer's new book will offer meditators a practical overview that can help us take up this paramount skill day by day in our own lives. Sofer shares in an engaging style with which ordinary people like us, trying to navigate the pitfalls of modern life, can relate with benefit."

—Michael Nagler, founder of
The Metta Center for Nonviolence

YOUR
HEART
WAS
MADE
FOR
THIS

Contemplative Practices for
Meeting a World in Crisis with
Courage, Integrity, and Love

OREN JAY SOFER

SHAMBHALA

Shambhala Publications, Inc.
2129 13th Street
Boulder, Colorado 80302
www.shambhala.com

The poem "Faith" is reprinted with permission by Patrick Overton, director of the Front Porch Institute, 309 Chestnut Street, Boonville, MO 65233. © 1975 by Patrick Overton.

Cover art: I Love Coffee dot Today/Shutterstock and Blue Cell/Shutterstock
Cover design: Daniel Urban-Brown
Interior design: Kate Huber-Parker

9 8 7 6 5 4 3 2 1

First Edition
Printed in the United States of America

Shambhala Publications makes every effort
to print on acid-free, recycled paper.
Shambhala Publications is distributed worldwide by
Penguin Random House, Inc., and its subsidiaries.

LIBRARY OF CONGRESS CATALOGING-IN-PUBLICATION DATA
Names: Sofer, Oren Jay, author.
Title: Your heart was made for this: contemplative practices for meeting a world in crisis with courage, integrity, and love / Oren Jay Sofer.
Description: First edition. | Boulder, Colorado: Shambhala, [2023] |
Identifiers: LCCN 2023012085 | ISBN 9781645472001 (trade paperback)
Subjects: LCSH: Meditation | Mindfulness (Psychology) | Mental healing. |
Self-help techniques.
Classification: LCC BF637.M4 S64 2023 | DDC 158.1/2—dc23/eng/20230404
LC record available at https://lccn.loc.gov/2023012085

In loving memory of my father,
who embodied courage, lived with integrity,
and loved unconditionally.

And for all who are seeking
wholeness, justice, and freedom.

Irrigators channel water,
Fletchers shape arrows,
Carpenters fashion wood,
The wise train themselves.
—*The Buddha*

What is life? It is the flash of a firefly in the night. It is the
breath of a buffalo in the wintertime. It is the little shadow
which runs across the grass and loses itself in the sunset.
—*Isapo-muxika (Crowfoot), Siksika Chief*

We need a vision that recognizes that we are at one of the
great turning points in human history when the survival of
our planet and the restoration of our humanity require a
great sea change in our ecological, economic, political, and
spiritual values.
—*Grace Lee Boggs*

Contents

Introduction

Your heart was made for love: for connection, belonging, and meaningful relationship with other people, beings, and the earth. Your heart was made to give and receive; to know joy, purpose, and freedom. All of this is possible for you and for each of us. Yet painful emotions, ignorance, and oppressive conditions disconnect us from our hearts' potential. The flow of this love has encountered obstacles from the beginning, but perhaps never more so than now. Our ancestors' village was not the global village of the twenty-first century with its seemingly infinite complexities and pressures, nor did we evolve to engage with social media algorithms or constant alerts of tragedy. How do we reclaim our birthright to love while navigating a complex world in crisis? How do we make love our guide?

The Buddha long ago taught that we can shape our inner lives: "Whatever the mind frequently thinks upon and ponders, that will become its inclination." Our thoughts, feelings, and intentions grow into habits and over time settle into our character. Contemplative practice roots itself in this power to mold the heart and thus renew ourselves. Today, we call this "neuroplasticity." If we do not shape the heart, the world will do it for us, and the world does not have our highest welfare in mind.

The tide of modern society floods us with incessant pressures, demands, and desires. On a personal level, urgency, confusion, and fear spin us in a blur, grind us down, and sap our energy. On a global level, war, social unrest, and a growth-driven economy sweep through our communities, setting us on a course for violence and ecocide. It takes steady, continuous effort to swim against these currents, make choices based on our values, and turn the tide together.

We are living through a mass extinction of our own making.[1] The climate crisis, the rise of fascism and the erosion of democracy, the COVID-19 pandemic, the ongoing trauma of injustice and oppression rooted in colonialism—these are our present reality. What will be our legacy? We are capable of beauty, but we destroy; we embody elegance, but are soaked in blood. Some days, it's a lot just to get out of bed in the morning.

At the same time, communities around the world are taking meaningful action, with those who have contributed least to the climate crisis often taking the lead. In the 1970s, shortsighted policies deforested vast areas of Nepal, leading to landslides and flooding. In response, a massive reforestation program enlisted millions of community volunteers who planted and tended to seedlings. Over several decades, they transformed barren, overgrazed hills into a revitalized ecosystem. Planting a tree for the next generation is a hopeful act, but by itself is insufficient for lasting change. Regenerating Nepal's forests required *structural* change: an innovative program coordinating international aid, legislation returning forests to village ownership, and forestry officers to protect the land. Yet even with its success, the program led to confrontations between people and wildlife, as well as violent conflicts over land use, with poorer communities struggling to maintain access to hunting and fuel rights.[2]

Examples like this show that, even with the best intentions, the challenge of living in harmony with one another and the natural world is complex. And still, our actions matter, individually and collectively. Every action plants a seed. Some seeds bear fruit in this lifetime, while others lie dormant for generations. We harvest the fruit of our ancestors' actions—for good and for ill—and our choices today shape the future.

How do we meet our challenges and choose wisely? To truly meet something is to encounter it with awareness, enter into relationship with it, and respond appropriately. How do we respond when we contact pain, sorrow, and injustice? Do we become broken, embittered, lost, or frozen? Do we lash out in anger, fear, or hatred, adding fuel to the fire? Or are we able to find the balance and clarity to meet the suffering of our world with tenderness, wisdom, and skillful action?

Responding effectively depends on training the heart and developing inner resources. We may not recognize it, but we are always practicing something. Our thoughts, words, and actions shape us. Each one creates a trickle of water flowing downhill, carving a channel in the fertile soil of our heart and mind. If you practice feeling anxious, stressed, and agitated, you etch those grooves deeper. If you practice patience, kindness, and ease, with every moment you grow stronger. In fact, these heart qualities can become your default orientation so that, when hardships arise, you draw not on old reactions but on new strengths.

The Buddha taught, "If it were not possible, I would not ask you to do it. But because it is possible, I say to you: cultivate the good, the beautiful; let it guide your life." Like an ecosystem recovering its innate balance, when we stop adding pollutants and seed the proper species, the process of awakening begins to flower in our hearts. Nourishing the heart is joyful. Remembering our potential and aligning ourselves with our deepest vision for life can happen in any moment, and can be filled with lightness and beauty. This is contemplative practice.

Such practice cultivates reflective, critical awareness and explores meaning, value, and purpose. It includes the arts, ritual, storytelling, relationship, and meditation, and it can provide the strength and clarity necessary to engage skillfully with the immense problems of our times—to mourn what we have lost, heal what we can heal, and transform what calls for change. If we are to adapt and grow, if we are to survive and create a better world, we need inner resources to meet our challenges.

Exploring the Qualities

This book guides you to discover and cultivate your best qualities. Some, like attention and energy, you may recognize as universal; others, like joy or devotion, may seem like things you either have or you don't. But contemplative practice and modern neuroscience agree that each of these is an innate capacity you can enhance just like any other skill.

Qualities are distinct, holistic patterns of energy, with their own signatures, functions, and behaviors. They are broader than emotions, intentions, or mental states. We feel them and they manifest as coherent states when cultivated. For example, kindness begins as an intention—the inclination toward goodwill—and develops into a stabler loving state, often accompanied by warm sensations, bright feelings, and expanding or lifting energy.

These qualities are complex and personal aspects of our humanity. I invite you to investigate how you experience them, using the practices at the end of each chapter to enrich and embody them. I find their resonances deeply nourishing, like harmonies in music. For me, energy, devotion, and resolve make a beautiful, soulful chord in the heart. Patience, rest, and wonder mingle into a melody of reverence for life. Joy, gratitude, and renunciation combine to quench an existential thirst.

Just as the qualities can flow into and resonate with one another, some of the contemplative practices discussed in this book overlap, differing only subtly, and strengthen multiple qualities at once. Each chapter emphasizes particular facets of the practices, but the whole is greater than the sum of its parts. When fully developed, these qualities have the power to catalyze a profound spiritual awakening. Rather than trying to make this happen, I encourage you to explore with a spirit of curiosity and adventure. See the qualities unfold and notice what they call forth in you.

Inner Transformation and Social Change

When I first started meditating as a nineteen-year-old in India, I asked my teacher Acharya Anagarika Munindra-ji about the social ills of our world. He replied, "Individuals make the family; families make a community; communities make states; and states make the world." Over the years, I heard the same logic repeated in many spiritual teachings: if enough individuals heal, society will heal, because society is a network of individuals.

While I respect the sincerity with which many teachers offer this theory of change, it fails to account for two essential factors. One is the impersonal, powerful momentum of systems like capitalism, militarism, and racism; the other is the existential threat of the climate crisis. To meet our collective challenges and avert disaster, we must also work at the societal level, applying these qualities globally. Communities and states include individuals, but social science has shown unequivocally that societies also exhibit network effects that transcend individual interaction. So, though the greater part of this book focuses on the *internal* cultivation of the qualities, we will also explore their *external* expression, collectively and in social movements, integrating them at all levels.

Many of this book's practices are rooted in early Buddhism, and my writing is inspired by nonviolent spiritual activism, specifically Engaged Buddhism, as pioneered by Thich Nhat Hanh, B. R. Ambedkar, A. T. Ariyaratne, Joanna Macy, and others. Engaged Buddhism teaches that we must apply the essence of Buddhist practice—understanding the causes of suffering and working to release ourselves from them—to society.[3] Teachings on compassion and wisdom naturally urge us to respond skillfully to injustice. Thich Nhat Hanh, the great Vietnamese Buddhist teacher (affectionately known as "Thay") who was nominated for the Nobel Peace Prize by Dr. Martin Luther King Jr. (himself a Nobel laureate), spoke of this choice to take meditation practice into the streets of Vietnamese villages where bombs were falling: "Mindfulness must be engaged. Once there is seeing, there must be acting. Otherwise, what is the use of seeing?"[4]

Personal and social transformation are inextricably linked. Focusing on internal transformation without also applying our love and wisdom to the world, we may fail to respond effectively to the suffering of others. Similarly, if we focus solely on external transformation without simultaneously healing our hearts, we risk re-creating the very ills we seek to address. How many revolutions have unwittingly replaced one domination system with another?

We strive for individual action and structural change to support each other. Individual actions can further the ethical evolution of culture, shifting the moral compass of society. Swedish environmental activist Greta Thunberg's undaunting advocacy for the climate exemplifies this, embodying so many of the qualities we will explore: energy, concentration, courage, patience, devotion, integrity, simplicity, and more. At the same time, pervasive systemic issues require systemic solutions. Global heating and climate feedback loops, and their ensuing scale of devastation on the planet, demand a different order of action than individual responses. Profoundly aware of this, Thunberg laments that—in spite of her celebrity and the enormous activism growing from it—governments have not acted meaningfully toward climate targets.[5]

In social transformation, we work for concrete results knowing that, despite our wholehearted efforts, the outcome may remain out of our hands (see chapter 13 on equanimity). Reflecting on the nonviolent campaign to end the Vietnam War, Thay wrote, "The conditions for success in terms of a political victory were not present. But the success of a nonviolent struggle can be measured only in terms of the love and nonviolence attained, not whether a political victory was achieved. . . . The essence of our struggle was love itself, and that was a real contribution to humanity."[6] Without knowing if the movement would succeed, Thay did the work. That same uncertainty is necessarily true for us, and still we do the work.

Tragically, many efforts for social transformation are subverted by right/wrong thinking, us/them mentalities, and cancel culture. Without an internal practice complementing our external work, we can unconsciously reenact patriarchy, white supremacy, and other forms of oppression. Service and social change work allow us to express our deep love and compassion for the world. Contemplative practices allow us to align means with ends, transforming internalized oppression and integrating our deepest values into social justice spaces. A truly nonviolent approach to social change sees no enemies, only fellow humans who might one day join us in Beloved Community. Cultivating the qualities shared in this book is one part of the journey to that community.

How to Use This Book

I wrote this book to accompany you in real life. If you devote two weeks to each of its twenty-six chapters, it will provide a year-long framework for learning and transformation. Each chapter explores a potent quality; offers suggestions for cultivating that quality through reflection, meditation, and action; and helps you work with difficulties that may arise. You can read this book alone or share your journey with a friend or small group. I encourage you to keep a journal, reflecting on what you learn.

The structure of the book follows a fundamental progression in the psyche that repeats naturally in the process of spiritual awakening. Each of the book's four parts begins with a foundational factor that uplifts the heart. Each part then follows the arc of this cycle: gathering momentum, consolidating and stabilizing energy, and culminating in freedom and release.

However, there are no hard-and-fast rules: let each quality reveal itself to you. I recommend you read part 1 first in order to establish some foundational principles and familiarize yourself with the cycle. Beyond that, if you get stuck, feel free to put a chapter aside and move on to another quality that feels more accessible. Though I've thought carefully about the qualities and the progression of the chapters, please know they are not exhaustive. Many beautiful qualities do not receive their own chapters: humility, creativity, discipline, intuition, and humor, among others. Their omission is primarily due to the limits of space, though I mention some of these as corollaries of related qualities.

I also must note that cultivating these beautiful heart qualities often reveals their opposite. Just as a tuning fork calls attention to how sharp or flat a note is, practicing mindfulness can highlight your distractedness. Focusing on kindness can uncover hatred and anger. Aiming for generosity, you may discover stinginess. Buddhists say, "No mud, no lotus." The pristine flower emerges from the decomposing muck of the pond. The work of liberation—both individually and collectively—shines light on our rage, pain, and fear, on the history of colonialism, land theft, genocide, and enslavement. Illuminating these personal and historical realities isn't an inconvenient downside of the work; it *is* the work.

So why does this book have no chapters on fear, anger, guilt, and the like? Because my aim is to help you establish a strong inner foundation—to develop the confidence and skill to meet all that arises, internally and externally. Especially when we carry trauma, we need to open to difficult emotions gradually. Thus I discuss these painful states within the context of the antidotes and supports that allow us to slowly metabolize them. Compassion, courage, and patience create a fruitful space within which to grieve. Mindfulness, kindness, and equanimity transmute fear and anger into generative power. Generosity and wisdom dissolve jealousy into love and belonging.

I offer basic meditation instructions in this text. If you have more meditation experience, you will find your years of practice helpful in applying the book's lessons. If you are new to meditation, I hope you will find the pointers I offer useful. You may also want to draw on other resources that are amply available today in books, in apps, and online. Start where you are and apply these instructions in whatever way best serves you.

Understanding the advantages and responsibilities of my position in our society has long been part of my own contemplative practice and teaching. While I have attempted to make this book as accessible, inclusive, and relevant as possible, my perspective is inevitably limited by my training and discernment. I may have unintentionally failed to consider others with different life experiences.

I invite you to take what is useful, adapt what may be culturally specific, and leave the rest aside. If you have feedback for me, I warmly invite you to get in touch through my website.

Our world is calling for healing and change. We each have a role to play in this transformation. Rather than a single path forward, the scale and urgency of the crises we face require us to follow many paths, all pointing in the same direction. I aim to provide as much nourishment as possible for you to discover and walk the path that is yours alone. Listen to the beautiful, quiet call in your heart, and follow it.

Let's dig in.

PART ONE

Part 1 explores six core qualities for training your heart, mind, and body to heal inwardly and guide your actions outwardly. The first is attention, without which we would be lost in a maze of habit and reaction. The remaining qualities are known in Buddhism as the "five spiritual faculties," essential companions on any spiritual path.

Chapter 1 presents the foundational skill of attention. What you attend to shapes your inner landscape and influences how you relate to the world. Chapter 2 examines aspiration, an orienting force and a powerful remedy for the despair of these times. Aspiration brings energy, the subject of chapter 3, which powers our lives physically, mentally, and emotionally. Chapter 4 applies energy to mindfulness, a quality that creates the conditions for clear seeing and strengthens our capacity to steer toward what is uplifting, true, and beautiful. Chapter 5 shows how to stabilize the energy and mindfulness we've cultivated. Continuous mindfulness brings concentration, allowing us to gather and apply our inner resources. Finally, chapter 6 explains how all these factors work together to produce wisdom—clearly understanding the nature of life and the challenges we face individually and collectively.

These six qualities form the foundation for our contemplative journey. Our hearts and minds are not fixed. We can hold ourselves with care, neither suppressing nor feeding the stress we experience. We can transform maladaptive habits we've accumulated. With the help of these qualities, we can heal the grief and emotional wounds we carry from personal or collective trauma. We can develop a clear, stable, loving, and bright inner life. And we can contribute through concrete actions to a more just and whole world that we long to inhabit.

It all begins with how we pay attention.

1. ATTENTION

A seed refuses to die when you bury it, that is why it becomes a tree. A seed neither fears light nor darkness, but uses both to grow. —Matshona Dhliwayo

When I was a kid, I would save the seeds from fruit—lemons, oranges, the occasional avocado. I soaked them in water and checked them until they sprouted. Watching them split open was like magic. From a hard, tiny shell would emerge a sensitive shoot feeling its way into the world.

Seeds create life. It's no surprise a battle rages over them. Heirloom seed stocks have been decimated. Farmers who saved seeds for centuries are forced to buy seed from agribusinesses that have patented nature's resources as intellectual property. As the author and activist Vandana Shiva argues, "... when you control seed, you control life on earth."[1]

Another battle also rages for a different kind of seed: the seed of attention. Each year, billions of dollars flow into research, marketing, and persuasive design to attract and retain our attention for profit. If you control attention, you can influence action. Because consciousness also contains seeds. The seeds in our hearts and minds govern our perceptions, intentions, and actions, in turn influencing the structures of society. We sow seeds of generosity, contentment, love, and joy as well as seeds of fear, greed, hatred, and ignorance. Whatever we cast in the fertile soil of the heart-mind will grow when watered with the seed of attention. Buddhists call this process of sowing seeds the four great efforts:

1. steering clear of unhelpful qualities not yet arisen
2. putting down harmful qualities that have arisen
3. cultivating healthy qualities not yet present in our lives
4. nourishing and sustaining healthy qualities already present

Buddhist psychology defines healthy or skillful qualities as those springing from the roots of wisdom, kindness, and compassion in our heart, benefitting ourselves and others. By contrast, unhealthy or unskillful qualities spring from the roots of ignorance, greed, and hatred, harming ourselves and others.

In South Asian thought, the heart and mind are not separate and so are referred to with a single word—*citta*, in the ancient Pali language of the Buddhist texts. Citta, the "heart-mind," is aware and sensitive; it feels and responds to the world.[2] Citta is where we live. You can experience the mercurial, sensitive nature of the heart-mind every day. You take a morning walk, feeling the sunshine, breathing fresh air. The light, temperature, and fragrance affect you. Perhaps you feel uplifted, energized, hopeful. If you notice this and allow your attention to linger on it, you can strengthen positive qualities such as gratitude, vitality, and joy. On a different day, you leave home in a heavy mood. Perhaps you've argued with your spouse or housemate, or feel distressed about our broken world. Unpleasant thoughts capture your attention. You barely notice the sky, light, and air. Even if you do, they don't register. Your heart-mind broods.

Our experience of the world depends on many factors: ancestral, collective, personal, momentary. These come together, coloring how we view the world, shaping the choices we make, and determining our responses. Without training, we move through life reacting to the world; we live as victims of circumstances and habits. With training, we can shape our interior and our relationship to life.

I grew up in a loving Jewish family, with two parents, a brother, and pets. My religion did not endanger me, as it had for so many generations of my ancestors. I had many blessings and privileges in my childhood, but the joy and wonder I felt were coupled with loneliness. When I was about ten, one member of my family had a psychotic break and spent the following years in and out of mental hospitals. To manage the emotional chaos that descended on our family, I kept busy. Already an overachiever, I dove into school even more and also became a child actor. My mom drove me to auditions in Manhattan until I was old enough to take the train myself. I filled my waking moments to avoid the weight of buried feelings. Mental illness carried a stigma, so I never spoke about it outside of our family. In high school my loneliness intensified and I discovered rock music and weed, distracting me further.

Things didn't crack open until I was a freshman in college. I was burning the candle at both ends, studying hard, doing drugs, and racing around the city, audition to audition. I don't know why it happened, but I remember the moment I stopped for what felt like the first time in ten years. I was standing in the bathroom, watching my belly move as I breathed. I felt a flutter in my core and a shudder of emotion—a mixture of anger, grief, and fear. I had become addicted to avoiding my feelings through incessant busyness. In that moment, my life shifted. Tears welled up as I remembered the wonder of my early childhood, and I saw that I was stuck. I wanted to stop running, and I yearned to feel my inner life again. So I started searching: reading meditation books, taking religion classes, and filling journals with my thoughts. *There must be a way out*, I told myself.

Unraveling the hurt we carry and finding our place in a world on fire start wherever we are. Directing attention begins to train the heart. Like a green shoot breaking through concrete, attention cracks the facade of the past so we are not prisoners of our habits or the programming of culture. Wise attention gives us the capacity to choose where we focus. To get a feel for this deliberate approach to focus, shift your attention from the sensations in your hands to your feet, or from seeing to hearing. We "change the channel" like this all the time, but we rarely notice it. Yet this capacity is one of our most valuable resources. Where we put our attention waters seeds in the heart-mind and shapes our ongoing reality.

Contemplative practice is one powerful way to reclaim attention. Rest your attention with an anchor, a home base for meditation such as the breath, a sensation, an image, a sound, or a mantra. An anchor is a primary meditation object to help steady your attention and limit mind-wandering, like an anchor for a ship. Choose an anchor that's easy to feel and either pleasant or neutral. (For example, if you have chronic pain somewhere in your body, use sound as an anchor. Respond to your needs.) Whatever anchor you choose, when you notice your attention drifting, gently return to it, letting go and beginning again. This mental action—recognizing that attention has wandered and then consciously redirecting it—strengthens your capacity to pay attention and develops a host of other skillful qualities, including patience, kindness, and concentration.

As we enter the inner terrain of contemplative practice, three principles can guide you in paying attention wisely. Bearing these in mind creates the best conditions for transformation and helps you stay regulated if you suffer from trauma or other acute distress. First, begin from a place of relative safety and relaxation. Try orienting to your external environment through your senses. Look around: notice sights, sounds, and smells. Connecting with your environment will ground you, send a signal of safety to your nervous system, and free your attention—at least temporarily—from traumatic memories.

Second, start small and take your time. We learn best when we are balanced and interested. Taking on too much too quickly can flood your nervous system and limit your capacity to learn new skills. Difficult emotions like fear, anger, and grief can overwhelm us. Explore this material in small and manageable bits. (In trauma healing, this is known as "titrating" intense states.)

Third, when working with difficult experiences, allow your attention to move back and forth between the difficulty and something supportive or nourishing. Moving rhythmically between these experiences stimulates our innate capacity for healing. (In trauma healing, this process is called "pendulating.")

Applying these principles depends on your capacity to choose where you place your attention. Where does your attention go each day? Screens often fulfill our need for self-regulation by offering a rabbit hole of endless distraction. How often do we reach for the screen at the slightest suggestion of boredom, anxiety, or discomfort? Tragically, the algorithms that drive our feeds respond to our brains' evolutionary tendency to focus more on what's negative or threatening than on what's positive or soothing. These algorithms capture our attention for others' profit, watering seeds of anxiety, fear, outrage, and other unskillful qualities in the process.

Even when we're not hooked to a device, what do we think about? Many of us ruminate on things that are distressing, incomplete, or "wrong." We dwell on aspects of ourselves we don't like, replaying our stupidities and feeling frustrated. We focus on things we can't control, feeling worried and helpless. Though once adaptive, this negativity bias has become a source of suffering, a habit that erodes our well-being and drains our energy. Whether you're on a device or just free-associating, without consciously tending to the heart, unhealthy seeds take over and distort your inner landscape. Similar to farmers fighting for the right to own the seeds of their crops, we must work to reclaim our right to the seeds of our attention.

Fortunately, it doesn't take a major life event to begin tending the heart. The next time you're doom-scrolling or caught in a mental loop, consider how to spend your time and energy. Are you oppressed by the habits of your mind, pulled along by negative rumination, subjected to whatever topic happens to have been planted in your feed by the latest headline or advertisement? With practice, you can change the channel, choosing where you place your attention instead of having it chosen for you. Can you notice and receive what is soothing and beautiful? The more you cultivate this quality of attention, the more you build inner resources. I am not encouraging you to avoid the painful realities of life and look only at what's uplifting. The idea here is to strengthen your capacity to choose what you attend to. Then—when you turn to face pain, distress, and hardship—instead of feeling helpless or demoralized, you will have more energy, confidence, and clarity to meet the challenge.

We direct attention both internally and externally. Internally, the process begins with awareness of *how we are living*. Track the states present in your heart-mind throughout the day, learning to water seeds of healthier, nourishing qualities as we've been discussing. Externally, the process begins with awareness of how we spend our time, making wiser choices about what activities we engage in. For example, there are countless ways to renew yourself instead of reaching for a screen: spend time with friends or in nature; learn a craft; make art; read poetry; exercise, dance, or explore other somatic practices; or broaden your views and open your heart-mind by studying social movements, history, ecology, or astronomy.

While I was writing this book, my wife gave birth to our first child. In our new family, we have the modest aspiration to make at least one half-day a week completely tech-free. Putting all screens and devices away makes it easier to connect with one another and the richness of life. Imagine the social transformation it would be if we collectively broke free from our entrancement with technology and came home to our own breath, to our bodies, and to one another? Imagine the wealth of community connections and inner resources social changemakers might discover in putting aside our devices and spending time building relationship?

On the collective level, directing attention can reframe a narrative, garner support, and mobilize resources. It thus has vast implications for building a better world. In 1963, for instance, the photo of a Black teenager, Walter Gadsden, being bitten by a German shepherd as a white police officer clutched Gadsden's sweater appeared on the cover of every major newspaper in the United States.[3] This image, along with those of dogs and firehoses attacking the young Black students of Birmingham, Alabama, drew national attention. The images evoked a deeper, inner attention to an underlying moral dissonance in the nation, arguably paving the way to the Civil Rights and Voting Rights Acts. When conditions are right, a moment of collective attention can tip the scales or spark revolution.

Vandana Shiva reminds us that seeds belong to the earth; they are the "repository of life's future evolution."[4] Just so, sowing the seeds of inner resources is our birthright. Rather than being swept away in a sea of consumption, rancor, or nihilism, we can choose to reclaim the natural right to our attention. What will you do with this powerful resource? To whom and to what are you paying attention? Who profits from that?

REFLECTION

Getting Started

Take time to contemplate the value of your conscious attention. How much of your day do you spend clicking and scrolling? How much are you lost in thought, daydreaming, ruminating, or brooding? How often do you choose what to think about and attend to? If you find that you're not choosing most of the time, don't worry—you're in good company. Almost everyone in modern life starts in that place, and some of us never leave. What conditions—internally and externally—support your choosing what you do with your attention? What *do* you control, and how can you move in that direction?

MEDITATION

Going Deeper

(In this section at the end of each chapter I offer meditation instructions. Read them first, then try it out. Do the instructions one at a time, opening your eyes to read the next instruction when you're ready.)

Set aside at least five or ten minutes each day for meditation exercises to nourish wise attention. Find a comfortable, balanced posture where you feel upright, relaxed, and alert. Sit, stand, or recline—whatever is most supportive for your body. Start with a few deep breaths to settle your nervous system. Set an intention to be fully present and let any thoughts, plans, or worries recede. Allow your attention to settle with an easeful anchor: the feeling of your body breathing, your hands in your lap, or the sounds around you. Rest your attention here, connecting with sensations or sounds, one moment a time. Whenever you notice your mind has wandered, appreciate that you remembered your intention! Gently return your attention to your anchor and continue. Notice the thoughts that capture your attention, and see if there are any patterns. Is there worry, fantasy, planning, remembering? In the moment you wake up from being lost in thought, notice your capacity to choose where you place your attention. Reclaim your power.

ACTION
Embodying Wise Attention

Notice what you're paying attention to. How much do you focus internally, on your own thoughts and feelings? How much do you focus externally, on the world around you? How much does the screen capture your attention? Notice where your attention goes and what you experience there. Are there topics, moods, or emotions that dominate your mind? Take some time to record what you notice in your journal.

Begin to pay attention to what you consume: news, entertainment, social media, and so on. Notice what happens when you pick up a device or turn on a screen. How do you feel? What are you looking for? Notice what engaging a device does to your heart-mind. How do you feel afterward? What qualities are stronger or weaker? With the news in particular, notice extremes: tendencies to block out information or to become obsessed with following a story. Again, what qualities of heart-mind does this consumption nourish? What purpose does media serve for you and when do you want to engage in consuming it? What would result from making more conscious choices in consuming media? Are there news sources that report on stories or projects that feed your heart?

IF YOU HAVE DIFFICULTIES

If you find it challenging to sustain your attention—or even to stay aware enough to truly notice anything at all—don't feel disheartened. Such challenges are entirely natural. Many of us have practiced for decades letting our minds wander and responding to media conditioning. Cultivating attention is like growing a garden. At first, nothing seems to be happening. But shouting at the ground or digging up the seeds to check on them won't help. To transform the habits of your heart and mind takes patience, consistency, and kindness. Try to cultivate an attitude of lighthearted adventure. Check the seeds every now and then, trusting they will sprout in their own time. The more you relax and enjoy the process, the more quickly you learn and the more fun you'll have along the way.

2. ASPIRATION

Don't ask yourself what the world needs. Ask yourself what makes you come alive, and go do that, because what the world needs is people who have come alive.
—Howard Thurman

I spent a few years in my midthirties training as a novice Buddhist monastic in England and Canada. After leaving the protected environment of the monastery, life came crashing down around me. I contracted Lyme disease and checked my father, then seventy-two, into the hospital with a life-threatening infection. I had to juggle my role as his primary healthcare advocate with my own doctors' appointments, while battling fatigue, headaches, and wandering joint and muscle pain. I recall lying miserably on the couch alone at my father's house, without energy, head hurting, body aching, sinking into despair.

Then I recognized what was happening.

I didn't feel well physically, but the rest was extra. My mind was clear, and I had enough energy to take care of myself in basic ways. I had been spinning horrific fantasies about the future, but I didn't know what the future would bring. The real suffering came from believing I actually *did* know the future. I took a deep breath and remembered my training: how I *relate* to this pain and uncertainty is up to me. I aspired to do what I could to help myself. I began doing qigong, bending and straightening my knees, lifting and lowering my hands in sync with my breathing. I could feel vitality begin to move through my body. My head still hurt, and parts of my body ached, but the worst part—the fear and despair—had begun to subside.

We all get trapped sometimes by the stories we tell ourselves about the future. Things can feel so intractable, politically and socially, that it may be hard to remember that *the future is not written*. Every day, every moment, can bring new possibilities—if we are open to them.

Aspiration connects us with a sense of what is possible.[1] It is a key that opens the door to healing, spiritual cultivation, and social transformation. Without aspiration—without the sense that things can be different—we don't bring forth the energy required for change.

Aspiration is not an attribute we either possess or lack. To aspire is a verb; *it's something we do.* To aspire is to connect with spirit, with the energy that animates our life. Indeed, the root of *aspire, spirare* in Latin, means "to breathe." Aspiration takes many forms, and it has both active and receptive aspects. The active component of aspiration brings us face-to-face with our responsibilities as individuals and members of our society. Aspiration calls us to question what's most important. How do you want to spend the time you've been granted on earth? What aspects of our world do you wish you could use your time, energy, or resources to change? What kind of world do you long to leave for your children and future generations?

Notice this longing. *This is aspiration*: a stirring of the heart that yearns for and trusts in something deeper, more fulfilling, just, or good in life. We can also have more than one aspiration.[2] It can be a calling to one or more vocations, an expression of our values, or an articulation of broad goals. Here are a few examples of aspirations:

- I want to parent with deep care, attention, and respect for my children.
- I wish to build and strengthen community wherever I go.
- I long to treat everyone I meet with love, dignity, and kindness.
- I aspire to stand against oppression and injustice, even when doing so may threaten my own comfort and safety.

Aspiration also can be more of a feeling than a specific goal—an uplifting glimmer that emerges when we feel moved, touched, or inspired. We witness this natural aspiration in small children whose faces light up and bodies thrill with energy as they encounter new possibilities in themselves and the world. I often feel the stir of aspiration, sensing the greatness of human possibility, when listening to a brilliant musician perform or seeing an Olympic athlete compete. But aspiration doesn't need to be so grand to lead us forward. If you feel sick, depressed, or overwhelmed, a skillful aspiration may simply be to eat a healthy meal, take a shower, or walk outside.

We may need to lean on others before finding our aspirations, borrowing their faith in us. For example, parents' and teachers' expectations support our academic achievement. Others' belief in us helps us believe in our own possibilities. Long-term, caring relationships with adults during our childhood give us the resilience to successfully face the societal, interpersonal, and physical challenges of life. Their care manifests as our aspirations, even when our external resources are strained.

Other times, aspiration is forged in the crucible of pain. When hardship strikes, how do you react? Do you grit your teeth, resist, or bear down, steeling yourself against the hurt? Do you collapse into numbness? Do you get stuck in anger, lashing out, passing your pain onto others? Do you turn anger inward, bitterly punishing yourself? If you can slow things down and find the inner or outer support you need to make space for your hurt and heartbreak, your rage and fear, then you have a choice. Rather than compounding pain into suffering, you can aspire to heal and grow. Aspiration is the seed of the lotus that grows in the muck of our suffering.

Aspiration is distinct from fantasy, expectation, and ordinary hope. Early in the pandemic, grappling with being in lockdown, I read about Vice Admiral James Stockdale, who spent seven years as a prisoner of war in Vietnam. In prison he noticed that overly optimistic prison-mates broke down as their imagined deadlines for freedom passed. Stockdale got through those painful years and came out more resilient through more realistic hopes. He spoke of "the need for absolute, unwavering faith that you can prevail . . . [and] the discipline to begin by confronting the brutal facts, whatever they are."[3]

Ordinary hope places our fulfillment and well-being in an imagined future, beyond our control. It ignores our agency and feeds craving. When our wished-for outcome isn't realized, we are crushed. The endless world of fantasy can provide temporary relief in an unbearable situation, but it ultimately leaves us hollow. Aspiration is a kind of practical hope that opens the heart to possibility. Aspiration becomes expectation when it fixates on a certain outcome. Expectation contracts around what we believe *should* be, attempting to control things. Aspiration expands into what *could* be, steering in a particular direction.

Aspiration can galvanize entire populations to place bodies on the line for change. In 1776, during an era of enslavement, servitude, and disenfranchisement for vast portions of the population, the US Declaration of Independence articulated an aspiration that for centuries has inspired citizens to hold their nation accountable to its values and has even sparked movements around the world for sovereignty, self-determination, and democracy. From the refrain of Dr. Martin Luther King Jr.'s famous "I Have a Dream" speech, to the rallying cry of the United Farm Workers labor union—"¡Si se puede!"—to the Movement for Black Lives' comprehensive and radical blueprint for a transformed nation,[4] collective aspiration waters the seeds of change in society.

From where does this active form of aspiration arise? It arises in part from a more *receptive* aspect of aspiration: the trust upon which our vision is founded. Allowing ourselves to feel held and supported by trust is essential for the arduous work of healing and transformation at all levels. For some, this may be the simple yet powerful faith that actions have effects. For others, it may be faith in the divine or the inherent goodness of life—an underlying sense of love, order, or moral justice in the universe. Cultivating connection with ancestors through ritual, prayer, reflection, culture, or research can create an abiding sense of trust and confidence. In her book *Faith*, the meditation teacher Sharon Salzberg writes of this quality as "trusting your own deepest experience."[5] What do you know to be true that you can rely on? What upholds you in difficult times? This trust relaxes the heart, which in turn allows us to orient toward the healthy longing of aspiration.

The author and educator Patrick Overton expresses this receptive aspect of aspiration beautifully in his poem titled "Faith":

When you walk to the edge of all the light you have
and take that first step into the darkness of the unknown,
you must believe that one of two things will happen—

There will be something solid for you to stand upon,
Or, you will be taught how to fly.[6]

Sometimes connecting with our aspiration just means taking the next step and trusting that the ground will appear beneath us or that we will discover new resources we didn't know we had. I struggled with Lyme disease for three years before fully recovering. There were many times—not knowing if the disease would ever resolve—when all I could do was take the next step.

The willingness to lean on our aspiration, to connect with a sense of possibility and walk into the unknown, sustains movements for nonviolent social transformation. When the Indian nationalist and spiritual leader Mohandas Gandhi began his famous march to the sea in defiance of the British salt tax, he had a clear aspiration for India's independence, supported by a deep trust in the power of what he called *satyagraha,* the force of truth rooted in nonviolence. Taking his first step, he could not know that the march would grow so large that more than sixty thousand people would be arrested, nor could he foresee that the journey to independence would take another seventeen long years. He walked into the unknown with aspiration and resolve, one step at a time.

Thirty-five years later, hundreds of demonstrators led by John Lewis and Hosea Williams set out across the Edmund Pettus

Bridge from Selma toward Montgomery, Alabama, in a march to demand equal voting rights for African Americans. Faith in the justice of their goal and training in the strength of nonviolence prepared them for adversity. As they set foot on the bridge, they did not know what violence they might encounter, who might live or die, or how pivotal their actions would become in the larger movement for freedom. Yet they walked.

When I speak with students and activists, they report the crushing effect of despair and hopelessness—the loss of aspiration. Seeing the deepening climate crisis, compromised politicians, ongoing structural violence, it is difficult to believe another world is possible. In these moments, we must call upon the receptive aspect of our aspiration. Perhaps we find trust in the innate goodness of the human heart. Perhaps we find it in our commitment to act with integrity helping others. As Paulo Freire famously wrote, "We make the road by walking." In the face of despair and hopelessness, if we take one step at a time and remain open to life, we will hear the call of our aspiration.

REFLECTION

Getting Started

Find a quiet place where you can feel centered and still inside. The process of reflection is one of *listening* more than actively thinking. Silently ask yourself, "Where in my life have I felt connected to aspiration, to the possibility that things could be better or different?" Ask the question, then allow different memories, thoughts, or images to come and go. Be open to whatever comes, however grand or mundane—an idea in a lecture or article, a moment in nature, a painting, a poem, a song. What uplifts you? What gives you a sense of possibility? Give yourself time to dwell with this memory, image, or feeling. If your focus drifts, come back to a stable center by feeling your body or breathing, then ask the question again.

MEDITATION

Going Deeper

Sit or recline comfortably and let your eyes close. Do whatever helps you quiet your mind and come to a place of receptivity and relative stillness inside. This might be feeling the sensations of your body sitting, the rhythm of your breathing, or noticing the sounds around you. (Remember to choose an anchor that feels pleasant or neutral.) As you become more aware of your sensory experience, reflect on being alive. Right here and now, this is the only moment you have to experience life. Take this in as you sit quietly.

Now ask, "What is most important to me? What is my aspiration?" Listen deeply to what comes, being open to different forms of your heart's intelligence. Welcome any images, thoughts, emotions, sensations, or memories that arise. Listen quietly and allow an aspiration to form. Aspiration doesn't need to be articulated verbally; it can be represented by an image, a phrase, a melody, or a feeling. Allow yourself to linger with whatever arises. When you're ready, open your eyes and shift your attention to the space around you. Repeat this practice periodically as you feel called to explore your aspirations in life.

ACTION

Embodying Aspiration

Nourishing an aspiration takes time and effort. In order to stay connected to your aspiration, renew your commitment regularly. After doing the reflection and meditation above, journal about your aspiration(s), or write one down on a small piece of paper. Alternatively, choose an image or object that represents your aspiration or aspirations. It can be anything that makes sense to you: a stone, a flower, a picture, a toy—anything at all that signifies your aspiration(s). Place this object in a special place: perhaps on a fine piece of cloth or in a little clearing on a shelf. For a week or longer, spend some time with this object daily. As you do, reconnect with your aspiration, repeating it silently, reading it aloud, or calling it to mind.

IF YOU HAVE DIFFICULTIES

You may struggle to sense your aspiration. If you feel stuck, blank, or discouraged, try to scale things back. Remember to start small and be patient. What's a reasonable aspiration for *this afternoon*? Work with aspiration in small steps, giving yourself time to hear a deeper aspiration inside. The more patient you are, listening and waiting, the more opportunity you will have to connect with genuine aspiration.

If this doesn't help, reflect on hardships you've endured. Notice how they eventually shifted. What got you through those times? Think of those who have faced similar struggles or worse. If you could offer something to others who are struggling, what would that be? Last, try reflecting on impermanence. Recall that everything changes—including the feelings and state of mind you're experiencing now. Can you trust the natural law of change as a reassurance that something else is possible?

If you notice clinging, striving, or tightness inside; if you feel a sense of brittleness, pressure, or grasping—check to see if your aspiration is being colored by expectation. Notice how the contraction feels in your body or mind and see if you can allow some softening there. Imagine that the breath can slowly dissolve any tightness or contraction. Recall that you can't control the outcome of things, but you can steer your life.

3. ENERGY

I get energy from the earth itself. . . . I feel that as long as
the earth can make a spring every year, I can. As long as
the earth can flower and produce nurturing fruit, I can, because I'm the earth. I won't give up until the earth gives up.
—Alice Walker

My childhood habits of avoiding my feelings didn't simply dissolve when I started meditating. In my midtwenties, I went to
India, determined to get enlightened. I did several rigorous ten-
day vipassana retreats, putting all of my energy into my practice.
Though I was pumping the gas full throttle, I barely knew what I
was aiming for, much less how to handle the power of meditation.
I pushed myself so hard that I broke down—crying on the shower
floor, alone on another continent, overwhelmed by a flood of repressed emotions.

I returned crestfallen and moved into my father's attic in New
Jersey, feeling like a failure. Still, I took a job as a cook at a Buddhist center, and I paid better attention to my spiritual practice. I
started to notice how much I was overexerting myself in all kinds
of tasks and situations—from too tightly gripping my toothbrush
to making excess effort in meditation.

Sustaining a meaningful life and responding to the urgent needs of our times takes energy. The Buddha urged his disciples to arouse extraordinary energy on the path, but he cautioned that we must do this wisely, applying effort with balance.[1] Transformation does not require some dramatic catharsis. It's almost always daily, patient, steady work that brings lasting transformation—both in the health and integrity of our psyches and in the justice and equity of our society.

Energy is precious, personally and collectively. Energy animates our lives and our relationships. It is the vital force that powers our bodies and minds. Energy either processes our emotions or suppresses them. Look closely: even thinking and awareness take energy. So how do we use energy?

Western society has an extractive, "all or nothing" orientation to energy. It prizes getting as much as possible, as fast as possible, for maximum productivity and accumulation. On the personal level, we may strive relentlessly, using willpower and caffeine to push beyond our limits, then we burn out and collapse. Notice the parallel with how we use our society's primary source of energy— fossil fuels. We burn it like there's no tomorrow. Though this fuel grows and transports our food, powers the vast majority of our vehicles, manufactures our clothes and products, and has helped pull billions of people out of poverty, its extraction, refining, and consumption are literally destroying the life support systems of our planet. For over a century, we have been overconsuming fossil fuels (especially in the global North), sundering ancient carbon bonds at an unfathomable scale without regard for the long-term effects on ourselves, other species, and future generations.

What would it mean to use energy mindfully? How do we

break out of the extractive fossil-fuel paradigm and develop a more sustainable relationship with our energy?

To become wise stewards of the earth, we must draw down carbon use and move to using more renewable resources. This will require a combination of policy changes, economic incentives, and shifts in lifestyle. To become wise stewards of our personal energy, we must care for our bodies. Balancing rest and exercise and eating a healthy diet are the foundations of healing, growth, and transformation. In the monastery, I valued the steadiness of the daily routine: going to bed and rising early, chanting and meditating every morning and evening, creating a rhythm of work and rest throughout the day. All spiritual traditions honor cycles of activity and rest in harmony with the natural cycles of the seasons, day and night.[2] Judaism teaches six days of work followed by rest on the seventh day. In the book of Leviticus in the Hebrew scriptures, every fiftieth year (after seven sevens) is a jubilee year, in which all prisoners are freed and all debts forgiven.

The effects of colonialism, capitalism, and patriarchy have disconnected us profoundly from the land and the natural cycles of our lives. Meanwhile, the pace of our lives and the immense economic pressure under which we live mask that disconnection. Working multiple jobs, raising children without adequate support, living in a food desert, or having poor access to nature all limit our ability to care for our bodies. Navigating the daily injuries of systemic oppression and personal discrimination—based on race, sex, gender, class, religion, or ability—demands extraordinary energy, making energy conservation and self-care all the more vital.

Becoming aware of the structural nature of these conditions helps us see that taking care of ourselves can be a radical act. This kind of self-care subverts the exploitative approach to energy, reclaiming our right to a more renewable, life-giving energy within. As the political activist and author Angela Davis has noted, "Anyone who's interested in making change in the world also has to learn how to take care of herself, himself, theirselves."[3] Start by taking even one step to take better care of your body, perhaps stretching for a few minutes in the morning or drinking more water throughout the day. For additional support in renewing your energy, call on friends and community and draw upon other qualities in this book (like resolve, patience, and renunciation).

Wise attention, which we explored in chapter 1, gives us another way to steward energy. Pay attention to patterns governing your life. The innovative movement teacher and author Moshe Feldenkrais beautifully expressed a fundamental principle of transformation: "You can't do what you want to do until you know what you're already doing." For example, if you regularly use a computer but want to move freely with less pain, you must first become aware of your posture: how you hunch over your screen, disconnected from the position of your pelvis and lower body. To feel more awake and free in your life, work through your resistance to difficult feelings like anger or shame just as you would work through poor posture: with patience, careful attention, and continual effort. Becoming aware of the prison of your mind's habits, you can transform them. This principle applies socially as much as physically and spiritually. The characters in George Orwell's prophetic novel *1984* are trapped in a society framed by Newspeak, a language in which they cannot confront their prisons. But we *can* confront ours, and when we do, we can envision a better society.

To direct energy more effectively, try doing less and feeling more. This will help you modulate how much energy you are employing and how to best direct it. Rather than clenching your jaw while you rush to do the dishes, become aware of the tension in your body; let it subside, and relax as you scrub. Balance and alignment conserve energy and create leverage. It's easier to move an object if you move from your core, standing with your feet firmly planted, hip-width apart, than if you lean over with your feet close together. Understanding this physically, you can translate it. Instead of raising your voice to make a point, you may discover more power when you speak clearly and directly at an even volume. It can be equally powerful and quite freeing in certain situations to remain silent and allow your presence to speak for itself.

As you pay attention to how you apply energy, you will notice where you are wasting it, pushing against things that won't move: growling at phone mazes that won't let you speak to humans, gripping the wheel while stuck in traffic, or trying to force loved ones to change when they aren't ready. Millennia ago, the Daoist philosopher Laozi wrote, "The soft overcomes the hard." Water flows effortlessly around obstacles, wearing them away slowly, singing all the while. The most efficient and powerful uses of energy channel our vitality naturally, aligned with our vision, values, and sense of purpose. This teaching is not a recommendation that we never use force. Force may indeed become necessary to prevent, interrupt, or mitigate harm in a clear and conscious way.

Here we encounter one of the most powerful vehicles for accessing energy in a quality we've already explored: aspiration. Aspiration evokes a sustainable energy we can draw on as we align our actions with our values. To discover this energy of willingness, we need to choose actively. Though our society inequitably determines access to external resources, we always have some measure of choice internally. When you question the things you tell yourself you "should" or "have to" do, you may discover that you *choose* to go to work (because you value providing for your family), do the dishes (because you value cleanliness), or obey traffic laws (because you value safety). Even though your options are constrained by external factors, you still have an inner choice you can embrace about how you relate.

We experience a profound difference between acting out of obligation and acting with an awareness of how it serves us. Obligation can destroy our spirit, leaving us drained, bitter, and resentful. Overriding our hearts, forcing ourselves to act out of obligation, we perpetuate the fossil-fuel model, extracting precious energy, strip-mining the contours of our spirits. Instead, let us liberate the sustainable energy of choice.

The global economy, valuing a financial bottom line over the health and well-being of the earth and community, depends upon obedience. At what point do we—individually and collectively—cease to cooperate with systems that are destroying the foundations of life? Examining ourselves, we may find the energy to resist. Energy derives from our values, not our obligations. The more consciously we choose what we do, the more energy we have to do it. Whether in labor organizing or love, awareness and choice magnify our energy and our power.

As with obligation, overstriving and other compulsive struggles lead to burnout. The extractive fossil-fuel approach rarely produces lasting results, differing entirely from the balanced, focused, and intentional struggle laying the long road to freedom. The energy needed to power true transformation—spiritually as well as socially—is sustainable and renewable. It is exemplified in the painstaking work of the suffragists, whose struggle for the right to vote in the United States lasted nearly ninety years—from its origins in the abolitionist movement in the 1830s—before succeeding. This is the energy of willingness that arises from a full heart, connected to aspiration, and guided by wise attention.

When we know our purpose, energy wells up inside as a spring emerges from the earth.

REFLECTION
Getting Started

Consider how you use your energy. What feels worthwhile and what feels superfluous? Notice when energy is present or absent. Explore the connection between your awareness of purpose, your level of willingness, and how much energy you have. When doing something you don't enjoy, step back and consider why you are doing it. What needs are you trying to meet? Are they truly yours? How does this awareness shift your available energy? Finally, what avenues do you have to replenish your energy? What do you need to sustain energy in your life?

MEDITATION
Going Deeper

Sit quietly in a comfortable position. Notice where your body touches the ground and give your weight to the earth, allowing it to support you. Appreciate any relief or rest coming from this. Feel the uprightness of your spine and the energy, the vitality, that brings. Notice how your breath enters and exits your body—attune to its rhythm. How do you experience energy in your own mind and body, right now?

Notice the experience of hearing. Let sounds come and go, listening as if you were enjoying your favorite song. Notice how much energy it takes to listen. Try to cultivate a natural curiosity in the sounds around you, sustaining the gentle, steady energy of wakeful awareness.

ACTION

Embodying Energy

Engage in an activity you can do wholeheartedly and willingly, in which you feel no sense of obligation or pressure, in which your motive is clear. This might be as simple as taking a shower or writing a postcard to a friend, something aesthetic like planting flowers or tidying a shelf, or something like connecting with a loved one or volunteering for a local group. Pay attention to your flow of energy as you engage in that activity. Can you modulate it evenly from start to finish? Where do you zone out or fall into habitual patterns? Where do you move consciously and steadily, with a full heart? After this, pay attention to the energy you exert during other activities, physically, mentally, and emotionally. How are you overexerting? Where are you sinking or collapsing? How do you notice this bodily? Pause and ask, "How much energy do I actually need to use here?"

IF YOU HAVE DIFFICULTIES

The world can be exhausting. When you feel burned out, it can be challenging to create any energy. When you are profoundly fatigued, it may be important to do nothing. What can you do to create time and space to rest? All things have cycles; if you've been going too long without downtime, it's likely you need rest. But due to social inequity, we don't all have equal access to rest. If you have less access to downtime due to work, finances, family life, or other circumstances, find simple ways to rest. Close your eyes when you have a spare moment or two, instead of looking at the phone or worrying about tomorrow. Feel your breathing for a few moments. Think of those who love you and remind yourself that you matter.

When rest isn't an option, or if you are so exhausted that you can't seem to get going even after you've rested, you may need a boost. A good friend or strong dose of joy can sometimes restart your energy system, bringing more willingness into the heart. Consider which friends or sources of joy you can turn to.

4. MINDFULNESS

Not everything that is faced can be changed. But nothing
can be changed until it is faced. —James Baldwin

While living at the Buddhist meditation center in Massachusetts,
I struggled with angst. Consumed by repetitive thoughts, I rumi-
nated about how best to contribute in life. I still recall clearly the
moment I finally recognized what I'd been feeling for months.
I was meditating, mindfully feeling my breathing, when all of a
sudden it became apparent: "Oh, I'm afraid." In that moment of
complete recognition, a weight was lifted. Instead of pushing the
fear away or trying to think my way out of it in an endless cycle
of oppressive thoughts, I faced it directly. Being mindful helped
me slow down enough to see beyond the planning and worrying
to how I truly felt. I stayed mindful of the fear, feeling it in my
body, and it began to unravel instead of surreptitiously driving my
thoughts all day.

Research on mindfulness has confirmed what meditators
have known for centuries: the untrained, wandering mind tends
to ruminate on things that make us unhappy. Without mindfulness, we move through the world on automatic pilot, a prisoner
to habitual thoughts, feelings, and impulses. We may sink into

unskillful patterns of boredom, apathy, agitation, self-loathing, or worry.

Godwin Samararatne, one of my first meditation teachers, was fond of a bold statement: "Mindfulness is the only way to be free."[1] Though there are many paths to inner freedom, each must include an aspect of mindfulness to be truly liberating. As we've explored, awareness is a prerequisite for transformation, revealing the forces that shape our minds and structure our society. When I first meditated, I felt like I was searching for something in the dark, without knowing what I was seeking. Mindfulness illuminates our inner life. The more it grows, the more aware we become in all aspects of life, creating a new, healthier habit of being wakeful moment to moment. Mindfulness works in tandem with other skillful qualities like concentration and equanimity, thereby opening the door to human flourishing and ultimately freeing our hearts and minds from reactivity and delusion.

When I began practicing mindfulness, I was so eager to make progress that I began silently narrating all of my daily activities with a tool called "mental noting": "Now I'm getting dressed . . . I'm drinking water . . ." It took a few years to understand that mindfulness isn't *thinking* about what's happening but *experiencing* it. Being mindful means being fully embodied, feeling the texture of the clothing as it touches your skin, sensing the coolness of the water as you drink. To illustrate the difference, try this experiment. First, deliberately think the thought, "I move my hand through space." Do it a couple of times. Got it? Now slowly and carefully raise one arm and move your hand through space, feeling all of the sensations. This direct experience is the difference between thinking about being mindful and actually being mindful.[2]

Mindfulness is more than just paying attention. It is our innate capacity to be aware in a balanced and curious way. Mindfulness is a fresh awareness that connects intimately with whatever we experience, just as it is, without the distortions of bias, expectation, and control. We're not judging what's happening, waiting for something else, or trying to get something. Thus mindfulness has two parts: awareness and equanimity. One is clearly and directly aware of present-moment experience and not reacting to it or getting lost in it. To be mindful is to return to a very open way of being, sometimes referred to as "beginner's mind." The Zen master Suzuki Roshi talked about mindfulness as a soft readiness. It is receptive, alert, and engaged.

The Buddha taught mindfulness as a cornerstone of the path to inner freedom, instructing his disciples to establish mindfulness of the body as a vehicle for being aware throughout life. You can practice mindfulness in any posture—sitting, standing, walking, or lying down. To cultivate mindfulness, one typically begins by using an anchor such as the sensations of breathing in and out, the sensations of your hands resting in your lap, your backside touching the ground, or the sensations of walking. Again, if feeling sensations in the body is fraught or stressful, as can be the case when there is a history of trauma, try using hearing or seeing as an anchor. From the anchor, progressively expand the scope of mindfulness to include more and more of your experience.

The Buddha instructs us to cultivate a direct experience of the body before the mental constructs through which we tend to view the world. So rather than "my hand," we learn to be aware of a changing constellation of sensations—warmth, coolness, pulsing, throbbing, tingling—that our mind recognizes and refers to conceptually as "hand." When practicing mindfulness, one endeavors to sustain this direct, nonconceptual awareness continuously, from moment to moment.

Developing mindfulness gives us back our life. We awaken from sleepwalking through the world and rediscover the richness and vibrancy of the world. We are present for the heat, aroma, and flavor of a cup of tea or coffee. We relish the presence of a loved one or a spectacular day, fully connected to life. A few years after my parents' divorce, I was helping my father in his basement. While on my hands and knees snapping floorboards together, I looked across the room at my dad, smiled lovingly, and said, "Hi, Ab" (short for Abba, "father" in Hebrew). It was the most ordinary of moments, and it was precious. Here we were, alive, healthy, working together. He looked back across the room and smiled, "Hi, Or." Life is made of moments. If we are not present, they slip by as in a dream. I'm so grateful for the moments of presence I had with my father before he died, and mourn the countless ones I was too preoccupied to cherish.

Although I practice and teach mindfulness, I'm also troubled by how the term has been commodified by the multibillion-dollar wellness industry. The latest feel-good fad, it is touted in pop magazines and advertisements as a panacea, suggesting if we are just present enough, everything will be okay. "Depressed? Stressed? Relationship woes? Climate anxiety? In debt or unemployed? Just be more mindful!" Mindfulness is a powerful tool, but it's not a replacement for wise action and can't cure all of our ailments on its own. What's more, popular mindfulness suggests that the sole source of our suffering is individual and internal, ignoring the vast influence of structural factors such as racism, sexism, and poverty on our well-being and our ability to access our inner resources.

Contrary to the hype, mindfulness doesn't always make us feel good. Sometimes slowing down to connect with life can feel like stepping on the wrong end of a metal rake—you get hit in the face with all you've been avoiding, like the fear I felt in my twenties. The insight meditation teacher Michele McDonald uses the metaphor of a flower to highlight the natural pace and radical inclusivity of opening the heart with mindfulness. A flower opens slowly, when conditions are right, and may close again at night. We don't try to force its petals open. So too, our hearts open in their own time, closing periodically for safety or rest. As a flower opens, it doesn't just open to warm sunshine and gentle breezes. It opens to all of the elements—to the wind and the rain, the heat and the cold. As we practice mindfulness, we don't just feel the pleasant, loving moments. We learn to feel *all* of life—the hurt and pain, fear and anger, contraction and numbness.

When mindful, we encounter the defenses we've built up over the years to protect ourselves from the raw vulnerability of life. It hurts to be alive in an unjust world of loss and change beyond our control. Without wholesome qualities to digest the stress and pain of a complex and often harsh world, we develop a kind of armor to stay safe emotionally and psychologically. This takes many forms: from always being chipper and upbeat, cracking jokes, to assuming the worst and being cynical so we're not disappointed; from staying chronically busy to disappearing into TV, video games, or substances. These layers of armor are informed by social factors like race, gender, sex, class, and ability. The more pain, the greater the perceived need for some way of insulating ourselves in order to manage the hurt.

Rather than being an obstacle, these defense mechanisms are a reflection of our heart's intelligence.[3] Imagine how untenable life would be if we lacked a means of protecting ourselves emotionally. In the absence of better strategies, we find a way to get by. Mindfulness provides a new way of metabolizing the challenges of being human, slowly dissolving and replacing the armor with more enduring qualities like wisdom, compassion, and equanimity—for armor comes with a price. The shields we put on don't just block out the pain; they also block joy and vitality, and they disconnect us from the truth. When we shut down the heart or put up a wall, we limit our capacity to be alive and to see clearly. What is the cost of the distractions we use to ignore the realities of climate chaos? What price in integrity, wholeness, or connection do those of us who benefit from society's current structures pay when we avoid or ignore the painful realities of oppression and injustice, or when we refuse to take action to address them?[4]

Mindfulness brings us into direct contact with all that needs to be healed, felt, and released, allowing us to slowly integrate what needs to be learned and to release all that no longer serves us. The fact that we must encounter our pain to heal it is one of the reasons why the popular narrative that mindfulness is about feeling good is so dangerous. It distorts mindfulness to another defense mechanism, abandoning the opportunity to transform our hearts and meet all of life.

Ignorance runs so deep that we sometimes need external support to become aware of our habits. However humbling or uncomfortable it may be to me in the moment, I recognize that there is a lot I can't see about my own conditioning as a straight white man, and I'm grateful when others point out how my words or actions may land as a microaggression or a manifestation of white supremacy culture.[5] One African American colleague gently pointed out that I had incorporated some of her points into my teaching without acknowledging her as the source, reminding me of the broader history of white people taking credit for the wisdom and creativity of Black culture. I felt simultaneously embarrassed and grateful, and now I always try hard to be mindful of acknowledging the source of material and practices I share.

For people in a dominant group in society—like those who have white-skin privilege in the United States—the very structures of our society are designed to prevent us from seeing certain aspects of the systems we live within.[6] As a result, we see less, not more. Without mindfulness, I won't notice how marginalized groups experience racism every day, because I don't experience it. I won't notice how the structures of our society favor those identified as white if I'm not even aware that those structures are there. Indeed, it's hard to notice a current that's carrying you forward. (Right-handed people rarely notice how well scissors work for them, while left-handed people experience the opposite their entire lives.)

Mindfulness not only reveals dynamics that we were formerly unaware of, positioning us to better address them, but also helps create the conditions to accept all that is unresolved in our hearts. Supported by the other qualities we are exploring in this book, mindfulness is an essential aspect of handling the inevitable hurt, loss, and pain in life. Sharon Salzberg, referencing a term coined by the psychoanalyst D. W. Winnicott, sometimes explains mindfulness as a "holding environment" that creates the space in which we can experience powerful memories, sensations, and emotions safely.[7] Within this space of mindfulness, we can learn how to feel and know anything without becoming overwhelmed.

Restorative justice (RJ) spaces offer a similar kind of holding environment on a collective level, bringing mindfulness to unresolved issues and harms in community in service of healing and repair. Some schools are replacing punitive disciplinary measures and armed security with RJ programs, supporting students to learn the critical awareness needed to see the web of causes that feed conflicts and the relational skills to resolve them. Many RJ groups are integrating somatic-based mindfulness practices to bring a more trauma-informed lens to this healing. Restorative justice is even offered as an alternative to the criminal justice system in some cities in the United States and Brazil, for instance. Implementing this kind of relational healing practice on a structural level could have vast repercussions for the collective psyche.

Mindfulness isn't just about getting calm, nor is it a replacement for action to address injustice. Calm comes from engaging with the truth of our lives and living with integrity, not through chasing bliss or blocking out pain. Mindfulness *does* reduce stress and enhance resilience, making us better positioned if we choose to work for social change. When mindfulness works together with other factors, such as equanimity and wisdom, it allows us to see the conditions around us clearly, relinquish our need to control things, and develop the strength, skill, and poise to respond skillfully to whatever is happening.

Mindfulness also reshapes our inner life. It has the unique property of withering unhealthy qualities and nourishing healthy ones. In the light of mindful awareness, afflictive, unskillful states are weakened, while supportive, skillful ones can grow. Being mindful of fear introduces a clear and steady energy to an otherwise contracted and frightened state, beginning to erode its roots. Being mindful of joy, we can choose to nourish and feed it. In this way, mindfulness is like a master key that opens the gates to all other helpful qualities on our journey.

Continuous mindfulness also strengthens concentration, which enhances our ability to see the world as it really is. When we have the humility to not know, to put aside preconceived ideas, views, and beliefs, we see more clearly things we haven't acknowledged personally or socially. On a personal level, the more directly we connect with experience, the more we begin to see its impermanent nature—how everything is continually changing, influencing and being influenced by everything else. On a social level, when we investigate our relationships and experiences with an attitude of mindfulness, we see how much history has shaped our roles, sense of self, worldview, and access to opportunity and resources. Life is rich, and fleeting. The more acutely we appreciate impermanence, the more our mindfulness matures into equanimity, a wise and balanced perspective (discussed in chapter 13). And with this wisdom, we may find ourselves disenchanted with chasing after pleasure and instead anchor our search for fulfillment in more meaningful pursuits.

REFLECTION
Getting Started

How present are you in your life, and how much time do you spend running on automatic or lost in thought? What emotional patterns govern your waking hours? What thoughts and stories play over and over in your mind? Pay attention to the habits and narratives that dominate your day. What themes do you notice? If your habitual thoughts were a playlist, what tracks would be in the top five? Self-doubt? Comparing with others? Worry about the future? Whenever you notice one of these mental loops playing, label it briefly ("planning," "comparing," "worrying") and, breathing evenly, notice how it feels in your body. For particularly persistent narratives, try giving the inner voice a pet name or making it into a silly cartoon character as a way to step back and see it more clearly. How does being more aware of your thoughts affect your quality of life?

MEDITATION
Going Deeper

Sit, stand, or recline comfortably. Take a few slow, deep breaths to settle your body and mind, setting a clear intention to put aside thoughts of the past and the future. Notice the sounds around you, taking time to be mindful of hearing. Connect with the direct experience of hearing: the pitch, tone, rhythm, and timbre of sound rather than the concepts of what you are hearing. Continue to practice in this way—or if you like, shift your attention to the overall sensations of your body. Feel its weight, warmth, and mass. Notice how it takes up space. What sensations do you feel clearly? Rest your attention with these sensations in the body, feeling them directly, from the inside.

Continue to practice in this way, or begin to notice the rhythm of your breathing. Let your attention settle wherever you feel the breath most clearly—at the tip of your nose, the rise and fall of your chest, or down in your belly. As you breathe in, know that you're breathing in. As you breathe out, know that you're breathing out. Let your breath be light, natural, and easy, quietly feeling the flow of sensations. Whenever you notice your attention has wandered, smile and appreciate the fact that you noticed. Mindfulness returned! Then gently allow your attention to return to sound, the body, or breathing. Try this for five minutes, ten, twenty minutes or more. Consider setting up a daily meditation practice where you can practice these and other exercises from this book on a regular basis.

ACTION
Embodying Mindfulness

There are countless ways to strengthen mindfulness during daily life. Getting creative with this process is a fun way to personalize your journey. Most methods are based around taking a daily activity and doing something differently to bring more awareness. For example, Thich Nhat Hanh suggested pausing to let the phone ring three times before answering it. During those three rings, you can breathe, notice how you feel, or recall deeper intentions (whether that's to be mindful or whether it's to cultivate any of the other qualities we're exploring). Put a Post-it on your laptop reminding you to pause and breathe, or set an intention to be mindful every time you open a door, drink water, or some such activity. To integrate mindfulness at work, try placing a meaningful photo or favorite object on your desk—something that reminds you to stay connected to your heart and be present.

You can also cultivate mindfulness while walking.[8] Whenever you walk from one place to another—be it to the bathroom or the grocery store—set aside thoughts, plans, and worries and give your wholehearted attention to the experience of walking. Feel the sensations of your feet touching the earth, your legs moving, or the play of your senses as you move through space. Rest your attention lightly with the flowing rhythm of your body moving. Whenever your mind drifts, come back to the sensory experience of movement. The more you practice, over time, mindfulness can become a new, healthy habit of its own.

IF YOU HAVE DIFFICULTIES

Being mindful takes practice, whether in meditation or the flow of life. It's not uncommon to set out at the beginning of the day with a clear intention to be mindful, only to notice, sixteen hours later when your head hits the pillow, that the day went by in a blur. Sometimes, in spite of our best intentions, the sheer volume of tasks and the pace of life make it hard to remember to stay present. Other times, we may be rushing around on high alert habitually, using busyness to avoid feeling what is true. Mindfulness of the body is the foundation for being aware and noticing where we place our attention. Try being aware of any physical sensations you experience throughout the day as a way of cultivating more present-moment awareness. Choose one or two simple activities (like walking, chewing, or drinking) and make an effort to do them with a clear and relaxed awareness.

If you experience strong emotions like fear, anxiety, overwhelm, or doubt, it can be very challenging to stay mindful. While mindfulness can help to process these feelings, it may require the support of other qualities like self-compassion, patience, concentration, and equanimity. The first order of business is to regain some balance and perspective by temporarily withdrawing your attention from the storm. Anchor your attention someplace else soothing, supportive, or just less disturbing. Notice your feet on the ground, the sky above you, the sounds around you. Take some deep breaths, shower, exercise, listen to some music, or talk to a friend. Do whatever you need to do to pull your attention out of the snag and reestablish balance. Then you can slowly reapproach the challenging emotions in small doses, feeling your body, and taking it one breath at a time. Remember as well the guiding principle to pendulate, shifting back and forth from whatever is challenging to something healing.

5. CONCENTRATION

When you develop concentration, you see things as they are. —The Buddha

When I was sixteen, I spent a month canoeing in the wilderness of northern Quebec, rising early and paddling all day, living simply. Being immersed in nature nourished me, and I learned a lot about myself from the rigorous physical labor. The portages—carrying our gear overland between rivers and lakes—challenged me the most. I hoisted the fifty-pound canoe onto my shoulders, using a traditional Cree leather tumpline to distribute its weight, and quickly realized that it took more energy to lift and the lower the canoe for breaks than to just keep going. It hurt, but I struggled over the muddy, mosquito-ridden trails, humming a nursery rhyme over and over. The trick to making it to the end of the trail was pairing the resolution to finish with moment-to-moment concentration—staying focused on a goal in spite of obstacles.

Without sufficient concentration, you may feel exhausted by life. You sit down to meditate and can barely stay with one breath before your attention jumps to the to-do list, ricochets off that to an argument from yesterday, then leaps to the next thought. At work, you can't focus, feeling worried or irritated. You return home depleted from trying to hold on to some shred of stability through the day. Embarrassing as it is for a meditation teacher, I've found myself reaching to look at my phone in the middle of a conversation with my wife! To live well, to be effective, focus, and connect deeply, we need concentration—a collected and stable heart.

Concentration gathers our inner faculties around the task at hand and filters out what's not relevant, in spite of resistance, difficulties, or prior failure.[1] Ordinary concentration depends on willpower, straining to subdue conflicting urges and shut out distractions. Such a state is brittle and exhausting because we must sustain it by force. Meditation teaches us to cultivate a holistic concentration that emerges naturally and sustains itself. This kind of natural concentration arises when the heart is interested and at ease, and it has several expressions: momentary concentration, continuous concentration, and deeper states of absorption. The more momentum behind this concentration, the more distractions fall away. We relax into a complete state of presence, catalyzed by interest, meaning, or pleasure. Moments linger and stretch out; hours slip by effortlessly.

Holistic concentration is akin to what's known as a "state of flow," or "being in the zone": full connection with an activity, characterized by enjoyment of the process and transformation of time. You experience this naturally when conditions come together in sports or music, physical intimacy, or rich conversation. You filter out distractions and irrelevant impulses. You collect attention naturally because you *want* to be present. In states of absorption, concentration merges with the experience and one loses the capacity to reflect and develop insight. In momentary and continuous concentration, which develop through mindfulness, you become deeply focused *and* aware, knowing what's happening moment by moment.

Perhaps you're thinking, "Sure—but I can't focus!" Regardless of the obstacles you face—from a hyperactive mind to a hyperactive child, from stressful thoughts to a stressful job—you still can enhance your capacity for concentration. Concentration did not come easily to me (in spite of my creative lullaby-mantra while portaging). In college, I would read the same paragraph over and over, frustrated at how quickly my mind wandered. Today, I am able to focus more easily on whatever I set my mind to. I learned through meditation how concentration arises and how to nourish it. Concentration depends on clear intent, interest, relaxation, and wholeheartedness. (We'll explore wholeheartedness, as "devotion," in chapter 22.) Clear intent means knowing our aim and simplifying our field of attention, setting aside everything else. When we're clear about what we're doing and interested in doing it, our minds focus naturally.

Consider the process of concentrating as being like speaking to a friend in a crowded, noisy café. You don't need everyone to leave or be silent to converse. You focus on your friend because you *want* to. Even if you look away, you come back and reconnect. You sustain attention moment by moment and concentration builds, like individual drops of water flowing into a stream. You can learn to steady your attention in any activity in the same way. Relax, be curious, and give yourself to a task or project. Explore how connection and willingness support focus.

Concentration itself is value neutral. Both surgeons and terrorists need focus, but the nature of their concentration differs due to their underlying intention. For concentration to benefit the world, we need to cultivate it together with qualities like integrity, empathy, and wisdom. Integrated with these qualities, concentration supports social change. Many of the freedom songs that echoed through the civil rights movement expressed this powerfully, perhaps none more plainly than "Keep your eyes on the prize. Hold on! Hold on!" These stirring words helped keep an entire movement anchored to its vision of human dignity and equity in spite of enormous setbacks and obstacles.

On December 10, 1997, the environmental activist Julia Butter-fly Hill ascended a thousand-year-old redwood tree in a campaign to stop clear-cutting. Her planned two-week tree sit turned into a 738-day vigil. Calling on steadfast commitment and concentra-tion, Hill set aside everything else in her life to bring awareness to old-growth forests. Her courageous act of civil disobedience garnered international attention not only for the trees but also for other social justice issues. With the support of both steelworkers and environmentalists, Hill's protest gained protection for three acres of redwood forest, including Luna, the millennium-old tree the activist at last descended in 1999.[2] In *The Legacy of Luna*, Hill describes the many challenges she faced during those two long years living in the tree canopy: from internal forces like fear and doubt to external forces like the hail and snow of El Niño and the threat of violence from security forces. Hill drew upon many qual-ities we are exploring in this book, including aspiration, energy, and a firm concentration that depended on handling challenges skillfully, rather than giving in to or suppressing them. No mud, no lotus.

Buddhism teaches that concentration minimizes the five hindrances—habitual, unskillful patterns that torment the mind: craving, aversion, restlessness and worry, sloth and torpor, and doubt. Craving is compulsive attraction toward pleasant sensory experience (see chapter 9, on renunciation). Aversion is the opposite: resistance to unpleasant experience. Restlessness is the uncomfortable, physical manifestation of excess energy, while worry is the unpleasant mental manifestation of excess energy. Torpor is a sleepy, heavy feeling resulting from a lack of physical energy, while sloth is sluggishness and apathy resulting from avoidance or a lack of mental energy. Finally, doubt, perhaps the slipperiest and most insidious of these forces, is an unhealthy vacillation in the mind that questions continually without leading onward in a useful way.

Handle hindrances by being mindful of them. The more clearly you see when hindrances influence your mind, the easier it is to set them aside and refocus. Become familiar with the hunger of craving that obsesses over something and the prickly texture of aversion. Learn to recognize the heaviness of sloth and torpor, the agitation of restlessness and worry, and the paralyzing spell of doubt.

Doubt presents a particular challenge to concentration, as it often appears cloaked in reason, sounding logical and helpful. But doubt agitates us, squanders our energy, and can stop us from pursuing our aspirations. Spinning and waffling endlessly, it distorts our vision. In contrast, healthy skepticism examines data in a careful way, without agitation, spin, or distortion, thereby bringing us into deeper relationship with reality.

It's easy to idealize concentration, create a project out of it, and then berate ourselves for not achieving it. I spent years worrying my meditative concentration wasn't good enough. But one's self-assessment is rarely accurate. Even when thinking stirs on the surface of the mind, the heart's power may be gathering and deepening. The best approach to strengthening concentration is to take things one moment at a time, being clear and deliberate about what you are doing and why. When it felt like everything was falling apart, Hill focused on her breathing one moment at a time—an example of how momentary concentration builds momentum. She reflects that she was not sitting in Luna for "two years": she was there *day by day, hour by hour, minute by minute.*

When the hindrances are at bay, even temporarily, we feel stronger, more at ease and confident. The Buddha likened this to paying off a debt, healing a disease, release from prison, freedom from servitude, and safe passage through a desert. Consider a time when your inner resources were gathered around an activity or task. How did you feel during and afterward? Did you recognize the absence of the five hindrances? It's common to feel nourished and refreshed by these periods of concentration. No longer pulled in a thousand different directions, we are freed from the agitation endemic to modern life. In a world where every click is tracked, online behavior molded, and attention commodified, developing a steady, collected mind is rare and radical. It relinquishes multitasking, increases our attention span, and heals our fragmentation and scatteredness. Concentration reclaims our innate wholeness and magnifies the power of the heart-mind. As we'll explore in the next chapter, with concentration we develop wisdom to see more clearly, make new connections, and cut to the root of a problem.

REFLECTION
Getting Started

Notice when any amount of concentration is present. Whenever you become engrossed in something, however briefly, notice how it feels inside. Experience your first sip of a cup of tea or coffee or your first bite of breakfast. Notice the first note of a favorite song or the first glimpse of a sunset. Appreciate this concentration to whatever degree it's present. Reflect on the conditions that support it. Are you relaxed? Clear about your aim? Willing to be present? Notice when concentration is absent, when your mind is scattered or beset by hindrances. Bring some gentleness to your experience and remind yourself that noticing the absence of concentration is the beginning of its presence, inviting more stability.

MEDITATION

Going Deeper

Devote a week or longer to cultivating concentration in meditation. Choose a simple method: mindfulness of breathing, walking, hearing, body, or lovingkindness (see chapter 10 for instructions on lovingkindness meditation). Start by doing nothing, allowing things to settle and relax on their own. Let your body be still, and let your attention rest in your body. Set a firm and clear intention to put everything else aside and give yourself completely to the meditation. Let meditating be the single most important thing in the world. Notice any compulsion to follow your thoughts, relaxing any tension in your body. One moment at a time, connect with your anchor, your object of meditation. Again, this can be the breath, a sensation, a sound, a word or phrase. Sustain attention on your anchor. Linger there, letting all else be like background noise in a café. Patiently set aside the thoughts, impulses, and feelings that arise, silently saying, "later."

At first, you may not be able to steady your mind for very long. This instability is natural. Thay likened the process of steadying the mind to pulp settling in a glass of apple juice. Moving the glass or pushing the pulp around with a spoon only stirs everything up. The more force and control you use in meditation, the more you agitate your heart and mind. Surrender to the process, giving your full and complete attention to the practice *for just one moment.*

Appreciate that moment fully. Then do it again. Whenever you lose track, let go and begin again with as kind a heart as possible.

Embodying Concentration

Once or twice a day, practice doing a simple activity with complete, focused awareness. Start with discrete, physical activities like brushing your teeth, going for a jog, or watering plants. Pause before you begin, set a clear intention, and put all else aside. Let this task be the most important thing in the world. Make your purpose not to complete the task, but to strengthen your capacity for concentration. Take your time and do the task with care, as if you were holding a newborn baby or a piece of fine art. Celebrate moments when you notice that your attention has drifted or that you're rushing, as these are precious opportunities to reshape the landscape of your heart-mind, to cultivate concentration, mindfulness, patience, and more. Journal about your experiences to deepen your understanding of concentration. Over time, explore doing more complex activities with complete attention: preparing a meal, eating, or having a conversation. Attempt to carry this singleness of intent into the flow of your day, using a simple reminder like "one step at a time." Descending from Luna, Julia Butterfly Hill encouraged us to "find your tree and take a stand." Where do you want to concentrate and take a stand?

IF YOU HAVE DIFFICULTIES

If you find yourself getting tied in knots, struggling, feeling frustrated or hopeless in your attempt at concentration, you may be trying too hard. Lower your expectations. Relax. We're aiming for one moment of complete attention. One moment of concentration is a powerful seed. If you water that moment, it grows, and you can aim for another, then another. Think of this as slowly adding molecules to a solution. Nothing appears to be happening until it reaches a point of saturation. Then it crystallizes.

Conversely, if your mind is continually drifting, floating in and out of daydreams, you may be *too* relaxed. Take a deep breath, sit up straight, and recommit to your object of concentration, applying energy and giving it your full attention.

Concentration is a magnifying glass for our consciousness: it intensifies what's present, including physical, mental, and emotional pain. If you feel overwhelmed by unpleasant sensations or disturbing memories, thoughts, or feelings, meditate for shorter periods of time, and perhaps with your eyes open. If you have a history of trauma, focus more on developing concentration in daily activities than in meditation. This will generate internal support for healing and eventually meditative concentration.

6. WISDOM

I am invisible, understand, simply because people refuse to see me. —Ralph Ellison

In one of my earliest memories, I am lying on a bed of pine needles in our small backyard, staring up at the sky. With quiet curiosity, I watch billowing clouds in a vast blue expanse. All of a sudden, astonished, I saw that *clouds move!* Before, they had been just fluffy shapes. My children's books were static, and I had never looked closer. It took me many years to recognize the significance of this insight.

Contemplative practice turns the power of observation inward to develop wisdom. How do we navigate an uncertain world with integrity and vision? When the stakes are high, as they always are in a personal or collective crisis, we must navigate carefully: slowing down, seeing clearly, and choosing wisely. We need clarity about what we see, who we are, where we stand, and what to do. Wisdom brings this clear discernment, helping us understand and release suffering at all levels—individually, relationally, and collectively.

Two core values animate the Buddhist path: wisdom and compassion. Wisdom understands directly how suffering arises and ceases. In this way it understands the natural laws of the heart and the world and, sensing what's needed, expresses itself as compassionate engagement. With wisdom, we awaken to our inner life and outer reality. We see how social, economic, political, and historical conditions affect us, how they function in our hearts, and how to create new possibilities for freedom.

Getting clear on what's happening inside can take some doing. I was nineteen when I began meditating. My parents were getting divorced, I'd had a falling out with some friends, and I was getting high daily. I felt lost. I ran to a Buddhist study abroad program in Bodh Gaya, India, where my meditation teacher Munindra-ji said, "If you want to understand your mind, sit down and observe it." I tried but felt restless, frustrated, and downright homesick. The harder I pushed, the more I tied myself in knots. When our other teacher in the program, Godwin Samararatne, gently invited me to *feel* my emotions (rather than try to *fix* them), I teared up. I realized that I hadn't stopped running, even though I was on the other side of the globe, seemingly sitting still.

That evening, Godwin spoke about the Four Noble Truths, the heart of the Buddha's teachings. Contrary to popular belief, the Buddha did not say "all life is suffering." Instead, his first noble truth offers the honest assessment that "there is suffering." Life can be hard. Freeing the heart begins with acknowledging this. Godwin urged us, "Look and see. Is it true? Do you suffer?" The second noble truth posits that there is a *cause* to the suffering we experience; the third, that this suffering can *end*; and the fourth, that there is a *path* to that end.

I felt a wave of relief. Finally, someone validated the hurt and anger I'd been carrying for so long—family mental illness, my parents' divorce, and my growing heartache over injustice and ecological destruction. Life includes pleasure and pain. The causes of my pain were external, beyond my control, but I saw that the causes of my *suffering* were internal, within my control. Turning toward my suffering, rather than away from it, brought some respite, and with it, a glimmer of freedom.

The second noble truth teaches that when we cling to or resist things beyond our control, we suffer. These reflexive desires are rooted in ignorance of impermanence. They take many forms: grasping, control, denial, avoidance, blame. The third noble truth promises freedom: when clinging and ignorance cease, suffering ceases. Finally, the fourth noble truth says that, to realize the cessation of suffering, we need to walk a path of skillful qualities like integrity, concentration, and wisdom.

I've been examining these truths ever since, trying to learn their lesson: grasping in a world of change hurts. On one meditation retreat, mindfully walking, I noticed another man sucking loudly on a hard candy. His unpleasant smacking noises stirred a wave of frustration and anger within me. I could have left the room, but I wanted to understand why this sound caused me to suffer. I carefully observed how the experience unfolded: hearing the sound, recoiling inside, blaming him, feeding the reactivity. I saw that the frustration and blame were extra, and my heart understood. Letting go of needing things to be different, I stopped suffering. All that remained was the sound, which even ceased to be unpleasant—it was just a sound.

I investigate the Four Noble Truths in ordinary experience, watching the mechanism of suffering operate. When my heart grasps pleasure or resists pain, I suffer. When I let go, simply feeling pleasure and pain, the suffering ends. Of course, challenging experiences test my capacity to let go. For instance, I bought a used car with many problems. Every time a part broke, my heart contracted, thinking, "I should've gotten a different car!" Resisting, I suffered. Letting go, I was released. A summer romance ended. Grasping at what had vanished, I felt shattered. Thinking of her, I wished things had been different, and I suffered. When I let things be, accepting the loss, I felt freer. The grief didn't vanish, but the anguish did. More recently, when I developed Lyme disease, these lessons helped me accept my present condition and an unknown future while taking steps to heal.

Not all holding on leads to suffering, and not all resistance is reactive. We hold on to our aspirations, our commitments, and our vision of equity and justice. We resist the forces of greed, hatred, and delusion. The generative resistance of social movements grows from seeing collective suffering and can be informed by profound love and compassion, rather than avoidance or denial. With careful attention and investigation, we can discern when holding on or resisting is connected to our integrity and wisdom and likewise when it's rooted in reactivity, ignorance, and producing suffering.

The Buddha talked about suffering that leads to more suffering and suffering that leads to the end of suffering. The former torments us in dizzying cycles of reactivity. The latter teaches us to feel fully, see clearly, and let go. With wisdom, we understand how ignorance and clinging create the first kind of suffering. We can then transmute it into the second. Everything changes; nothing is ultimately reliable. Ignoring this truth creates underlying anxiety, to which we react by clinging or resisting. These reactions are our hearts' way of trying to protect us in an uncertain world. Clouds move. Our bodies, hearts, and minds follow the laws of all energy in the universe. Every feeling, sensation, thought, mood, and impulse is like a passing cloud, an accumulation of energy, rolling in, rolling out.

As we sustain mindfulness, our hearts relax and we see that our effort to control life and attain happiness prevents us from receiving it. We realize grasping itself is just another cloud; we can allow it to float through us. This understanding can mature into a peace and freedom independent of conditions. Instead of trying to reshape, resist, or avoid things beyond our control, we can allow them to unfold. When we understand that even our most deeply rooted emotional and mental habits are like clouds, we can let them roll through or respond with appropriate support when helpful. In this spacious, responsive way, peace and well-being no longer depend on outer circumstances but instead arise from an intimate, relaxed awareness.

My childhood insight into the impermanence of clouds points to some of the conditions necessary for cultivating wisdom: relaxation, curiosity, mindfulness, concentration. With an acute awareness of the inequities in our world, I also recognize how the tremendous blessings of my childhood are embedded in that memory: access to nature; sufficient safety to relax; time to daydream. While cultivating the heart-mind is not dependent on external conditions, having our needs met—from basic material needs to social, emotional, and psychological needs—supports the process immensely.

You can develop wisdom by being mindful of your intentions, your actions, and their effects. Intention is the motivation or volitional push behind action. Skillful intentions arise from helpful qualities like kindness, generosity, and compassion. They uplift the heart, bring beneficial results, and may feel bright, clear, or grounded, expansive, steady, brave, or vulnerable. Unskillful intentions arise from harmful qualities like ignorance, greed, cruelty, and hatred. They contort the heart-mind, produce pain and suffering, and may feel dim, blurred or ungrounded, contracted, unsteady, scattered, or urgent.

Wisdom discerns this felt tone and chooses skillful intentions that steer our lives, shaping our inner and outer worlds. Following a reactive, irritated impulse, sending someone a sharp email, I feed that irritation and strain the relationship. Mindful of irritation, I can recognize its potential for harm and restrain myself from acting out. Wisdom is precisely this *felt knowing*. It knows directly the difference between a clear, empowered intention and a self-righteous or dismissive one.

Mindfulness connects to life and creates the space to relate differently; wisdom senses what's needed. As a seasoned surfer uses focus, body weight, and position to ride a wave, wisdom employs mindfulness, energy, concentration, and more to ride the swells of sensation, reactivity, and memory. Wisdom assesses the ethical valence of our impulses, helps us handle them, and guides our responses, both internally and collectively.

Because Buddhism emphasizes meditation as a vehicle for wisdom, some may believe that meditation will reveal all our ignorance. But the Buddha mentioned *two* causes for the arising of wisdom: our own careful attention and *input from others*. We need feedback to accurately see our conditioning and actions at all levels. Learning how social, political, and historical forces shape who we are—how they grant or deny us access to resources, advantages, and opportunities—requires reading, study, and difficult conversation. Combining such input with self-reflection can bring us transformative awareness regarding our relative position in society, in turn helping to uproot both unconscious bias and internalized oppression. We can apply these wisdom teachings to every area of our lives: internal, relational, and social.

Recently, I've been contemplating how they apply to unlearning racial bias.

For years, I struggled with unrealistic standards of perfection and independence, clinging to an image of how I should be. Friends and mentors encouraged me to question those standards and ask for help. Investigating, I saw how my conditioning as a man instilled a myth of independence and how the intellectual, performance-driven, white culture in which I was raised idealized perfection. Holding myself to that standard, I suffered. Seeing the cause of my suffering, I began to let go of believing I should be a certain way and felt freer to make mistakes and seek help. I came to see my sense of entitlement and my need for perfection as a reflection of the continual messages I received as a white male from teachers, community, and media, telling me I was bound for success.[1] Seeing these factors brought some humility, some understanding of those with different life experiences, and a resolve to use my advantages to address inequity.

It's normal to miss our own blind spots, especially with respect to privilege, so we need to cherish advice and feedback that help us see ourselves more fully through the eyes of others. For example, some years ago at a residential training, I noticed an African American woman sitting next to me coloring in her notebook. Appreciating her art and seeking to connect, I gently placed my hand on her shoulder and struck up a conversation. She tensed up and later shared that my making physical contact without asking permission had violated a boundary and brought up painful past experiences. Though I had intended my gesture to be friendly, I hadn't considered it from *her* perspective. I felt disturbed by the low awareness and high entitlement that led me to feel free to touch her. In that moment, I had been completely unaware of being both white and male, and the intrusive power those identities might carry for someone living in a Black female body. What I had intended as a friendly gesture carried a world of different meaning for her.[2] I had failed to notice (let alone *respond to*) our divergent experience as social beings—in particular, the history of male violence against women, as well as the specific intergenerational trauma of white male sexual violence against Black women that started in slavery and continues to manifest in present-day objectification and violence.

Seeing the harmful effect of my ignorance in that situation continues to motivate me to remain aware of my positional power and its undesired consequences. Without prior contemplative training and inner work, I doubt I would have been able to constructively receive her pain or hear her input, much less allow it to help me change. To heal the racialized trauma that drives white supremacy, the author and trauma specialist Resmaa Menakem distinguishes between "dirty pain" and "clean pain," which are akin to suffering leading to more suffering and the suffering leading to the end of suffering. Feeding dirty pain, we react to our wounds. We deny, avoid, or blame, compound pain or pass it on to others. Feeling clean pain opens us with courage, metabolizing hurt. Menakem writes, "Clean pain hurts like hell. But it enables our bodies to grow through our difficulties, develop nuanced skills, and mend our trauma."[3]

Wisdom also connects individual to collective experience, allowing us to understand suffering, its cause, its end, and the way leading to its end. In the last years of his life, Dr. King spoke out against the Vietnam War, describing how the oppressive forces of militarism, racism, and materialism operated so similarly in America and Vietnam. Accused of stepping out of his lane and hurting the movement for civil rights, he responded, "Such questions mean that the inquirers have not really known me, my commitment or my calling. Indeed, their questions suggest that they do not know the world in which they live."[4]

As Ralph Ellison makes clear in the epigraph opening this chapter, ignorance of social realities is not passive. To avoid seeing the illnesses of greed, hatred, and delusion that are destroying our communities and our planet, we must actively ignore them. Conversely, to address them, we must turn toward them. Contemplative practice studies and *relinquishes* the inner causes of individual suffering. Engaged practice studies and *responds* to the outer causes of collective suffering. Inner choices of attention intertwine with outer awareness and action. We know our own heart fully only when we know the world in which our heart lives, just as we know the world around us fully only when we know our own heart.

In *The New Jim Crow*, Michelle Alexander asks her readers to use wisdom to see how the dehumanization of slavery evolved into debt peonage, Jim Crow, redlining, and mass incarceration. Isabel Wilkerson's *Caste* similarly urges us to employ wisdom in analyzing the structural conditions that feed oppression in our contemporary lives. Seeing the underlying forces driving oppression alters the nature of the struggle for freedom and equity from superficial change to holistic transformation. The kind of transformation needed toward healing the hundreds of years of oppression, terror, and brutality inflicted upon African Americans, and toward rectifying the generations of genocide, land theft, and marginalization of First Nation peoples, must go deeper than policy reform. Thus Alexander argues for a multiracial, multigenerational movement to root out supremacy and caste from our social fabric. Likewise, Menakem speaks of "culture work" and the healing of embodied trauma to address the wounds of history in our collective psyche.

Every moment of life offers a choice. With wisdom, we understand that what we say and do creates the conditions for our future, both personally and collectively. The interlocking challenges of oppression, ecological crisis, social unrest, and political gridlock arise from specific historical conditions, actions, and decisions. Wisdom gives us the clarity to respond effectively.

Getting Started

Wisdom grows from being mindful of experience, rather than being caught up in it. Choose an area of your life where you're struggling or a social issue that you feel strongly about. Step back a bit, acknowledging thoughts and attending to feelings as they come and go. Try to observe your inner landscape with a kind and curious attention. Can you witness what's happening inside rather than resisting or getting lost in it? What messages have you internalized about this, either through life experiences, media, or otherwise? How do those messages relate to different facets of your identity or other aspects of your social conditioning?

Review what you already know about the underlying causes and conditions of this struggle or issue. How can you develop more insight into suffering here? Personally, where are you contracting, holding on, or trying to control what is beyond your influence? Socially, who else is working on this issue that you can learn from or connect with? What skills or resources can you offer? Listen quietly to discern what you need. What does your own wisdom say? Journal about what you've learned from this reflection, and what questions you wish to pursue further.

MEDITATION
Going Deeper

Settle your mind and body, resting your attention with an anchor. When you're ready, turn toward any habitual afflictive force:

craving, anxiety, agitation, sadness, anger, despair. Acknowledge any negative mental narrative and whether this is connected to larger social forces. Honoring the truth of those conditions, drop below the surface of the narrative. What do you experience directly in your body? Is it pleasant or unpleasant? Tight, loose, hard, soft, something else? Where do you feel it? Breathe mindfully, attending to your entire body, allowing sensations to move through you. If it feels like too much, anchor your attention with sounds or sights while you let things move inside.

Observe different thoughts, feelings, impulses, and intentions as they come and go: an urge to shift posture, an impulse to pick up your phone, a wave of frustration, a judgment about a social condition. How does each thought, emotion, or intention feel in your body? Whenever you notice any resistance, try opening to this entire experience—the feeling and the resistance itself. What shifts inside? If you begin to struggle, use that difficulty as an opportunity to study the mechanism of suffering. Breathe naturally; open to the discomfort of struggling. Get curious, bringing a friendly, patient attitude to this exploration. Ask, "How's this working? What's driving this?" Carefully feel your way through. Where are you contracting, resisting, or holding on? What happens if you allow yourself to feel that contraction? Is it possible to release or relax it, even a little? What happens when you do?

ACTION

Embodying Wisdom

Track intentions during your day in one particular arena of your life: individual actions, the interpersonal sphere, or your experience as a social being. Note the felt tone of each intention you notice. Then pause and consider, "Is this helpful? Will this lead toward more well-being, peace, and happiness or toward entanglement, stress, and difficulty?" Reflect on your intentions before a conversation. Emphasize skillful intentions; remain aware of unskillful intentions. Track intention carefully for the first five minutes or more of the conversation, staying aware of how it feels. After the conversation, reflect on how it went (you can also seek input). Did it lead toward more well-being or less? Were there any unexpected outcomes? Take notes in your journal about what you learned.

IF YOU HAVE DIFFICULTIES

Though it may be challenging to notice intentions before acting, you can develop discernment at any point. Investigate your actions whenever you become aware of them—even if it's after the fact. Trace an action back to your underlying intentions. What were the results of acting on them? What was the effect on your heart? Did it benefit or harm you and others?

If you feel caught in afflictive states, sinking in suffering, try to be patient and compassionate with yourself. Wisdom develops slowly. Emphasize moments of awareness, however brief. Draw on any resources available to bring balance and perspective. When you feel more grounded, investigate what drives the suffering. Suffering isn't your fault; it occurs naturally when conditions are present, and it dissolves when those conditions cease. Take things one moment at a time, attending carefully to internal contraction or resistance. Even when you bear responsibility for unskillful actions that have harmed you or others, try to bring tenderness and compassion to your reflection and learning. Understanding and releasing the causes of suffering are wisdom.

PART TWO

Here we begin another progression of qualities. Now that you're familiar with the overall cycle, you can enhance your practice by attending to patterns of mental, physical, and emotional energy. The more you understand the way energy moves, the more skillfully you can modulate it as you cultivate qualities. I've observed three ways energy commonly unfolds.

RISING AND FALLING Energy rises and falls. The underlying progression of qualities within each cycle flows like a wave: initiating, building, and then settling. Emotions frequently come in waves, too. You may experience rising as an increase in physical energy, alertness, a bright feeling, or upward movement in your body. You may feel falling energy as settling or calming in your body, evenness of affect, or quieting of your mind. Cultivating energy, curiosity, or courage arouses vitality. Honing concentration, ease, or rest may soothe you. Attend to the swelling and subsiding of energy, sensations, and feelings in your mind and body.

EXPANSION AND CONTRACTION Energy expands and contracts. Just as breathing opens and closes your lungs, different qualities may broaden or consolidate your outer awareness and your inner landscape. Gratitude, generosity, and wonder expand us, while concentration and resolve gather and focus our resources. See if you can notice these signs as you cultivate different qualities.

YIN AND YANG In Daoism (Taoism) *yin* and *yang* represent two natural principles and the dialectic between polarities in the universe. The *yin* is the receptive, soft principle, often associated with darkness, quiet, the moon, the womb, and water. The *yang* is the active, hard principle, often represented by light, the sky, the sun, and linearity. Yin and yang exist in relationship, cocreating one another. They are naturally present within your body and heart-mind. Your back, the outsides of your arms, and the front and outsides of your legs contain more yang energy—the tissues have a harder, more protective nature. Your belly, the insides of your arms, and the backs and insides of your legs contain more yin, bearing a softer, more receptive quality. Compassion, creativity, and emotion usually express more yin, while wisdom, rational thought, and action usually express more yang.

Rather than existing in a state of purity, these energies occur on a spectrum, each containing a seed of the other as represented by the light and dark in the yin-yang symbol. Even so, many qualities contain aspects of both yin and yang. Play invites us to participate *and* to observe. In generosity, we give *and* receive. Certain qualities balance each other, just like yin and yang. Arousing factors like curiosity, energy, and joy balance calming factors like ease, rest, and equanimity. Some qualities complement others: the potential of aspiration complements the experience of wisdom; the vibrancy of energy complements the stillness of concentration; the strength of resolve complements the repose of rest. Explore the presence and relationship of these energies in the qualities as you practice.

Beneath these patterns, the qualities remain in motion. Our cultivation of them never ends. Explore your experience with a spirit of curiosity and discover how the energies arise and change within you.

7. CURIOSITY

The important thing is not to stop questioning. Curiosity
has its own reason for existence. —Albert Einstein

Our cat Lexi picks her way carefully through the front yard. Primarily an indoor creature, she relishes time outdoors. It warms
my heart to see her captivated by life. The breeze kicks up and
she grows intensely still and focused, receiving every smell, sound,
and movement with rapt attention. Parenting a newborn, I see
this natural curiosity abounding. As our son grows riveted by a
string of colored lights, I see them dazzle in a new way.

Curiosity is the gateway to understanding. It is a strong desire
to learn or know, an open, interested attention that seeks to understand. We all possess this quality (or its analog, interest), and
can develop it.[1] Humans have harnessed the potency of curiosity
to uncover vast knowledge of our world, from the mind-boggling
expansion of the universe to the intimate reality that atoms are
almost entirely mere space.

Contemplative practice turns the immense power of curiosity
inward. Integrating interest with energy, mindfulness, concentration, and wisdom, we can open to transformative realizations
about the human heart, consciousness, and the nature of existence.

Collectively, curiosity can help us navigate and address long-standing patterns of intergenerational trauma and suffering.

As with aspiration, curiosity has both receptive and active components, integrating yin and yang energies. The yin aspect of curiosity is receptive and open: the sensitive attention that arises when we close our eyes and lean in to smell a rose. Curiosity arises from mystery and humility. Real learning flows from a willingness to not know.

The active yang aspect of curiosity focuses. When we lean in to smell the flower, our attention gathers immediately and effortlessly around a single point. When we study a problem, the yang aspect of curiosity consolidates and magnifies attention, giving a penetrative focus to the inquiry. To truly smell a rose requires both receptivity and one-pointed interest.

Like aspiration, genuine curiosity brings energy. Ever stay awake late into the night reading a gripping novel or talking with an old friend? Interest energizes us and nourishes awareness. As we explored in chapter 4, healing and transformation at any level (individually, relationally, and socially) begin with awareness. We can only engage with problems we are aware of. Privilege and oppressive power are often invisible to those they benefit. This invisibility is why being racially "color-blind" is a trap and why pretending the glass ceiling for women doesn't still exist perpetuates sexism. We must nurture curiosity about the realities of injustice if we ever want to end them.

Beautiful and pleasing things naturally hold our attention, but can you be curious about things you dislike? Try getting interested in boredom, back pain, or headaches. True curiosity includes interest in what repels us: physical pain, conflict, psychological suffering, political difference, and unearned social or economic advantage. This kind of radical interest nurtures empathy, insight, and skillful action. The author and nonviolence teacher Kazu Haga practices listening mindfully to podcasts and news media from the opposite side of the political spectrum as a way to strengthen empathy and nonreactivity. To really hear the deeper needs of people with whom you disagree demands curiosity.

Indeed, curiosity plays a pivotal role in nonviolent approaches to conflict, creating bridges to common ground. Through the power of curiosity and respect, the blues musician Daryl Davis persuaded over two hundred members of the Ku Klux Klan to leave that organization.[2] Similarly, in *Search for a Nonviolent Future*, Michael Naegler tells the story of Michael and Julie Weisser, a Jewish couple who befriended a former grand dragon of the KKK in a series of phone conversations that were guided by simple human regard and curiosity.[3] The transformation of these relationships grew from a deep faith in our shared humanity, accessed through true curiosity about others.

In 1931, while visiting Britain to discuss India's future, Gandhi met with British textile workers whose livelihoods were jeopardized by the noncooperation campaign he was leading in India; the workers took note of Gandhi's interest in "frank and friendly discussion" of their economic relationship.[4] His willingness to engage them in discussion embodied his view that both parties in a conflict hold pieces of the truth. Though Gandhi and the mill workers appeared to be opponents, he stayed with them and listened to their plight, embodying the fundamental value of curiosity. Even seeking to win over an opponent, curiosity remains open to their truth.[5] In this case, Gandhi ultimately helped British laborers understand that the Indian workers' struggle was also their own.

Curiosity can become unbalanced by grasping, obsessiveness, or self-centeredness. You may recognize this, for instance, in the probing questions of a friend prying to satisfy a compulsive curiosity instead of connecting empathetically. On the social level, white folks' interest in Black friends or colleagues can arise from grasping for approval, exoticizing difference, or performatively trying to prove their lack of racism, rather than from genuine, respectful curiosity.

To sustain interest in unpleasant experience depends on skillfully employing the core qualities we examined in part 1. We seldom remain curious about something unpleasant out of sheer willpower. Instead, to bring attention, energy, and concentration, we must have a vision of something larger, be it greater love, understanding, or freedom for all beings. Our contemplative practice shifts fundamentally when we can move beyond cringing or feeling defeated when we uncover unhealthy patterns or unconscious habits. Instead, we need to grow interested, recalling that awareness is the beginning of transformation. What would it be like to *actively long* to become aware of these areas? With mindfulness and interest, we can understand, heal, and transform these patterns—be they personal habits of control, harshness, or avoidance, or more socially conditioned dynamics like unconscious racism or internalized oppression.

In this regard, support from good friends and caring community is indispensable. For myself, talking with white friends who are further along in their process of unlearning racism has eased the shame and confusion over my own privilege and helped me grow in anti-racist capacities. It's been supportive to examine the ways I habitually take advantage of even small benefits of being white (anything from asking for exceptions to a policy to cutting across private property without fear) and the way I at times resist others experiencing me through the lens of race and gender, insisting on being seen as an individual rather than as a white man.

Curiosity guides us to look deeply into a single moment, and flowers in a process of sustained inquiry. It fuels our attention and powers the inquiry, probing, exploring, and gathering data on a particular theme, pattern, or phenomenon. For both Gandhi and King, engaging in noncooperation campaigns began with thoroughly investigating the facts. Collectively, this kind of inquiry unearths an issue's causes, stakeholders, and leverage points, informing strategy for nonviolent action. Relationally, curiosity opens new avenues for connection and empathy. Individually, meditative curiosity sustains inquiry through quiet observation rather than cogitation. It's like examining an indoor plant to see if it's real or fake. Curiosity asks, "Is that real?" and draws our focus to the plant. We can ponder all day, but to know for certain, we need to inquire. We observe the color of the leaves, the way they reflect light, the joints of their stems. We may need to touch or smell the plant. At a certain point, we will have enough data to arrive at a conclusion based on empirical observation, not assumption or rationalization.

We've already explored how mindfulness and concentration work together to reveal insight. Curiosity provides a key ingredient in this process, supporting us to release mental concepts and explore direct experience with nonconceptual awareness. Returning to the example of "my hand" (from chapter 4), the concept and corresponding visual image reify a world of changing sensations: pulsing, throbbing, tingling, moisture, pressure, heat. To see the nature of things, we cultivate a clear curiosity. We let go of what we think we know and open to the mystery of being alive.

The mind is slippery. It can rationalize and justify anything. In conflict, how quickly do we assume we're right? How much openness do we experience toward those who have different views or who occupy a different position in society? Transforming our heart, relationships, and social structures requires deliberate, careful curiosity about our own assumptions: why this rather than that? In my early twenties, when I first studied in India, I awoke to how relative nearly everything was about my life—from social norms of physical distance and eye contact to the way one uses the toilet.

True curiosity allows us to see beyond the structures, messages, and roles we have been handed by society and history—roles that can feel so innate we may have never examined them. Curiosity holds a mirror up to nature, questioning what we believe and why, how we behave and why. It invites us to step back and consider how these notions arose. Do they align with our values, our deepest truths? This curiosity is radical. When combined with strengths like resolve, courage, mindfulness, kindness, and equanimity, curiosity can reveal and transform deeply unconscious patterns of bias.

I recall the first time I noticed how I had internalized sexism: I was coteaching a workshop with a female colleague and repeated a point she had just made (an unfortunate habit in men that most women will recognize immediately). What astounded me in that moment was not only seeing my need to repeat what she had just said but also *why I felt it*: I wanted to be sure that an important point landed. In that moment I saw that I believed my deeper, male voice carried more weight and power in the room than hers. After an initial wave of embarrassment, I named what I had noticed and felt thrilled that it opened the potential for a more equitable way of sharing the space. Curiosity—particularly about the self—aligns us with our values.

At the deepest level, curiosity leads us to the profound investigation of our own identity. Almost every spiritual tradition prompts us to ask some version of the question "Who am I?" A Rinzai Zen koan—a potent question we contemplate over time—asks the student to show their original face, the face they had before their parents were born. During a *sesshin* (Zen meditation retreat) I attended in Japan, meditating late at night in the zendo, the teacher bellowed through the darkness, "Who am I? What am I? What is this?" The words cut through me to a stark, tender not-knowing. I sat perfectly still, feeling my whole being—open, sensitive, and alert. In that curiosity, I received one of my most powerful lessons in how to shed all ideas, concepts, and preconceived notions and meet the moment freshly, with a true beginner's mind.

REFLECTION

Getting Started

Allow yourself to become curious about anything: personal, relational, or social. Notice what it's like to step back from the sense of routine and question your habits, choices, and roles with a fresh eye. In particular, begin to notice when repetitive thoughts or habitual narratives occur. Instead of jumping on board or avoiding them, can you shift your attention out of the momentum of the story and get curious about it? How old is this story? Whose voice is speaking in it—your own or someone else's? What's happening in your body and your heart? Who would you be without this story?

MEDITATION

Going Deeper

Relax the mind and body in a comfortable posture using an anchor or any other supportive method. As you settle in, invite one or more of these questions: "How do I know I'm breathing? What lets me know? How do I know I'm breathing in? How do I know I'm breathing out? What's the breath without the label or concept 'breathing'?" Can you bring curiosity to the experience of breathing in and breathing out?

We can also cultivate interest through meditative inquiry. First, listen carefully for a question, letting it arise from the deepest place. What does your heart long to know? In many ways, inquiry is a practice of learning to ask better and better questions, ones that spring from wisdom and draw you into the heart of the matter. Reframe your question until you feel a sense of settling, of openness, or even of slight discomfort and edginess.

"What do I need to focus on in my life right now?"

"How can I access more kindness?"

"What is beneath this anxiety?"

Let your own question emerge.

Now ask that question sincerely. Hold it in your awareness without seeking an answer. Sometimes the asking of a powerful question is the true gift, rather than any discrete cognitive response. Instead of seeking an answer, keep listening with a heartfelt wish to learn, to experience the question fully. Include everything that arises: emotions, sensations, images, memories. Open to the flow of experience without trying to make sense of it. If your mind wanders, return to a grounded presence, then ask the question again, listening to what follows. Finally, put the question down and consider what you have received or learned from this process.

ACTION

Embodying Curiosity

Over the course of your day, try listening to others with a spirit of curiosity. How interested can you be in their world? What is the effect of sustaining curiosity in a conversation? Study social interactions, roles, and other cultural phenomena as if you were an observer from another place. What unspoken agreements are operating? What is assumed and why? If difficult or unpleasant experiences arise during your day, get curious: investigate what is actually happening in your heart, mind, and body. What are you telling yourself? Are there other ways of looking at this situation? What would it be like to let go of everything you think you know and meet this experience with a beginner's mind?

IF YOU HAVE DIFFICULTIES

As with other skillful qualities, curiosity is supported by safety, relaxation, and confidence. If you are having trouble being curious, check out your unmet needs. If you are tired, hungry, in pain, or afraid, curiosity might hold a key to your freedom. How can you address these conditions? Call a friend, ask for support, or try engaging with an activity of healthy pleasure. Listen to music, be in nature, eat delicious and nourishing food. Explore the pleasure of this experience as a way of reconnecting with natural curiosity. If you still are struggling, consider getting curious about conditions that you cannot shift immediately (such as chronic pain or social injustice). With genuine curiosity, you may discover within yourself the power to hold these conditions with clarity and compassion.

8. COURAGE

When I dare to be powerful, to use my strength in the service of my vision, then it becomes less and less important whether I am afraid. —Audre Lorde

When my wife Evan told me that she wanted to have a child, I hesitated to say yes. I worried about the disintegration of social institutions, the fraying of the social fabric, and the future habitability of our planet. Yet I sensed the possibilities of her invitation and had faith in our ability to contribute through child-rearing. Having chosen to bring new life into this world, I wondered if it's always taken this much courage, or if the trials ahead have taken natural, protective parental fear to a new level. Before our son was born, I had a palpable feeling of standing on the edge of a cliff, not knowing what was coming. It takes courage to stand on that edge with awareness, open to everything.

Looking ahead, I see courage as essential in meeting our collective challenges. Courage takes many forms: the courage of the activist, standing in the way of systems of domination and extraction; the courage of the teacher, elected official, or scientist, speaking unpopular truths to power; the courage of the family member, swimming against the stream of business-as-usual life choices that don't align with their integrity.

A great myth about courage is that it means not feeling afraid. But in fact, far from being the absence of fear, courage is the willingness to be present and vulnerable, meeting what is happening with an open heart, in *spite* of fear. Sometimes I feel terrified about having a child, not because I'm worried about the inevitable mistakes I will make but because I fear the intensity of grief and pain that I know accompanies any depth of love and joy in this life. They are inseparable companions, as necessary as up and down, left and right, and it takes courage to acknowledge that.

It takes courage to love—which is to risk loss. It takes courage to grieve, to open to pain. To find the will and resources to transform society, we must come to terms with the grief of loss: the clear-cut forests, the polluted rivers, the dried lakes, the extinct species that will never reappear on this miraculous planet. When I read about increasing teen depression and suicide and their causes—climate despair, social media addiction, anxiety, and more—my heart contracts in fear for how I will parent our son who will need to find his own response to the heartrending changes we are living through.

Courage requires wisdom and compassion, two primary Buddhist values. Wisdom offers understanding and perspective, so that we don't freak out when things go haywire. Compassion softens the heart, so that we don't deny reality and pretend everything is okay. Courage also draws strength from self-compassion, which soothes us during difficult moments.

When I was a child, my mother often brought me with her

to run errands or go food shopping. I enjoyed those little trips. It was a cherished opportunity to spend time together and for me to help with small tasks. I remember once, however, waking up in the passenger seat with Mom nowhere to be found. At first, I just felt confused. But the longer I was alone the more frightened I became. Finally, I panicked and began to wail. *Where's Mom? Why did she leave? What's happening?* I was overwhelmed by the shock of being alone and the fearful stories my mind created to make sense of things, and too young to recognize what had happened: I'd fallen asleep while we were driving, and rather than rouse her sleeping son, my mom had dashed into the store for a few minutes. Of course, she returned and comforted me, and all was well. But before she did, I was in sheer terror.

Fear is a natural response to danger. We all received a lesson in fear and courage when the COVID-19 pandemic hit. Something as simple as grocery shopping became frightening, especially for those at higher risk or with vulnerable loved ones. In the midst of danger, it's natural to be on high alert. From an evolutionary perspective, the fight-flight-freeze response makes complete sense. Movies and television often valorize a kind of primal courage: the heroic counterattack against a threat. When there's pain, hardship, or discomfort, our hardwired tendencies are to resist: to fight it, to look for someone to blame, to turn and run the other way, or to shut off altogether. These adaptive responses can keep us alive in extreme circumstances.

But when our minds amplify a threat or simply imagine one, that evolutionary mechanism makes things worse, adding spin to an already tense situation. There's a difference between feeling afraid and panicking or freezing. Discerning this difference is where contemplative practice shines. It takes courage to be with things as they are, to turn toward and be with the truth of each moment—

pleasant or painful. Contemplative practice opens the door to a more versatile, morally nuanced courage in meeting what is.

For courage is protective. The first step toward not succumbing to panic is recognizing what's happening (a function of mindfulness) and stepping back (a function of wisdom). Courage begins with one moment of awareness and the possibility of taking a pause. We can ground ourselves in the present moment, breathe, and bear with the discomfort of fear without letting it take over. The word *courage* comes from the Latin word *cor*, for heart. It takes heart to meet life on its own terms, rather than through the illusions of safety, comfort, and predictability that we crave as humans. It takes a heart full of courage to face the truth and act in alignment with our values, just as it takes tremendous courage to look squarely into the horrific, violent history of racism, terror, land theft, genocide, and broken treaties in the United States.

History offers countless examples of humans mustering courage in extraordinary and deeply inspiring ways, often placing their bodies on the line to confront unjust systems. The unrelenting activism of Mamie Till-Mobley forced the nation to confront the brutal murder of her son, Emmett Till, in 1955—often recognized as a galvanizing event in the civil rights movement. In 1957 the Little Rock Nine needed protection from the federalized National Guard and the US Army as they entered Little Rock Central High School, and three years later six-year-old Ruby Bridges was escorted by federal marshals as she walked into an all-white school in New Orleans. Many activists draw strength from the model of Archbishop Oscar Romero, the "voice of those without a voice" in El Salvador, whose sermons openly criticized the military regime, its death squads, and human rights violations, ultimately making him the target of assassination in 1980. The Tiananmen Square protesters for democracy in 1989 in China, the water protectors encamped at the Standing Rock Sioux reservation beginning in 2016, and the prodemocracy activists who took to the streets in Hong Kong beginning in 2019: all embodied immense courage.

The more awake we are to the suffering in our world, the more courage we must call forth. The courage to act in the face of danger or crisis is supported by a deeper kind of existential courage: the courage to allow ourselves to be seen just as we are. Roy Duran, who became a nonviolence trainer while incarcerated for murder, spoke of how his understanding of courage changed from the ideology of toxic masculinity to the true courage of vulnerability:

> I realized later that it didn't take any courage for me to commit murder. That was . . . based on fear. . . . I was afraid of being judged, of being seen as weak, of not being accepted, of letting people see my emotions, of letting people see the real me. I ultimately learned that being my truest self is what takes the most courage. True courage is about being willing to stand up to fear, expressing how I truly feel and being vulnerable. Learning to talk about what we are ashamed of, and transforming that shame into power by speaking about it.[1]

How much courage does it require to remove the masks we wear every day and allow ourselves to be emotionally naked? What does it take to say, with clear eyes and a steady voice, "I don't know?" What does it take to trust that who we are in this life is enough, just as we are? That we aren't defined by what we do, how much we accumulate, or even how much we give. That sometimes we need to set limits and say no to people we love. That each of us belongs here, deeply and intimately, just by virtue of our being part of the human family, and that alongside all of the good we can do in the world, one of the most valuable things we can offer is our capacity to keep feeling. We can give the gift of walking through the world with a courageous heart.

I was fortunate to have a mother with enough love and wisdom to soothe me when she found me terrified in the car that one afternoon. Truly growing up is about having the courage to be here for ourselves and for one another when things get difficult and we're frightened. I'm grateful for my years of contemplative training as well as for the hardships I've endured that taught me how to have courage so I can offer it to my own son. We can each learn to be that steady, loving presence for ourselves—and open the door to being there for others. Then our action comes from a courage deeper than fear, stronger than doubt, and greater than grief.

REFLECTION

Getting Started

Part of developing courage is building on the places where we already have it. Consider one or two challenges you've faced in life—physical, emotional, or spiritual; personal or professional. (Try not to pick the *most* difficult thing you've experienced. Choose something that was challenging enough that it took some doing to get through, but not so challenging that it overwhelmed you.) What helped you rise to the occasion? Allow yourself to acknowledge the range of factors that played a role: the support of others or a stroke of good fortune, as well as your own internal resources. Then focus on what helped you to face any fear or anxiety you felt as you lived through the challenge. See if you can recognize the courage it took to walk through that difficult time in your life, in spite of the fear and without knowing how things would work out.

MEDITATION
Going Deeper

Find a comfortable meditation posture and give yourself some time to settle. Allow yourself the gift of putting everything else down for a spell and being with the simplicity of this moment. An essential part of courage is having time and space to rest the heart. What would it be like to trust that you can be exactly as you are, right here, just for the time being? Rest like this for as long as you like. Stay alert enough to receive this nourishment without drifting off to sleep.

Then, when you're ready, bring to mind something slightly challenging for you—a situation, circumstance, relationship, or feeling. (Again, recall the trauma-informed principle to start small and not choose anything overwhelming.) As you bring this challenge to mind, notice any resistance to it. Ask yourself, "What am I not willing to feel or face? What am I avoiding?" This resistance might manifest as a feeling of contraction, rigidity, or tightness. It could appear as fogginess, or a floating sensation, or even a flurry of thoughts distracting your mind from the situation.

Try to bring the loving, wise, and patient attention of a parent to whatever you notice and however you feel inside. It's natural to want to avoid discomfort, to pull away, resist, or ignore it. Notice the strength of heart it takes to acknowledge that resistance. Notice also that you have the capacity to turn toward this challenge and to feel whatever comes in response. Recognize as courage your innate capacity to turn toward what's difficult and stay engaged with it. Recall that courage is not the absence of fear, but the willingness to be present in the face of fear. How does it feel to recognize the courage in your heart?

Finally, consider if there is anything you want to do, say, or ask for in relation to this challenge. When you're ready, allow the challenge to dissolve in your awareness, and return to the basic simplicity of being present.

ACTION

Embodying Courage

Consider where you are in your trajectory of developing courage and what amount of challenge will be most supportive in deepening this development. Do you need to build a foundation and muster courage for a small step? Are you in a middle range, looking to build your heart's courage muscle with some more substantial lifts? Are you in a more advanced place, ready to take on the biggest challenges in your life?

Wherever you are on that spectrum, choose carefully the *next thing* that is just beyond your comfort zone. What is something you've been avoiding out of fear or resistance that you would like to call forth the courage to act upon? It might be starting a new project, getting involved in a local issue, reaching out to someone to apologize or engage in repair, or taking a bold step to pursue a dream. What is one specific first step that you can take in the next week? If you're concerned about following through, consider sharing your step with someone close to you. Ask them to follow up with you as a way of holding yourself accountable.

IF YOU HAVE DIFFICULTIES

If you feel stuck, lost, or confused, try dialing things back. Choose a task that doesn't appear quite so challenging, and develop some strength and momentum there. Slowly work up to bigger challenges. Or try reaching out to a friend. Share what's important to you about this action, task, or project, as well as the fears or concerns that are getting in your way. Ask them to reflect on and share the strengths or resources they already see in you for this task. How does their reflection on your strengths affect you? Alternatively, journal about your strengths, resources, and challenges in this area. How does it help to put this down on paper?

If you still feel stuck or overwhelmed, try taking things more slowly. Feel your feet on the ground. Breathe. When things are really difficult, courage is often about taking them one moment at a time. In *this* moment, right here and now, are you okay? Give yourself the space to feel however you feel. Keep putting one foot in front of the other, recognizing and practicing the courage of showing up for even one moment.

9. RENUNCIATION

Renunciation is not giving up the things of the world, but accepting that they go away. —Shunryu Suzuki Roshi

Toward the end of my "enlightenment or bust" episode in India, I was so crestfallen that I found myself sitting in a sweets shop, binging to numb the pain. A few months later, living at a meditation center in the US—but still miserable—I would sneak into the dining hall late at night to eat cake, cookies, whatever I could find. I'd always had a sweet tooth, but this was out of hand.

I don't know if all that sugar had harmed my microbiome, but within a few months I noticed blood in my stool. I had ulcerative colitis—a painful, chronic digestive disorder. Reluctant to take immunosuppressants, I learned everything I could about alternative approaches to treatment, most of which centered around rebuilding gut health through diet and supplements.

All goodies were suddenly off-limits: sweets, ice cream, bread, pizza. My body demanded a more balanced relationship with carbs and sugar. I did my best, but still ended up yo-yoing between abstinence and indulgence. These wild swings continued for years and peaked during my time at the monasteries in England and Canada, where—in addition to my restrictive diet—I'd vowed to remain celibate, wear simple robes, and refrain from music, entertainment, and eating after noon. The hardest days were when lay supporters brought enticing foods. I'd walk through the food line with my alms bowl, fighting the urge even to *look* at the desserts. One afternoon, cleaning bowls in the ablutions block, I saw in the compost bucket, atop a heap of half-eaten food, a perfect, square brownie and I broke down. When no one was looking, I thrust in my hand, snatched the brownie, and absconded to the bathroom to gorge on it. So much for austerity and restraint!

Looking back, I can see myself with a mixture of humor and empathy. My diagnosis was hard to accept, and it took me time to understand that letting go of certain foods wasn't something I *had* to do because my doctors said so, but that I *could* do because it was truly beneficial for me. I had a lot to learn about letting go.

So much of the ecological devastation in our world is due to unchecked consumption without either regard for natural limits or understanding of true satisfaction. Entranced in a collective delusion of limitless growth, the advertising industry and global economy prey upon craving. An unquenchable thirst for more, an utter lack of corporate responsibility, and the absence of sane regulations are destroying habitats, depleting the soil, polluting our water, and cooking all of us alive. What skills can we bring to bear on this insatiable hunger? Individual action can't solve collective overconsumption. In fact, the term "carbon footprint" was coined by a public relations firm working for British Petroleum to obfuscate responsibility for climate change.[1] We need radical, collective action to hold corporations accountable and make structural changes to the global economy.

That said, there is no single, bright line between individuals and collectives—our actions do affect others, especially if we uphold them with clarity and integrity. Practices of renunciation can empower us to recognize and communicate the wisdom of limits. In freeing us internally, renunciation can clarify our priorities, creating time and energy to engage more fruitfully with external challenges. While renunciation cannot directly solve our collective challenges, it can help us adapt to a world in crisis and forge a new path forward—one that honors the natural limits of our planet.

Renunciation expresses the heart's innate capacity to let go and experience inner richness. Understanding directly how less is more, renunciation strips away distraction, reveals the improbable miracle of being alive, and fulfills us through contentment rather than accumulation. Renunciation checks the flood of craving and unlocks a door to our inner wealth. I believe it is one of our most overlooked inner resources.

Many of us associate renunciation with deprivation, repression, or asceticism. Yes, renunciation entails restraint, but in Buddhism its aim is fulfillment, not self-mortification. What happens if you think of it as simplicity, nonaddiction, letting go, or relinquishment? (Each of these terms highlights a different facet of renunciation, so I will use them interchangeably.)

Renunciation opposes the often-unquestioned assumption that happiness comes from having *more*: more wealth, more pleasure, more accolades, more of anything. It reminds us that we have the capacity to feel deeply fulfilled with relatively little. Looking back over my own life, the times I've felt happiest had nothing to do with *more*. Many such times arose through relationships and occurred when I lived with the minimum necessary to meet my needs: camping in the wilderness, living out of one bag on the road in my twenties. There's nothing romantic about being poor, but beyond bare necessities, real happiness and fulfillment are never about how much stuff we have.

Renunciation creates the possibility of simplicity, a value cherished over millennia by communities as various as the Christian desert fathers, Gandhi's lineage of nonviolence, Dorothy Day's Catholic Worker movement, and contemporary back-to-the-land movements. In 1973, E. F. Schumacher's influential book *Small Is Beautiful* advocated for an economy rooted in human needs and natural limits. Mark Sundeen's 2016 book *The Unsettlers* explores inspiring present-day examples of living with less, like the Possibility Alliance, an off-the-grid educational family homestead devoted to simplicity, service, and gratitude.[2]

Valuing renunciation begins by reflecting on what we actually need; this is distinct from a performative minimalism.[3] How much is enough? Buddhist monastics live on four requisites: food, clothing, shelter, and medicine. What remains when you relinquish the never-ending pursuit of bigger, better, faster, and more? You might find that choices like living car-free, or eating vegetarian or vegan, can be personally transformative and have social impact as well.

These choices only seem radical in the face of the messages that bombard us daily, asserting that satisfaction comes from getting, doing, or being more. Over two millennia ago, the Buddha described his teachings on letting go as going *against the stream*. How much more so today, when advertisements constantly manufacture new desires. I recall a car billboard that said, "To be one with everything, you need to have one of everything." So much for the sacred! Like a strong undertow, this current of craving can pull us through an entire lifetime and keep us chasing unattainable rewards. Unattainable because craving is always about something *we don't have*. Craving can never be fulfilled through consumption, because the nature of craving is always to need more, like a bucket with a hole in it.

There are of course healthy desires in life: wanting to be happy, to help others, to learn a craft, to protect and enrich one's community. By contrast, *craving* or *clinging* involve an unconscious thirst—a reflexive hankering for something to fill us up. If you've ever been obsessed with a purchase or a lover (or—*ahem*—a dessert), you know this terrible thirst. Part of what we crave is pleasure and the rush that comes from obtaining the object of our desire. But there is a difference between *enjoying* pleasure and *craving* it. Opening to the experience of healthy pleasure nourishes us. Let it in. But caught in the throes of craving, we grasp at experience, trying to possess it or make it last. Ironically, the contraction of craving curtails our uninhibited enjoyment of pleasure.

Indeed, it's not our yearning for happiness, pleasure, or fulfillment that's the issue but our assumptions about where we'll find these things. Craving *can* be satisfied temporarily, but has any object or experience ever fulfilled you completely? Where does real satisfaction arise? Craving co-opts our natural longing for fulfillment and points us in the wrong direction. When we long for what we don't have, we overlook what we do have and rob ourselves of contentment.

Renunciation offers us a way to study craving, instead of pursuing it. Observe carefully and you'll discover that all pleasurable experiences follow the same, wavelike pattern: a lift of anticipation, a hit of pleasure, and then dissipation. When we understand sensory pleasure for what it is—a temporary rush of sensation—we can appreciate it without snagging. Freed from the spell of craving, we can survey our situation—personally and collectively—and wisely assess our response.

To be clear: we can never fulfill craving, but we can release it. This takes practice. It requires the *skill* of renunciation. To study craving, we must be able to stand in the flood of sense desire, feel its pressure, and resist the urgency to act on it. If we suppress desire, we often act out, as I did with sweets. But when we steady ourselves and bear with the discomfort of craving without trying to gratify it, we see that craving passes. Like everything else in this world, it too comes and goes like a cloud.

To practice renunciation intelligently, we need resilience and proper support. I needed to feel my sadness, anger, and disappointment—which, in part, required help from others—before I could find a balanced relationship with sweets and my digestive condition. Only then could my renunciation arise from love and care for my body rather than suppression of craving.

Trauma can interfere with our ability to distinguish unhealthy cravings from healthy needs for nourishment. Doctrines that repress or shame desire confuse things further. Skillful renunciation requires wisdom to discern what to let go of, when, and why. If you're lost at sea, gripping a lone piece of driftwood, you don't let go until something sturdier comes along. Just so, the Buddha taught a gradual process of renunciation, relinquishing one kind of happiness for progressively more refined, wholesome, and enduring happiness: from healthy sense pleasure to the joy of good deeds, from the happiness of concentration to the peace of awakening. Thus, relinquishing craving for sensory pleasure helps us go deeper, renouncing unhealthy tendencies such as the desire for control, dogmatic views, beliefs in not being good enough, even rigid notions of who we are.

It's taken time for me to learn how to allow letting go, rather than forcing it. When my parents divorced and sold my childhood home, in my newfound Buddhist zeal I sold my cherished childhood belongings in a garage sale. Later, I realized I had pushed these reminders away in a futile attempt to avoid our family's pain and grief. I hadn't actually let go. True healing and growth come not from rejecting anything but instead from engaging with the truth.

At the monastery, I initially struggled against my vows and chafed against rules that seemed arbitrary. It took resolve to be patient, to be curious, and to sustain mindfulness. Over time, surrendering to this form of life bore fruit. The training revealed and diminished my incessant need to have things conform to my preferences or to keep busy with distractions. In their place grew presence and contentment. I began to discover a freedom that came from working with my mind's reactivity and releasing its constrictions.

Relinquishing this fixation on having our way allows us to open to something even deeper: freedom from unhealthy wanting itself. We come to see that the coveted object, state, or experience is only a ripple on the surface of a wave of craving, driven by deeper forces: the thrill of the chase, the meaning an object holds, the yearning to be released from the tension of wanting. We may even find that part of our mind is addicted to the experience of craving itself—wanting to want.

Perhaps the most tenacious form of clinging is our tendency to grasp views and identities. Being convinced that we are right or know "the truth" blocks dialogue and learning. Renunciation invites us to let go of being right and move into more generative spaces of not knowing and curiosity. The poet and activist Audre Lorde observed, "There are very real differences between us. But it is not those differences between us that are separating us. It is rather our refusal to recognize those differences."[4] Those (like myself) in privileged social positions often downplay difference, retreating to the more comfortable, color-blind terrain of our shared humanity. To meaningfully collaborate, we must honor our differences—of race, class, culture, religion, political affiliation, and beyond—neither erasing *nor* solidifying them. We can do this without pitting ourselves against each other, obscuring our common ground, or limiting our potential for collective action. How freeing would it be to relinquish any insecurity driving us to put others into boxes, and instead to cultivate a receptive and engaged curiosity about one another?

Renunciation allows us to embrace the relative and open beyond it. By releasing the tendency to contract around *anything*, we realize a wider perspective, very much including the diversity at the core of a just society. Renunciation creates the possibility of holding multiple—even conflicting—perspectives simultaneously. If we are to form bold, diverse coalitions in service of our shared liberation, we must be able to affirm our differences as unique and beautiful while also making common cause with one another.

In 1676, 100 years before the American Revolution, people from all classes and backgrounds—small landowners and nobility, workers of European and African descent, bond and free—joined in Bacon's Rebellion to demand political and economic freedom in Virginia.[5] After British imperial forces crushed the rebellion, ruling elites instituted new laws aimed at breaking the people's solidarity by creating rigid racial categories and intensifying chattel slavery laws.[6] Using terms like "white" and "black" for the first time, the key strategy aimed to make now "white" workers feel an allegiance with "white" rulers. Over three hundred years later, this divide-and-conquer strategy still fractures the popular majority and pits us against one another—especially by race—undermining coalitions for radical change.

Renunciation makes possible a beneficial inner flexibility—sometimes actively embracing aspects of our identity, other times transcending these in service of solidarity and collective action. Knowing when to engage in each takes investigation, sensitivity, and wisdom. For example, discernment helps me to hold my Jewish identity skillfully, using it to lean into my ancestors' strength, unlearn white supremacy, and draw on Jewish peace and justice teachings to challenge oppression and violence against Palestinians. But renunciation also carries us beyond such identifications. Roshi Bernie Glassman, founder of the socially engaged Zen Peacemakers Order, led street retreats combining meditation with living unhoused in urban settings without money. Practitioners had to relinquish comfort, predictability, control, and ultimately their familiar identity. Glassman also created a series of retreats bearing witness to the pain of genocide—another practice of renouncing comfort and the illusion of separation—with programs addressing atrocities carried out in Auschwitz-Birkenau, Rwanda, Bosnia-Herzegovina, and the Wounded Knee and Pine Ridge reservations. In fostering intimate contact with suffering, Glassman helped those of us who have more than we need act on behalf of others by realizing that *there are no others.* As Glassman taught:

> When we bear witness, when we become the situation—homelessness, poverty, illness, violence, death—the right action arises by itself. We don't have to worry about what to do. We don't have to figure out solutions ahead of time. Peacemaking is the function of bearing witness. Once we listen with our entire body and mind, loving action arises.[7]

REFLECTION

Getting Started

Pay attention to the advertisements you see this week. What are their underlying messages? What do they suggest will bring happiness? Notice which images and messages entice you as a way of uncovering your own assumptions about happiness.

Reflect on the difference between wants and needs. Is yearning for an object or experience driven by habitual craving? Ask, "Do I really need this?" What is the difference between wanting something (say, the latest phone) and needing something (a replacement because yours broke)? When you want something, investigate what your heart longs for, beneath the craving. Ask yourself, "If I had that, what would it give me?" Are you longing for rest? Fulfillment? To belong? Something else?

MEDITATION

Going Deeper

Sit or recline comfortably, and settle your attention in the present moment. Connect with an anchor like your breath, the sensations in your hands, or the sounds around you. Notice when any kind of craving arises: an impulse to move, to get something, to do something else, even to entertain or distract yourself with thoughts. Shift the focus of your attention from the *object* of craving to craving *itself*. Notice any restlessness, agitation, or tension inherent in wanting something you don't have. Every time your mind snags on a thought, impulse, or judgment, practice renunciation by disengaging your attention and gently returning to your anchor. If you notice a particularly strong thought or impulse, step back and ask, "Who would I be without this?"

ACTION
Embodying Renunciation

Choose a habit or activity that you would like to relinquish (or limit) for a period of time: eating sugar, watching TV, scrolling through social media, or some other indulgence. Set a realistic goal: What is a pleasure you can live without for a week or two? Alternatively, choose a material object(s) you don't need and would like to part with. If you're not ready to give it away just yet, put it in a box and store it somewhere out of sight for a month or longer. Practice living without this item(s) for a period of time. Then return to it and see if you're more willing to give it away (or whether in fact you really need it). Take this investigation deeper. What is a wise and balanced approach to living with less and learning to free your heart from habits? Record your reflections in your journal.

IF YOU HAVE DIFFICULTIES

Wise renunciation develops slowly, with layers of subtlety. Don't go to war with yourself. If you find yourself struggling, swinging back and forth between abstinence and indulgence, something is out of balance. Try dialing back your renunciation. Go for low-hanging fruit, something not too hard to put down. Then you can more effectively explore the discomfort of the process and the spaciousness of feeling free once the heart lets go.

We need wisdom and balance to release fixations of view and identity. Explore how your relationship to your beliefs, views, opinions, and identities opens or closes down the possibility of dialogue and learning. Whenever you encounter fixation or over-identification, investigate what this energy of clinging protects. Are there other ways to honor the truth of your experience without contracting or shutting down the space of connection?

10. KINDNESS

The moment we choose to love we begin to move towards freedom, to act in ways that liberate ourselves and others.
—bell hooks

Kindness arises from love and flows naturally from an undefended heart. We sometimes overlook the many ways kindness is present in our lives every day: a genuine smile at the store, a text message or surprise visit from a friend, one neighbor lending a hand to another.

Small moments of kindness add up. Even one comment can make a difference in our sense of belonging and self-worth. As a teenager, I went through my share of social anxiety and insecurity. After being shunned by one group in high school, a new friend remarked, "*They're* the ones missing out—they don't get to hang out with you." Hearing that, I could relax, instead of worrying there was something wrong with me. Years later, working at an outdoor education center, I felt exposed and vulnerable in a similar way when I shaved the beard I'd been growing for over a year. The first person I saw that morning was the director, who lit up and said, "Nice face!" Small moments like these stay with me, warming my heart for years.

Kindness comes from *kin*, highlighting the fundamental truth of our interdependence. Kindness connects us to the human family. A universal quality, kindness nourishes the heart, heals isolation, and brightens our lives. It sees the potential for good in all and serves as a potent guide for collective transformation.

Kindness softens the harshness of the world. Without kindness, life can feel bleak and lonely. When present, kindness soothes us, creating space to handle our reactivity and relate wisely to uncertainty, change, and loss. Grasping for stability in a chaotic world, the untrained heart tries to control the flow of life, pursuing pleasure and resisting pain. Kindness protects the heart from the trembling of fear, the distortion of ill will, and the poison of cruelty. In moments of kindness, we connect with the beauty of our potential and temporarily free the heart from afflictive states.

It's easy to become so consumed by tasks and troubles that we believe we don't have the bandwidth to be kind. We may postpone it with a vague notion: "I'm too stressed out to be kind." Yet being kind *generates* energy and goodness. Think of the last time you smiled at someone, offered a kind word, or gave someone a hug. A librarian my wife once knew tried to make every patron he served feel seen and cared for, because, he said, the endeavor filled him with delight. Research confirms what we know from experience: it feels good to be kind. Lovingkindness meditation produces measurable increases in positive emotions leading to a wide range of benefits, from increased purpose and satisfaction in life to reduction in depression and symptoms of illness.[1]

Kindness also helps us metabolize hurt and return to balance when we're caught in the throes of suffering. After years of striving, perfectionism, and self-criticism, I slowly learned the healing strength of kindness through lovingkindness practice. When I felt achy, depressed, and fatigued during my struggle with Lyme disease, turning toward my symptoms with kindness brought relief. When I couldn't find kindness for myself, offering it to another or receiving the warmth of a friend softened the pain like a gentle balm.

Initially, kindness may arise randomly, a passing state dependent on conditions. With practice, kindness becomes a skill, a firmly ingrained character trait. We can develop kindness as a baseline attitude, an orientation to life that informs how we relate to ourselves and the world.

Kindness is born of love. Just as the bubbles on the crest of a wave are made of water, kindness expresses a deeper love in the heart. What is love? Fairy tales and media idealize love as a kind of ecstatic, joyful emotion exemplified by sexual encounters. Reducing love to this romantic feeling compounds the disempowerment and spiritual impoverishment so endemic today. We fetishize love as something intense and exciting, and thereby misconstrue it as an unattainable state.

Love expresses itself in so many ways. Millennia ago, the Greeks recognized many kinds of love: *eros*, erotic love, yearning for union and the divine; *philia*, the intimate love of friendship; *storge*, familial bonds of affection; *ludus*, the playful love of children; *pragma*, deep, hard-won love of life partners; *philautia*, self-love, which can take the form of unhealthy narcissism or of healthy inner kindness; and *agape*, an unconditional, selfless love for all. Love in one's own culture may not fit these ancient categories, but we can see that love takes many forms. Love is at once a feeling, a need, and a skill. As a feeling, we may experience love as warmth, openness, or connection. It lights up our faces when we see an old friend; it opens our hearts when we pet an animal.

We need love. Raising our son has made real for me what I previously knew theoretically: we depend on love for our survival. Modern medicine has observed what any parent or caregiver knows intuitively: babies need to be held and loved. Lack of love and connection early in life has a range of harmful effects, from delays in cognitive function, language, and motor development, to emotional and psychiatric disorders.[2] It can even kill an infant. Our species has evolved to depend not only on the physical sustenance of the earth, but on loving, emotional connection. Research studies with adult meditators have shown a range of promising changes in both neurological function and behavior through lovingkindness meditation.[3]

The Buddha urged his disciples to cultivate an expansive love called *metta*, or what we have been calling "lovingkindness." His Holiness the Dalai Lama defines *metta* as "basic human warmth." Metta sits at the core of kindness: it is our innate capacity for goodwill. When developed, metta—like agape—opens into a boundless, unconditional love for all creatures.

This love is not sentimental. It doesn't demand we put on a happy face or act politely when we're upset. Nor does it require us to be doormats, abandoning our needs and allowing others to walk all over us. Love does not ask us to like those who would harm us, whose actions we oppose, or whose views we abhor. Rather, metta shifts our attention to a deeper level. Recognizing both our shared condition and our potential for goodness, metta appeals, persistently and unfailingly, to our best nature. Living from a foundation of love, we embody kindness and help naturally, from compassion.

This impartial love that lends itself to simple kindness also lends itself to revolutionary love on the stage of social transformation. It animates social justice as a force for change, nourishing our courage to face collective pain and the energy to act for its healing. Gandhi was known for this kind of love through down-home kindness and amicable communication with opponents. In South Africa, when he learned that the railroad workers had called for a sudden strike, Gandhi suspended plans for mass civil disobedience in order to spare his primary political opponent, a South African military commander and chief minister named Jan Smuts, and the local police from being overwhelmed. Moved by Gandhi's kindness, General Smuts's secretary wrote:

> You help us in our days of need. How can we lay hands upon you? I often wish you [Indians] took to violence like the English strikers, and then we would know at once how to dispose of you. But you will not injure even the enemy. You desire victory by self-suffering alone and never transgress your self-imposed limit of courtesy and chivalry. And that is what reduces us to sheer helplessness.[4]

Dr. King, in his vision of Beloved Community, his teachings on agape, and his tireless organizing for justice, called us to broaden our understanding of love into a universal force of connection, a true kinship binding us together. Challenging the assumption that some people are more worthy of our love than others, he urged us to learn how to treat everyone with a dignified and impartial love: "Love is the most durable power in the world," he said. "It is the only force capable of transforming an enemy into a friend."[5]

But why? Why love those with whom we have fierce and irreconcilable differences? Why love those who seek to dominate, harm, or oppress us? The reason lies in the nature of reality: our future is shared, and violence can never yield peace. The Buddha taught: "Hatred never ceases through hatred. Through love alone does hatred end."[6] In 1967, during his last Christmas sermon, moving beyond the horizon of racial justice, King called for an international commitment to nonviolence and radical love. He explained, "All life is interrelated. We are all caught in an inescapable network of mutuality, tied into a single garment of destiny. Whatever affects one directly, affects all indirectly. We are made to live together because of the interrelated structure of reality."[7]

Wisdom reveals to us the nature of reality and expresses itself as love. Our time here is too short to withhold even a moment of our love. The more we see how our lives intertwine and the more we understand how hatred only begets hatred, the more we are called to love—be it in daily acts of kindness or in the challenge of transforming our hearts and our world through loving our enemies.

REFLECTION
Getting Started

Consider how bleak the world would be without kindness. Imagine going through an entire week without experiencing even a glimmer of kindness from or for anyone. (If things are hard right now and this feels too close to home, skip this reflection.) Think of the small moments of kindness you've offered, received, or witnessed. With each instance that comes to mind, notice how you experience warmth, care, or goodwill in your body. How does kindness affect you? How has your kindness affected others?

MEDITATION
Going Deeper

Allow your mind and body to settle naturally. To practice loving-kindness meditation, begin by bringing to mind someone for whom it's easy to feel a sense of warmth—a dear friend, a relative, a mentor, or a beloved pet. (Choose someone living, lest you slip into grief.) See them in your mind's eye or imagine being with them. They're happy, smiling at you. Allow yourself to receive their love. Like remembering a favorite melody, allow your heart to recall their kindness. Now shift to offering them kindness, letting it flow freely from your heart to theirs. Practice sustaining a genuine intention of kindness. If you feel any warmth or connection in your heart, let your attention dwell there, inviting the warmth to grow.

You may find it helpful to silently repeat a few phrases that express your wish for their well-being—for instance, "May you be safe and happy. May you be healthy and at ease." Offer each phrase like a gift, expressing your sincere wish for their happiness. This won't magically improve their state, but it will actively strengthen the love in your own heart-mind. Repeat the phrases, or dwell with the quality, savoring any sensations of warmth, openness, or relaxation in your body. Finally, focus on yourself, offering these phrases to your own heart. Linger with each phrase, receiving it completely. Sometimes trying to practice kindness can bring up opposite feelings like anger or self-judgment. This reaction is natural. Remember that practicing the qualities in this book can reveal their opposites. Don't try to force kindness. If you aren't able to get in touch with it, tune in to the *wish* that you could. That too is a wholesome intention that may help you sense your good heart.

ACTION

Embodying Kindness

At the beginning of each day, set an intention to treat yourself and others with kindness and to notice and celebrate any moments of kindness that occur. Throughout the day, as often as you re-member, ask yourself, "How can I be kind to myself right now?" Pay particular attention to how you speak to yourself, aiming for gentle words and a kind inner tone. When engaging with others, look for the goodness in them. Rather than trying to perform a grand deed, aim for simple and honest expressions of your heart. Mother Teresa famously advised, "Don't look for big things. Do small things with great love, sometimes the smaller the thing, the greater the love."[8] Anytime you notice a moment of kindness—in yourself, from another, or between others—pause and let it regis-ter: "This is a moment of kindness." Allow your attention to linger there, noticing how it feels in your body, appreciating the beauty of kindness.

IF YOU HAVE DIFFICULTIES

If you're feeling down or having a hard day, kindness can feel far away. Remember that lovingkindness allows things to be just as they are, meeting life on its own terms. You don't have to change how you're feeling, pretend, or be chipper to be kind. True kind-ness can be as simple as wishing someone a happy birthday, or meaning it when we say, "Drive safely." Listen for the genuine care in your heart, trusting it's there even if you can't feel it all the time.

When we're suffering, compassion can be a helpful first step, and it may be more appropriate medicine than kindness. How do you relate to a friend who is suffering? Offer that same tenderness to yourself. If you are struggling to find kindness for someone with whom you are in conflict, consider cultivating compassion for your own pain first. Explore the chapter on forgiveness as a way of freeing your heart from resentment. Then use your imagination to connect with the other person's potential for goodness, training your heart to see their humanity. Expand your view beyond the conflict or harm you have experienced from them. Picture them cuddling a pet, cooing with a baby, or sleeping peacefully. Remember that cultivating kindness doesn't condone harm or dictate any specific action or behavior. It doesn't require becoming friends, or even having a relationship. Instead, kindness frees your heart from animosity and opens the door to new possibilities.

11. EASE

Within you there is a stillness and a sanctuary to which
you can retreat at any time and be yourself.
—Hermann Hesse

My anxiety from living with a mentally ill family member ramped
up when I was a young adult. I recall incessantly pestering a friend
during a summer drive: "What'll we do when we arrive? Where's
the best place for lunch? Where'll we park?" He finally shot back,
"Geez, will you *stop*?" "Stop *what*?" I asked, clueless about my neu-
rotic planning and the anxiety driving it.

When I first started meditating, I could barely sit still, let
alone feel at ease. On my first silent meditation retreat, being with
my own mind felt like being locked in a room with someone high
who couldn't stop talking! It took patience and persistence with
meditation and other forms of healing before I began to experience how much transformation is possible. In spite of our personal or ancestral trauma, even alongside the legitimate anxiety
about the intersecting crises we face, this can shift. It is possible to
cultivate calm.

When at ease, we feel relaxed and comfortable. Stress dimin-
ishes and difficulties recede. Ease supports flow, effortlessness, and

contentment, a spectrum from ordinary relaxation to meditative calm to deep tranquility.[1] But ease must also include integrity, empathy, and wisdom if it is to be skillful; otherwise, it can become a vehicle for harm, amplifying any tendency to exploit others, extract resources, and accumulate wealth for its own sake.

We have countless reasons to feel uneasy, including a profound mismatch between our ancestral social conditioning and the current structure of our society. We evolved in small tribes with shared senses of place and meaning. We soothed our nervous systems with rhythmic activities like walking, grooming, threshing, weaving, and toolmaking. For almost all of us, life now differs entirely from that prehistoric existence. Of course, certain things have improved dramatically (longevity, physical safety, food security), but others have disintegrated. Instead of being born into the warm, familial comfort of a close-knit community, we find ourselves in a disorienting and strained world that's beset by conflict and addictive stimulation. Understanding this can help depersonalize our uneasiness and point toward ways to relieve it.

As with many of the qualities we are exploring, finding ease depends on feeling safe enough externally and internally to slow down. Yet many families and communities feel increasing economic, environmental, and societal pressures; the resulting uncertainties feed distress and push us to speed up. Teens and young adults feel increasing anxiety.[2] Among marginalized communities, the chronic stress of oppression adds an additional hurdle. Here in the United States, centuries of structural racism have led to people of color having starkly higher rates of illness and worse health outcomes than their white counterparts.[3] All of this has a cumulative effect, instilling a low-grade panic in our nervous systems. Many of us have to swim faster just to keep our heads above water. Even if we're privileged, we often counter this mountain of stress with a manic energy that avoids looking inward (as I did, growing up). It works for a while; then we crash in a heap.

How do we develop a tool kit for soothing our troubled nerves when so much is out of our control? How do we find more ease, so life is not such a struggle? One thing is certain: we don't unwind by placing more demands on ourselves. Ease can't become another item on the to-do list, despite the products the wellness industry peddles.

I invite you to begin to find ease by noticing any moment when your body relaxes or settles the smallest bit. For example, we usually feel well after finishing a meal or taking a shower. Instead of scrolling through your feed or jumping into the next activity, pause. Take a breath. Appreciate being satiated. You are an animal: notice how it feels to be at ease in your body. Try easing into a soothing activity. If you're hungry, eat. If you're tired, sleep. Eating grounds and comforts us, signaling safety to the body and relieving stress through sensory pleasure. Some feel more at ease alone; others appreciate social contact. A walk in a natural setting can bring perspective and quiet the heart. Time spent playing or relaxing with pets, listening to music, or enjoying a craft or hobby often brings ease, as do embodied activities like exercise, stretching, or yoga.

You can also access ease by spending time with others who tend to be more relaxed than you are. When I was an attendant for the Thai forest monk Ajahn Sucitto and our flight was delayed, I got agitated and prepared to storm the check-in counter to complain. Meanwhile, my teacher exhaled and enjoyed some extra meditation time. We can learn new ways of being when others respond with ease and we truly see it.

When we regulate our nervous system, we establish ease and restore balance by sending a hardwired signal of safety to our bodies. Encourage ease by using your senses to orient to your environment (a natural mechanism for assessing safety). Look around in a relaxed manner, letting your eyes, head, and neck take in your surroundings.[4] Notice if you take a spontaneous deep breath—indeed, anytime you find yourself taking such a breath, it can be a cue that your system just registered something as safe or easeful. Orienting yourself in a relaxed way like this, you may feel more settled and present. Orienting, along with other ways to register physical safety, is especially helpful if you suffer from trauma. Try firmly patting your body from head to toe—especially the powerful muscles in your arms and legs—thinking, "I'm here, I'm okay now." A long, slow exhalation engages the parasympathetic nervous system, easing stress. Try this: take a deep breath through your nose, then purse your lips as you breathe out through your mouth long and slow. Other activities that coordinate slow, gentle movement with breathing can also soothe your nervous system, inducing calm and relaxation.

The meditation practices in chapters 1 and 5 develop calm: return to them by setting everything else aside and resting your attention on a single, soothing aspect of your experience. This practice (in Buddhism called *samatha*: calm abiding meditation) effectively changes the channel within. Instead of ruminating on worries or worst-case scenarios, encourage ease by focusing on a single aspect of your experience (preferably something pleasant, like the warmth of your hands, sounds around you, or the rhythm of your breathing).

Through meditation, you can learn to release the fixations that keep your mind spinning and rest in the present moment. Cultivate ease by calming your thoughts, fostering the spaciousness to accommodate stress, and allowing tensions to unwind. Progressively relax different parts of your body with a body scan or visualization. Slowly sweep your attention through your body from head to toe, part by part, feeling the sensations in each area just as they are—subtle or gross, pleasant, unpleasant, or neutral. Alternatively, focus on softening areas where you may hold tension: jaw, eyes, neck, shoulders. Imagine your mind and body like a snow globe, each thought, emotion, or sensation a floating snowflake. Allow the particles to settle simply by doing nothing except being still. The more you *try* to calm down through control, the more you agitate your heart-mind. Use the exercises in this chapter and elsewhere in the book to learn how to let fears, hurts, and worries come and go through your awareness, feeling them fully without getting caught up in them. The less you push and pull, the more still and quiet your mind becomes. The Buddha likened this process of mental and emotional downshifting in meditation to the physical transition from running to walking, to standing, then sitting in the shade, then lying down.

Ease is not only about feeling calm but also about moving through the ups and downs of life without getting rattled. As you practice, you can cultivate calm in the very midst of activity. "Real calmness should be found in activity itself," wrote Shunryu Suzuki. "We say, 'It is easy to have calmness in inactivity, it is hard to have calmness in activity, but calmness in activity is true calmness.'"[5]

Growing our capacity for ease isn't about dissociating from the world, micromanaging our environment, or pretending that all will be well if we just breathe. On its own, no amount of breathing will get us out of an abusive relationship or a toxic work environment, nor will it stem the tides of racism and climate change. But calmness does support skillful action, which itself offers an antidote to anxiety and a catalyst for ease. Activism, service, and volunteering relieve stress through community connections and the gratification of taking a stand. Ichiro Kawachi, a professor of social epidemiology, notes, "Research suggests that these community social connections are as important for resilience to disaster is as [sic] physical material like disaster kits or medical supplies."[6]

Wisdom thus reminds us of the true purpose of calm: clear seeing in service of action. If we panic, we cannot help others. Thich Nhat Hanh likened the precarious position of our world to that of refugees attempting to cross a stormy sea: "If even one person aboard can remain calm, lucid, knowing what to do and what not to do, he or she can help the boat survive. . . . One such person can save the lives of many."[7] Our clarity and calmness can assure others. Integrated with wisdom, ease rejuvenates us, supports clear seeing, and creates conditions for effective action.

Knowing that we are doing *something* can bring us a measure of ease—*and* begin to heal the wounds of the world.

REFLECTION
Getting Started

Where in your daily life do you experience ease, calm, or relaxation? What interferes with that ease? How much interference is personal, relational, ancestral, or social? Rather than searching for an ideal state of complete ease, attune to small moments of settling down—a sigh of relief after catching the bus, a smile as you look up at the sky, the way your body melts when your head hits the pillow. Review this chapter's suggestions for accessing ease. Which methods already work for you? Which could you develop? Without making a project out of it, jot down in your journal a few activities that help you feel at ease, so you have them handy when you need to unwind. Review things that do *not* put you at ease and create a "not-do" list!

Going Deeper

Sit or recline in a comfortable position. Take a few deep breaths and choose a suitable anchor. Appreciate that in this moment there is nothing special you need to do, fix, accomplish, get, or have. Notice the space around you, the absence of pressure or demands on your body and mind. Give yourself time to be still, letting things settle on their own like those particles in a snow globe. As you breathe in and out, try repeating a couple of words or short phrases: "Calm . . . peaceful." Or "It's okay . . . May I live in peace."

If you have time and want to take another step, sweep your attention through your body, starting at your head, working your way down to your feet. Part by part, invite your muscles to soften. Visualize a soft light or golden liquid flowing down your body, bringing ease and relaxation to your cells and tissues. Finally, be gratefully aware of any pleasant aspect of your experience: the weight of your body, the warmth in your hands, the sensations of breathing, the sounds around you. Notice thoughts, feelings, and impulses, gently letting them come and go as you return to your anchor.

Embodying Ease

Choose a specific activity like getting dressed, leaving the house, or walking to the store. Practice moving through it easily. Avoid struggling or forcing yourself to move in an unnaturally slow way. As I once heard Thay suggest on a retreat (in Ascutney, Vermont, in the late 1990s), "Walk like a free person, free from the past and free from the future." What is it like to give full attention to your movements, inviting ease in your mind and body?

If you have the time and energy, get involved in a social issue that you care about as an antidote to anxiety and a vehicle for catalyzing ease. Serve those who need the most support. Appreciate the ease you feel in working with others. We *can* contribute in meaningful ways, and it serves all of us.

IF YOU HAVE DIFFICULTIES

You may feel so wired or anxious that nothing seems to ease you. First check: are you judging or criticizing yourself for not unwinding? If so, recall the array of forces contributing to your state. Bring yourself some compassion and acceptance, recalling how many people suffer from anxiety. Your experience is entirely normal. Track your daily tension and stress. Notice when your anxiety reduces, even a tiny bit, and relish the relief you experience in those moments. Try other methods to deactivate stress. Coordinate your breathing with simple, slow, rhythmic movements like lifting and lowering your arms as you breathe, or gently circling the index finger of one hand in the palm of the other, going clockwise on the in-breath and counterclockwise on the out-breath. Review this chapter, looking for just one suggestion that feels doable and helpful. You can find ease.

12. PATIENCE

Patience paves the road to freedom. —Sayadaw U Pandita

My Lyme disease lasted for three years before resolving. I took loads of antibiotics, gave myself injections, induced controlled fevers in a UV bed, and more. Through the ups and downs, I drew upon many of the qualities we're exploring: aspiration, energy, mindfulness, compassion, resolve, and—perhaps most of all—patience. When I felt like giving up, patience allowed me to tolerate the physical discomfort and the mental anguish of the disease without losing heart. In moments of pain and fear, it helped me take things one step at a time, conserving energy for the journey ahead.

Whether or not you've had a chronic illness, you already know something about the challenges and benefits of patience: sitting in traffic, navigating a corporate phone maze, dealing with a difficult relative or coworker. Though religions around the world recognize the supreme value of patience, in a world on fire (literally and figuratively), this can feel fanciful. How can having patience with the climate emergency, war, or political chaos be useful?

Patience allows us to open to and bear with any experience, to tolerate difficulty and discomfort without reacting. Patience is not gritting one's teeth, tensing up, or resisting the unpleasant while we wait for it to end. These are all forms of contraction and aversion. Inwardly, patience works at the level of our tension and reactivity to life, easing the heart with spaciousness. Outwardly, it perseveres. Patience offers us the long view and works synergistically with resolve, conferring strength. It transforms the heart by relinquishing impatience and clinging, and it sustains us to move both our psyches and our societies toward more health and wholeness.

Patience is absolutely not passivity. Patience does not mean standing idly by in the face of harm, allowing others to engage in abuse, or quietly enduring the destruction of our planet. We can cultivate patience and still take a clear stand against harmful actions, refusing to tolerate systemic violence. Far from preventing our powerful response, patience supports us to respond clearly and deliberately. It confers time to reflect and choose wisely, enhancing our efficacy rather than robbing us of agency.

Transforming the heart is a bit like growing a garden, with the twist that we are both garden and gardener.[1] Gardening takes time and energy—we have to cultivate the ground, plant seeds, water, and weed. It takes patience; we can't rush the process. I've mentioned how, growing up, I buried myself in schoolwork and auditions to cope with difficult emotions. It took years to realize how angry and hurt I felt. Although meditation revealed and softened some of the suppressed emotions, I needed more help to heal. I remember one somatic therapy session in which I was filled with frustration and impatience, tired of feeling trapped inside, wanting to move past the pain I'd been carrying for so long. My therapist looked at me with great warmth and said, "The slower you go, the faster you go."

In that moment, I was able to hear the message: *you can't rush healing*. Healing requires loving attention, care and understanding, and space to breathe. Impatience stalls the process. Consider the last time you got a scrape or a cut. How did your body heal? It began at the edges, and it took time. You may have tended it and kept it clean, until it healed on its own. So it is with the heart. First we must recognize the injury. We can spend years—even a lifetime—avoiding pain, burying it, running away from it. Only when we turn toward the hurt and acknowledge it do we open the door to healing and transformation. Next, we do our best to create supportive conditions: we clean the wound, carefully setting aside any shards of the past. Then we nourish it and wait. Just as our cells know how to mend, our hearts heal, open, and recollect their wholeness with the right support.

Patience runs counter to a culture of instant gratification. It invites us to release our fixations on efficiency, speed, and clock time and instead attune to organic time—to the cyclical, nonlinear rhythms of nature. Neither the process of spiritual awakening nor the tipping points of social change follow a linear progression. A flower blooms in its own time, not on a schedule. It opens naturally in accordance with conditions. Here, patience relies on wisdom, which understands that all things unfold due to causes and conditions.

Creating the specific conditions necessary for transformation—spiritually or socially—takes careful and deliberate action. Indispensable to this process, patience integrates yin and yang energies: soft and hard, yielding and engaging. It lets go *and* holds on—we relinquish clinging but hold fast to our vision. An analogy here may be illustrative: to start a fire by rubbing sticks with a bow drill, one must run the spindle over the fireboard continuously for a long time. This requires both the suppleness (yin) and perseverance (yang) of patience. Without suppleness, we grow tense and burn out. But without perseverance, we take a break every time our arm feels tired and never generate enough heat to ignite the fire.

In this way, patience bestows infinite strength, the enduring strength of water, so soft and gentle, that over centuries wears away even the hardest stone. Combined with energy and resolve, patience confers tremendous power to the heart-mind, creating an unshakable basis for the work of personal and collective transformation. On a personal level, its gentle perseverance opens pathways to deep transformation and healing. On a collective level, it sustains bold and creative movements as they challenge and dismantle oppressive structures. Like a spindle rubbing against the fireboard, patience aids sustained nonviolent resistance to generate the continuous friction needed to bring the powers that be to the negotiating table.

When we turn our attention to the realm of social action, it is vital to acknowledge the deeply important difference between patience and complacency. Dr. King steadfastly decried those who postponed change out of fear, bad faith, or inconvenience, and he urged freedom fighters to cultivate a healthy *impatience*, refusing to consent to oppressive conditions and persevering against the way things are. King illustrated this powerfully in his famous "Letter from Birmingham Jail," writing, "For years now I have heard the word 'Wait' . . . This 'Wait' has almost always meant 'Never.'"[2]

King's admonition in no way contradicts the wisdom that real transformation requires time. During the Vietnam War, the socially engaged Buddhist activist Thich Minh Duc spoke candidly of the patience the struggle required. "We did not think that by demonstrating we'd turn things around immediately. Rather, we had to look to the long-term process . . . today one inch, tomorrow another inch . . . For one hundred years, we were controlled by the French. We knew that it would take years to untie the knot."[3]

In his decades-long struggle for racial equality in South Africa, Nelson Mandela embodied the potency and wisdom of patience. Mandela reflected how his twenty-seven years in prison transmuted the impatience of his youth. He warned against "an illusion of urgency forcing us to make decisions before we are ready."[4] Like Thich Minh Duc, Mandela understood that an unjust edifice that took decades to build, and that rested on centuries of colonialism, would not be eradicated in a few months or even years. Mandela's life stands as a testament to the enduring value of patience.

The applications of patience are endless, from handling daily irritations to soothing the agitation of a fast-paced life, from processing grief, anger, and despair over our world to sustaining an engaged response against powerful odds. As a new (and older) parent, tired and achy, I call on patience daily. I practice patience with my exasperation as our son thrashes in bed at 2:00 a.m. I practice patience, breathing deeply, as my wife and I muddle through another tiff. And in my many moments of impatience, I practice patience with my own limitations, calling forth self-compassion and forgiveness.

To establish a foundation of patience, I encourage you to start with the inevitable, smaller difficulties of being alive. Begin by investigating how you relate when you experience a benign irritant. Choose something unpleasant that is neither harmful nor urgent—for example, an annoying sound, an unpleasant odor, an itching sensation. Notice any reactivity in your heart, bringing your focus right to the point of contact where the external object (an image, sound, odor, or taste, for example) touches your sensory awareness. Can you breathe right there, bearing with any tension, tightness, or contraction? The word *patience* comes from the Latin *patientia*, meaning "suffering." Patience creates space to understand suffering: witness how resisting your direct experience creates struggle. Hold your attention at the point of contact, softening and widening, until the heart concedes its argument with reality. Notice the relief of letting go, even a little. Once the wave of reactivity has softened, you can attend to the unpleasant circumstance with more clarity, choosing if or how to engage. Do you act? Make a request? Exit gracefully? Let go?

Thus, in contemplative practice, patience relinquishes clinging and resistance, reclaiming wasted energy. This inner surrender at the core of patience is not a collapse or defeat; it is a merging with the flow of life. Instead of suppressing your life energy, a few moments of patience can create the space to bear with the internal pressure of a reaction and offer the freedom to choose your response. Over time, patience wears away the chains of reactivity until—like a ship cut loose from its mooring—it releases us, free to sail in the direction of our choosing.

In a moment of greater tension or reactivity, if you feel unsettled or disturbed, soothe and regulate your nervous system. Modulate your breathing, shift your attention to something more neutral, do a visualization or a silent mantra. Then return to applying patience to the discomfort.

Contemplating an image can offer inspiration to patience. Where I live in Northern California, a few stands of old-growth redwoods remain, some more than three thousand years old (thanks to the resolute and patient work of many conservationists and activists). These living, breathing giants exude a stable, grounded presence. You can learn to embody this steady, quiet strength of patience by spending time with any tree—an oak, maple, or pine in your neighborhood will do just fine. Trees teach us the immense strength of a slower pace. As the Buddhist monastic Thanissarro

Bhikkhu teaches, "Good things always take time. The trees with the most solid heartwood are the ones that take the longest to grow."[5]

A greater challenge to our patience comes when we are wronged, harmed, or insulted by others. Here again, patience does not encourage us to be silent or ignore our needs but rather to respond from wisdom and compassion rather than reactivity. One Buddhist text sees patience as the shore of a great lake, encompassing the forces of hatred and anger. Just as the shore surrounds the water, patience holds the tumult of our hatred in a wide, open embrace. With patience, we are not rattled. It provides a steady container whether the lake is calm like glass or stormy with waves.

This kind of patience opens a space of great possibility. As King famously wrote, "Somehow we must be able to stand up before our most bitter opponents and say: 'We shall match your capacity to inflict suffering by our capacity to endure suffering. We will meet your physical force with soul force. Do to us what you will, and we shall continue to love you.'"[6] When married with resolve, wisdom, and love, patience lifts us to the heights of the human spirit.

Surviving chronically difficult situations—unhealthy relationships, ongoing health conditions, the dynamics of oppression—relies on the endurance of patience. Build your foundation on the moment-to-moment level of feelings and sensations, while challenging the mind's tendency to project into the future with thoughts such as "This will never end." Patience allows us to tolerate fear, sadness, and despair and recall a broader perspective: "This too shall pass. I have borne this before and can do so again." Recollecting our empowerment can dislodge the stuck places we hit in long-term challenges. Though the future is always unknown, we do have the ability to shape it in meaningful ways with our present actions.

Healing and transformation—of the heart and our world—are

a marathon, not a sprint. They demand we dig deep and persevere. Without patience, we falter, forget, or grow disheartened. It takes patience to begin again over and over, coming back with love and resolve, with interest and forgiveness. Persevering patience allows us to bear with the heaviness of setbacks, to drain away the agitation of impatience, and to wither the harshness of self-judgment. It opens the heart's capacity to give ourselves to the journey. The richer our patience, the more joy we can take in the process, knowing every step brings us closer to the goal inside and out.

REFLECTION

Getting Started

What assumptions do you have about patience? Do you associate patience with weakness, passivity, or detachment? Can you imagine an experience of patience that feels open and spacious, that dissolves agitation and resistance while including all of life? Explore the idea of moving through life with even a small measure of this kind of patience. Consider times when you contract, resist the flow of experience, or rush. Investigate the times you compulsively resist something unpleasant or cling to something pleasant. What happens when you soften that inner tension and open to the complexity of your experience?

MEDITATION

Going Deeper

Find a quiet place and connect your mind and body through breathing naturally. Invite patience with the rhythm of your breathing, taking all the time you need for each in-breath and each out-breath. In your own time, choose an image that represents patience for you: an immense mountain, the vast earth, a great lake, an ancient tree—any image that evokes the steady, enduring presence of patience. Let the image become clear in your mind's eye, picturing it in front of you. You might try saying silently to yourself a simple phrase, like "infinite patience" or "boundless patience." As you regard the image (or say that phrase), notice the effect on your mind and body. Allow this visualization to linger with you. When you're ready, let the image dissolve, but stay with the presence, spaciousness, and depth of patience. Let its effects nourish you. Notice the sounds, sensations, thoughts, or feelings that are present. Allow things to arise, be known, and pass away without resistance.

ACTION
Embodying Patience

In the flow of your daily life, observe how the concept of linear time feeds impatience while presence opens the door to patience. Pay attention to when you are fixating on deadlines, schedules, or linear progress. Notice the effect of rushing on your mind and body. Take a short pause. Use the pace and depth of your breathing to relax any sense of straining against the clock. "Rushing" is a way of trying to arrive at a point in the future, while "moving quickly" can be done with full presence and relaxation now. See if you can shift from rushing to moving quickly.

Notice when you jump from one task or project to another without awareness or reflection. When you finish a task, do you feel a sense of completion, or does your goal keep receding to a new point in the future? Experiment with allowing yourself to pause between activities, taking a few moments to feel any sense of completion that comes from truly finishing one thing before you begin the next. Invite this spaciousness into your relationships and conversations, patiently giving others your full attention in a conversation. In work for social transformation, create space to pause with colleagues and appreciate any progress or results from your efforts. Notice the effect of taking time to celebrate along the long road to freedom.

IF YOU HAVE DIFFICULTIES

Self-judgment, striving, and inaction often trip us up in practicing patience. Try not to hold yourself to unreasonable standards. Remember that we're all works in progress, and that it will take time to unlearn the impatience we've cultivated. Bring a spirit of kindness, self-compassion, and play to your self-exploration. If you find yourself becoming rigid, forcing yourself to be patient, or contracting inside, remember to breathe. Try directing your attention to an easeful place before turning to a difficult or unpleasant challenge, and then slowly moving back and forth between the two. When exploring patience, work right at the edge of contact between your awareness and the resistance, breathing, softening, and widening your attention to include what's happening, rather than trying to stop it or make it go away. Finally, if in the name of patience you find yourself allowing others to take advantage of you, remind yourself that patience is not the same as passivity or inaction. It transforms our relationship with life so that we can make conscious choices instead of reacting. Lean on your aspiration, energy, and courage to stir you to act.

13. EQUANIMITY

You may not control all the events that happen to you, but you can decide not to be reduced by them.
—Maya Angelou

When I was growing up, on Saturday mornings my dad and I used to watched cartoons together in bed. I helped him with projects around the house whenever I could: building garden beds, cutting the grass. His smoking habit cast a shadow over these moments, and I begged him to stop. One year, he finally promised to quit for my birthday. Not understanding addiction, I was heartbroken when I discovered him smoking again. He eventually kicked the habit, but my heartbreak continued as he struggled to care for his health in other ways.

I felt angry, helpless, and disappointed in the face of this. I oscillated between a resigned indifference and idealistic attempts to help, before discovering a more balanced attitude. I never stopped caring for my father and did my best to accept the limits of my influence over him. The more I could accept his choices, the more I could love him for who he was, rather than for who I wanted him to be. Only when my father suddenly passed away did I see how much I still had been resisting my pain and helplessness, recoiling from his choices and withholding some of my love for him. We can't fake equanimity or skip the hard road leading to it, but we can grow in wisdom, learn to let go of things we can't control, and thereby find balance.

Our hearts can feel so much: from exquisite sweetness to the most devastating anguish. Equanimity helps us navigate this expanse without losing our bearings. Born of wisdom, equanimity is a resilient, nonreactive inner balance that lives in our bones as a felt understanding. We find it in the knowing gaze of the elder who's seen it all and doesn't lose perspective when tragedy strikes or windfalls occur. A subtle and often misunderstood capacity, equanimity offers us the space to feel all of life fully without drowning. It steadies us in the face of change and supports a clear, empowered, and sustainable response to injustice.

We have an innate capacity for equanimity. We begin developing it when we are born and meet the harsh reality of a sensory world of pleasure and pain beyond our control. Caring for our son, I've been amazed at how utterly raw and vulnerable we all are when we arrive. As newborns, our unadulterated reflexes are viscerally obvious: wailing when uncomfortable, hungry, or tired, smiling and cooing when content. As we grow, our senses adapt, our understanding matures, and so our resilience increases. With support, we handle challenges with grace: the flat tire, unexpected bill, or canceled plan doesn't faze us. We might feel annoyed, worried, or disappointed, but we don't lose perspective—today's worry becomes tomorrow's memory.

Equanimity connects intimately with life. Its steadiness comes not from cutting ourselves off, but from having the perspective to see a bigger picture, enough space to include all that we experience.

The Buddha pointed to eight conditions blowing through our lives like winds: pleasure and pain, gain and loss, praise and blame, fame and disrepute. Experiencing only the pleasant side is as impossible as breathing in without breathing out. Contrary to the messages we get from culture, our hardships are not personal failures. A wise heart knows the truth: conditions change without end. The more deeply we understand this, the less agitated we grow when things fall apart or change unexpectedly. We discover instead a spacious and grounded openness. Equanimity steadies us like the keel of a ship at sea.[1] Storms may shake us, but we don't capsize.

The more we develop equanimity with small things, the more our capacity for balance grows into a profound nonreactivity—a vital, dynamic poise. The civil rights activist David Hartsough, threatened at a lunch-counter sit-in in 1960 by another white man holding a knife to his heart, drew on his training and his deep faith in Jesus's instruction to "love your enemies." Though a moment of doubt flashed through his awareness, he reacted neither to the external danger nor the internal fear, instead performing a remarkable feat of nonviolence. "I turned around and tried to smile," he writes. "Looking him in the eye, I said to him, 'Friend, do what you believe is right, and I will still try to love you.'"[2] The other man's mouth and hand dropped, he turned away, and left.

Hartsough's response was creative and intentional, and it resulted from long-standing commitment to and training in nonviolence and equanimity. Equanimity operates at two levels: the momentary level of our internal experience of pleasure and pain, and the larger level of our external circumstances, relationships, and social conditions. Buddhist equanimity training begins at this granular, moment-to-moment level, where pleasure and pain may consume the mind.

The Buddha taught that, at the moment of contact between awareness and any sensory or mental experience, a particular "flavor" or "feeling tone" of pleasant, unpleasant, or neutral arises. We habitually react to this flavor. Look closely and you may notice how quickly you latch on to anything pleasant, wanting more; how you resist anything unpleasant, trying to make it stop; and how you ignore anything neutral, growing bored or distracted.

Equanimity attends carefully to that moment of contact, interrupting reactivity. In the Sallatha Sutta, the Buddha likened unpleasant sensations to being shot with an arrow, affirming we all experience this *first arrow*. The untrained mind reacts, resisting or becoming consumed with irritation, anger, sorrow, or self-pity. We thus shoot ourselves with a *second arrow*. We make uncomfortable experiences worse by adding unpleasant reactions, arrow after arrow.[3] Understanding the nature of the first arrow, equanimity lays down the quiver.

During one meditation period, I grew tense with knee pain. I was anxious for relief, waiting for the bell, as the ache increased and waves of resistance washed through me. Mindfully observing, I noticed the difference between the first and second arrows—between the discomfort in my knee and the contraction throughout the rest of my mind and body. All of a sudden, I understood both the nature of the aching sensation and the futility of reacting. The pain was temporary: when I moved or the bell rang, it would end. With this understanding, the resistance dissolved completely. My knee still hurt, but my heart was still. (Here too was the wisdom of the Four Noble Truths: with the cessation of resistance, suffering ends.)

This little example can teach us important lessons. Equanimity grows at the edge of our capacity to bear with reactivity. We develop inner balance by tolerating what throws us off—be it an unpleasant sensation, an irritating coworker, or an unjust event. We witness directly the suffering of struggling with our direct experience. The more we resist, the more it hurts, until the heart surrenders. When we finally understand and acknowledge the truth—*that this is how it is right now*—our capacity for balance grows. When we are mindful of reactivity, it becomes the grain of sand that forms a pearl of equanimity.

Of course, I could have chosen to shift my meditation posture. What happens when we *don't* have a choice? How does equanimity function with chronic pain or illness? What can equanimity offer a single mother who can't afford to lose her job, and so feels unable to report inappropriate advances from her boss? How does equanimity help someone from a historically marginalized community who feels unsafe responding to a racist comment on public transit? Importantly, for those who experience ongoing discrimination, whether or not an external threat is objectively present, its pervasive possibility may be enough to function as a psychological or emotional constraint. The persistent *likelihood* of discrimination—for those who have long felt it—can challenge equanimity.

It's easy to get the mistaken notion that equanimity encourages indifference. But equanimity is distinct from passivity, collusion with harm, or consent to oppression. Rather than inhibiting action, equanimity informs a wise response. It saves us from denial and engages the painful realities of our lives, personally and collectively. Equanimity recognizes: "Right now, this is the world I live in." Engaging what is, the heart opens. For balance doesn't come from suppressing our feelings, detaching from the world, or passively accepting harmful conditions. Indifference and apathy may appear cool and even-minded on the surface, but they only mimic equanimity. Equanimity encompasses our *internal relationship to what is actually occurring*, rather than a blanket approval of external conditions. This inner balance (a synonym for equanimity) includes our feelings, senses our boundaries, and has the capacity for decisive action.

In the face of injustice, equanimity honors the full range of our emotions: helplessness and dignity, anger and comprehension, shame and hope. Accepting the complexity of our inner life provides the breathing room to act clearly in our outer life. As the psychotherapist and Holocaust survivor Viktor Frankl wrote, everything can be taken from us "but one thing: the last of the human freedoms—to choose one's attitude in any given set of circumstances, to choose one's own way."[4] Equanimity arises from wisdom, from knowing what we can and cannot change, and helps us understand that we create the future through our present actions.[5] It also draws upon the compassion that urges us diligently to transform harmful conditions like depression, conflict, marginalized work, poverty, hunger, oppression, and abuse.

In this way, equanimity sustains our work for change in the world. It helps us commit to our vision of a healthy, equitable future while letting go of controlling the unfolding of life. I meet many activists who are exhausted and disillusioned. If the uphill societal battle to achieve concrete, systemic change hasn't worn them down, the closer-to-home internal politics of antagonism, bitterness, and cancel culture has left them feeling battered. Equanimity protects the heart from burnout, embodying the age-old wisdom of total effort toward a goal without attachment to the results. We know the results of our actions are in many ways beyond our control. As Vandana Shiva once told an interviewer, "The context is not in your control, but your commitment is yours to make, and you can make the deepest commitment with a total detachment about where it will take you. You want it to lead to a better world, and you shape your actions and take full responsibility for them, but then you have detachment."[6]

On a larger scale, equanimity brings the composure, poise, and stability necessary to fierce truth-telling. After the home of a local Black attorney was bombed in 1960 during the campaign to desegregate Nashville's lunch counters, thousands marched to city hall. Surrounded by the crowd, a heated exchange ensued between the city's white mayor, Ben West, and a young Black minister, C. T. Vivian—until the Black student activist Diane Nash intervened. Clear and collected, she challenged Mayor West: "Do you feel that it's wrong to discriminate against a person solely on the basis of his race or color?" West prided himself on his principles and admitted he "could not agree that it was morally right to sell someone merchandise and refuse them service." Nash then asked if West thought the lunch counters should be desegregated. West waffled, but she pressed him: "Then, Mayor, do you recommend that the lunch counters be desegregated?" In a shocking concession, West broke with the conventions of his time and admitted "yes." The crowd erupted in applause, celebrating a key victory in desegregating the city.[7]

The latest report from the International Panel on Climate Change (IPCC) warns that we only have until 2030 to make radical reductions to greenhouse gas emissions to avoid catastrophic climate change. (Note that the IPCC assessment is widely viewed as *optimistic*.) The suffering and devastation we already see from climate change are immense, but this pales in comparison to what could unfold. How can we find balance in the face of this existential threat to our biosphere?

We must dig deep. We might think nothing could prepare us for this unknown, yet, also, every challenge we've ever faced has prepared us for it. Equanimity will not shield us from the pain of loss, but it can help us open our hearts to see beyond our lifetimes. Our individual time here is so fleeting. Decades pass like dreams. Integrity demands we value the needs of future generations—human and nonhuman—in our choices. Holding this perspective, we may find gratitude for the wondrous gift of living on this planet, compassion for the hubris and ignorance of our species, and tenderness for the suffering unfolding through climate disruption. Equanimity helps us accept both the known present and the unknown future. We need all of the other qualities we are cultivating (and more) to meet this peril—from courage to compassion, from joy to forgiveness.[8] We need the strength of our ancestors, a connection to future generations, and our deep love for one another and this planet. With steady hearts and clear eyes, we do all we can and then we let go. The destination may be beyond us, but the journey is ours.

REFLECTION

Getting Started

Bring your attention to a neutral sensation in your body—for example, a tingling or sensitivity in your hand. Notice how it is to feel this sensation without resisting it or getting lost in it. Now bring your attention to a pleasant sensation in your body (a relaxed arm, warmth or coolness somewhere). Notice any tendency to lean into the pleasure or want more. Can you return to a balanced awareness of what is pleasant? Repeat the same exercise with something unpleasant, noticing any resistance or contraction. Can you find a place of nonreactive, balanced awareness with this sensation?[9]

Apply this exploration to the events of your life. Imagine an unpleasant or irritating situation—running late, having a meeting be inconveniently canceled, spilling coffee on your favorite outfit. Witness any feelings and reactions that come up. Steady your awareness until the reverberations settle. Notice the quality of balance and acceptance that remains. Repeat the reflection with something pleasant—an award or recognition at work, a wonderful gift, a perfect date. Again, witness feelings and reactions that arise, letting any excitement flow through you. Notice the space and balance that remain within when it all passes.[10]

MEDITATION

Going Deeper

Settle your mind and body in a comfortable, upright posture. Bring to mind an image that embodies or represents the depth, wisdom, and spaciousness of equanimity: a massive mountain, the view of our planet from space, a great river, the open sky, the knowledge of your ancestors gazing lovingly upon you, or any other image meaningful to you. See this as clearly and vividly as possible. (If you have trouble visualizing, imagine being there; *feel* what it's like to be on that mountain, near that river, or whatever image you choose.) As you visualize, notice any sense of balance, depth, or perspective the image calls forth. Notice where and how you experience this on the level of sensation, in your body, allowing it to grow. When you are ready, call to mind a situation, person, or circumstance for which you'd like to have more equanimity. (Recall the training principle to start small, taking care not to choose the most challenging thing first.) Evoking the situation, keep coming back to the felt sense of perspective and balance instilled by the image of equanimity. With its support, you can silently repeat a phrase that captures the essence of equanimity's wisdom. Some possibilities include the following:

- This is how it is for me right now.
- May I be at peace with things just as they are.
- Everyone has their own path.
- I care about you and know you must make your own choices.

ACTION
Embodying Equanimity

Throughout the day, notice ups and downs of pleasant and unpleasant experiences, your mood, internal states, events and conditions around you. Keep coming back to a wise and balanced perspective, recognizing that change is natural. Pay attention to the flow of gain and loss, praise and blame, fame and disrepute. Notice when you shoot a second arrow—chasing pleasure or resisting pain. Can you bring even the smallest measure of equanimity and acceptance to this reactivity? Use this as an opportunity to grow in equanimity: pause, breathe, and bring your attention to the inner tension and agitation of reactivity. How does it feel to pursue or try to control pleasant things? How does it feel to avoid, resist, or try to eliminate unpleasant ones? Allow your heart the space to feel what is real, bringing patience and acceptance to whatever you experience. Note any observations, insights, or experiences in your practice journal.

IF YOU HAVE DIFFICULTIES

Just as we grow in patience by learning to be with impatience, recall that we mature in equanimity through learning to be with reactivity. Equanimity ripens slowly, at the edges of our reactivity rather than in the throes of a meltdown. Recollect the fundamental, trauma-informed principle of starting small. Attend to minor annoyances and breathe patiently. Notice any grasping after mild pleasure and practice letting both the pleasure and the grasping sensations flow through you.

If you find yourself stuck in reactivity, find ways to step back from its intensity. Lean into external resources such as friends, art, music, or nature to get perspective; lean into community especially if you are reacting to social inequity. Next, allow yourself to feel a small amount of your reactivity for a moment or two, then shift your attention back to something neutral or grounding. Move back and forth like this between resource and reactivity. As you feel able, make space for your feelings, remembering that all emotions are natural and temporary.

PART THREE

So far we have focused on the internal cultivation of qualities and have also explored how those around us help us learn to embody them. As we begin the third leg of our journey, I'd like to consider more directly the central role that friendship plays in growing these beautiful qualities in our relationships and our society.

Have you ever felt inspired to give by witnessing another's generosity? Have you ever called forth courage seeing another's strength? Or found greater kindness after feeling another's goodness? Those we spend time with shape us. Being with people who speak or behave in certain ways, we may find ourselves slowly drawn to those behaviors. Habits create a subtle, gravitational pull that affects others. This malleability can be an asset or a liability, depending on whom we associate with.

For this reason, the Buddha repeatedly emphasized the central role of friendship and community in his teachings. He once even remarked that "good friendship" constituted *the entire spiritual path*.[1] Time and again, recounting the many steps leading to awakening, the Buddha traced them back to the same initial cause: being with wise companions.[2] Spending time with decent folks, we observe, learn, and emulate their good qualities.

Friendship plays an important role in activism. The sociologist Doug McAdam has shown how building relationships can lead to high-risk, high-cost activism. His analysis of the 1964 Freedom Summer determined that committing to the movement followed from having strong ties with others already involved, and he traced those ties back to initial involvement in lower-risk, lower-cost campaigns.[3] Who we spend time with matters not just individually, but collectively.

Growing deep friendships is neither fast nor easy. To have our needs met, we must first reveal them: allowing ourselves to be vulnerable and to be seen. Inevitably, we hurt one another or let each other down. True friendship does not grow from being perfect, but from trusting that we can reconnect and repair things we've messed up. Learning the value of real friends, we cherish them.

The more diverse our friendships, the richer our lives and learning. We find comfort and reassurance in a close-knit circle of like-minded friends, drawing strength and reassurance from those with whom we share views, values, and life experiences. Such friends can nourish our belonging and bolster our sense of mattering. But wisdom guides us to use such friendships as a secure home base to support venturing into spaces and relationships of real difference. In this, we break our bubbles and escape our echo chambers.

Our lives are increasingly isolated, even as we depend on a vast web of fellow beings for our basic needs. Loneliness hurts, and its roots go deep: children interacting with screens don't learn essential social skills like empathy and conflict resolution. How are we to engage these teachings on the qualities that nourish and awaken us amid such impoverishment of community life? With creativity and inspiration, we can make new connections. Service creates opportunities to meaningfully engage with others. Online spaces offer valuable ways of building relationship with people around the world.

The Buddha's words on friendship point to deeper connections: friendship is also a way of relating. We can befriend ourselves, and all that is within our hearts: including our pain, our anger, even our loneliness. In learning to be good friends to ourselves, we grow our capacity to befriend others, including those we have never met. Ritual, research, and reflection open pathways to connect to ancestors we never knew.[4] Time spent with particular landscapes and ecosystems can build relationships rich in companionship, extending beyond the human.

As you make your way through part 3, notice the places where your relationships have taught you important lessons about the qualities. Draw on the support of those close to you, and choose wisely the people with whom you share your precious time.

14. EMPATHY

The only way to survive is by taking care of one another.
—Grace Lee Boggs

When I was practicing Buddhism intensively in Asia in my early twenties, years of repressed anger and pain from the chaos of mental illness in my family tore through my heart. Even sitting quietly, voices of rage and violent images gripped me. The staff guiding my practice were not trained to respond to such intense emotion, and I eventually became overwhelmed and dysregulated (crying on the floor of the shower, as I mentioned in chapter 3). I was deeply fortunate to make a friend who invited me over, offered tea, and listened. His empathy helped me to realize I needed more support. With a mixture of relief and defeat, I booked a flight home.

Seeing the suffering and violence in our world, we need empathy at every turn, on every issue. In response to the pain and desperation of those people—nearly always men—responsible for mass shootings; the grinding effects of poverty, racism, and other forms of oppression; and the cruel impact of human activity (including factory farming, deforestation, habitat destruction, ocean warming, and acidification) on nonhuman species, empathy brings home the suffering of others. It fosters healing and helps spark our capacity for compassionate action.

Empathy opens our hearts to one another. It heals the pain of isolation, gathering us back into the human family just as we are—with our fear, shame, and woundedness; our anger, confusion, and despair. Empathy bridges the divides of racial, ethnic, national, political, and other affiliations. And being innate to all social animals, it unites human and nonhuman species, breaking down the barriers we create between ourselves and the rest of life on the planet. In the early 1980s, a chimpanzee named Washoe, who had learned some American Sign Language from her trainers, displayed touching empathy toward one of her caregivers, Kat Beech, who had just had a miscarriage. Washoe had lost two babies of her own, and learning of Kat's loss, she signed the word for "cry." As Kat was leaving that day, Washoe caught her attention, signed "Please person hug," and embraced her.

Our hearts feel. We vibrate in harmony with others. Babies begin crying when nearby babies cry. Mirror neurons in our brains echo others' physical movements and emotional expressions. Empathy and connection soothe the nervous system through coregulation when we attune to what's alive in others. When equanimity protects us from being overwhelmed, we can connect with the full range of one another's emotions: joy, sorrow, ecstasy, and anguish. Success and happiness are sweeter when shared, just as pain and hardship are softened by companionship.

As a fundamental capacity of the heart, empathy gives birth to a host of other potent healing qualities. Appreciating connection, empathy begets generosity. Attuning to goodness, empathy blossoms in kindness. Knowing harm, empathy feeds our integrity and serves to guard our body, speech, and mind. Orienting to the success and happiness of others, empathy nourishes celebration. Witnessing loss and sorrow, empathy opens into compassion.[1] Understanding regret, empathy helps us forgive.

Empathy begins with inner resonance and develops into understanding. Empathy heals us: when our hearts break, empathic connection eases our pain. One moment of true empathy may offer years of reassurance, comfort, and strength. The memory of my friend in India pouring tea and listening helped me through many difficult months upon returning home. Conversely, our empathy for others releases us from self-centeredness and expands our capacity for emotional care.

Empathy begins early in life, through mirroring and healthy attachment between caregiver and infant.[2] It develops through social learning, becoming a key aspect of our emotional intelligence. Even as adults, we can enhance empathy and increase attachment through friendship, therapy, emotional intelligence training, and what psychologists call "corrective experiences." In fact, research shows that empathy between client and therapist is the primary indicator of positive therapeutic outcomes.[3] Connection heals.

Many of us—particularly (although not exclusively) people socialized as women—face the challenge not of cultivating empathy but balancing it. We may have been trained to take care of others at our expense, even to feel so much empathy that we over-identify with others' emotions, disregarding our own feelings. While empathy dissolves barriers between self and other, crucially, it also includes empathy for ourselves, honoring our own needs and boundaries so we don't become flooded with another's emotions.

Empathy allows us to be side by side with others' experience, maintaining both our own and their autonomy. If you sometimes become dysregulated by empathy, balance it with healthy differentiation. Explore somatic exercises that heighten your awareness of your body's physical boundaries; reflect on perspectives that reinforce your sovereignty; investigate your emotional wounds and limiting beliefs that cause you to seek safety, love, or belonging through caretaking.[4]

As you strengthen and balance your capacity for external empathy, you can also turn this quality inward with self-empathy. Self-empathy brings love and understanding to your heart. When we are well, self-empathy appreciates happiness, savors joy, and deepens gratitude. When we struggle, it nourishes tenderness and self-compassion. Throughout, it brings warm, caring awareness to your emotions and needs. Yet we live in a world often devoid of true empathy. How often do you feel fully seen, understood, and accepted? Our economy pits us against each other, and the dominant social narrative fetishizes individualism, further isolating us from one another. Empathy allows us to stand in each other's shoes. How would our political and social landscape shift if we had more empathy for those of other classes, races, and political affiliations?[5]

Empathy offers a radical approach to relationship- and movement-building, with immense potential for collaboration despite our multiple, intersecting crises. Tragically, even activists who greatly value inclusion sometimes dehumanize those with opposing views, through shaming, cancel culture, and binary "us-them" narratives. In an effort to champion a cause, such dynamics echo the very dominating systems they seek to transform. Empathy offers another way forward, shifting the focus to our shared humanity. Sensing shared feelings and underlying needs, it sees beyond surface differences into the core of our hearts. It honors others' experiences without necessarily agreeing with their views or condoning their actions.[6]

In this way, empathy sits at the heart of nonviolence, refusing to hate the oppressor but rather seeking to see their humanity and to embody the vision of Beloved Community. We can strongly oppose another's actions or neutralize their influence without losing touch with their potential for goodness and their place in the human family. Again, Gandhi's empathy for the plight of English mill workers offers a cogent example (see chapter 7). His friendliness and empathy disarmed them. They, in turn, began to understand that their economic challenges paled in comparison to the abject poverty of Indians suffering under the Raj. Empathy won many of them over to Gandhi's cause.

Mindfulness, curiosity, courage, and wise attention all support empathy, opening our eyes to the lives of others. Though we have evolutionary tendencies toward in-group bias, these qualities help us unlearn the habit of "othering." As we nourish empathy, it grows to its full potential. Throughout modern history, dialogue and relationship-building projects across ethnic and political lines have worked to bridge differences with empathy: from Israel-Palestine to Bosnia-Herzegovina, from the Rwandan genocide to gang violence. Dialogue at the personal level then opens the door to more powerful, collaborative struggle for structural change. In Nigeria, the American psychologist Marshall B. Rosenberg, founder of Nonviolent Communication, had success mediating a conflict between Muslim and Christian tribes that had killed nearly a quarter of the area's population. Believing firmly that all violence is an expression of unmet needs, Rosenberg offered empathy to both sides, receiving their pain and rage and helping them hear one another's needs. Within two hours, one of the chiefs exclaimed, "If we know how to communicate this way, we don't have to kill each other!"[7]

Empathy reweaves connections among the human family, restoring our sense of belonging after profound dislocation. Around the United States, organizations like the Ahimsa Collective hold restorative dialogues (sometimes referred to as Victim-Offender Dialogues). In these processes, facilitators might spend months preparing participants to offer and receive one another's stories— sometimes between an incarcerated person serving a life sentence for murder and the family members of the person who was killed. One sibling reflects, "I saw his side of life and better understand the reasons why this man was filled with rage and anger when he killed my brother. But most importantly I was able to release my feelings and allow him to release his. When our meeting ended, we both felt overwhelmed with a true peace and goodwill toward one another."[8] Healing conversations like this explode our assumptions about the limits of empathy and forgiveness, and they reveal the radical potential of restorative practices to transform our justice system.

What kind of world could we create if empathy were woven into the fabric of our society and the core curricula of our schools? How would our justice system, immigration policy, and policing look if restructured with empathy as a core value and guiding principle? How would an economy built on empathy function? How could we redirect international resources currently spent on war if empathy were our guide?

REFLECTION

Getting Started

Reflect on a time when someone showed you empathy, listened with heartfelt presence, offered a caring remark or tender gaze. If nothing comes to mind, *imagine* someone showing empathy in this way. Make this recollection or imagination as clear and detailed as you can. Imprint this connection on your heart by noticing the feelings and sensations arising within you. Now think of a time when you *wish* someone had showed you empathy. Allow yourself to imagine the other person responding with care and understanding. Let yourself be nourished by this.

MEDITATION

Going Deeper

Find a comfortable posture and let yourself become still and quiet. Anchor your attention with your breath or a neutral sensation such as your hands in your lap. Bring to mind something emotionally pleasant or unpleasant from the last few weeks. (If choosing something unpleasant, start small to avoid getting flooded.) Let the event or circumstance come to life, staying loosely connected to your anchor. Regard thoughts, feelings, and sensations with a kind and understanding gaze, as you would for a good friend. Silently name any emotions, bringing tenderness to sensations, images, and feelings. Recall that they are natural, universal human experiences. Now listen for what is important to you in this recollection. What did you need then? What matters to you now? Can you bring tenderness to the needs in your heart?

ACTION

Embodying Empathy

Set an intention to listen with empathy during an interaction. It could be your first or last of the day, in person, on the phone, or by video. Open your heart to this person, sensing the feelings and needs beneath their words and actions. What emotions do they feel? What matters to them? Allow genuine curiosity to guide you. Respond authentically, showing empathy in whatever way feels natural. If you are already skilled in empathy, try stretching your capacity by listening to someone with whom you strongly disagree. Can you connect with the universal feelings and needs beneath their views and opinions?

In addition to practicing empathy for another, consider asking someone to listen to *you* with empathy. Let them know you value them and that it would be meaningful to have them listen and show understanding of something you're going through. Check if they have the time, energy, and willingness to offer this kind of listening *before* you dive in. If they offer advice or respond in ways that are not helpful, thank them for their care and remind them that what you are asking for is just for them to listen and understand. Allow yourself to take in any nourishment or connection from the interaction.

IF YOU HAVE DIFFICULTIES

If you find it challenging to offer or receive empathy, take your time. Many of us have been trained to hide our feelings so we can protect ourselves or conform to expectations. It takes a combination of trust, safety, and courage to extend empathy or share vulnerability. There's no rush and no need to pour your heart out if you don't feel safe or ready. Remember that empathy doesn't need to be a grand emotion: it's the simple, direct connection we feel with another's experience. Notice the ways you naturally express empathy. Notice the ways others naturally do so and the ways you're able to take that in. Practice placing your attention on others' emotions, spoken or unspoken. Silently consider what they might need. What matters to them? What kind of world would we have if we all practiced this daily?

15. INTEGRITY

The idea that some lives matter less is the root of all that is wrong with the world. —Paul Farmer

During the height of the trans-Atlantic slave trade in the 1800s, two sisters from a slave-owning family in South Carolina began advocating for abolition and women's rights. Horrified by the brutality of slavery, Sarah Moore Grimké defied the law and taught the enslaved girl assigned to her personal care to read. She and her sister Angelina became two of the first American women to participate publicly in any social reform movement, as they leveraged their status to reach women around the country, arguing against slavery on both moral and religious grounds.[1] With aspiration, courageous energy, and resolve, Sarah and Angelina Grimké stood against the tide of their times and embodied integrity.

Integrity means living into the world as we long for it to exist. For decades in the United States, right up to and even during the Civil War, the idea of the abolition of slavery seemed distant if not impossible to most people. The integrity of the abolitionists—foremost, enslaved people themselves, and also white allies such as the Grimké sisters—was an act of remarkable aspiration, resolve, and ethical fortitude. (I will use the terms *integrity* and *ethics* synonymously here.)

Living with integrity uplifts our hearts and brings truth, beauty, and goodness to our lives. Widening the scope of contemplative practice to include how we live every day, we honor our dignity, offer others the gift of safety, and guide all to a more just and equitable society.

Ethics can be a charged topic. What do you associate with the following words? *Morality. Ethics. Integrity. Righteousness. Character. Discipline.* Do some hold connotations of fear, control, or repression? Many of us associate our early ethical training in our faith traditions with pain. How tragic that something so beautiful as the ethical sensitivity of our hearts becomes tarnished by experiences of coercion.

Integrity is not about repressing our impulses or following arbitrary rules; nor is it based on guilt or self-loathing. Instead, integrity is a natural expression of our love and a coherent movement toward happiness and collective liberation. Integrity aligns our conduct in the world with our values: firmly committing to refrain from causing harm, and generating the strength to swim against the forces of greed, hate, and delusion in our world. Living with integrity engenders trust, offering others the gift of fearlessness. Honesty and integrity are the bedrock of healthy relationships and are foundational tenets for a better society.

Two powerful complementary qualities animate a commitment to ethical integrity: conscience and concern.[2] Conscience turns our awareness inward with dignity. It gives our actions a moral compass. As we've explored, our actions leave imprints in our hearts: speaking harshly violates the heart; dishonesty separates us from the truth. Even if no one ever sees or learns of our unskillful actions, such actions injure us. What we know in our hearts matters; this is the gift of conscience. On the other hand, concern moves our awareness outward with compassion. Being alive, aware of the pain we each have encountered from hurtful words or acts, concern urges us to move through life with care.

Committing to integrity encompasses our entire life: livelihood, action, speech, even thoughts. Given the certainty that ignorance, greed, and animosity will challenge our integrity, religions contain ethical guidelines to help us. For example, lay Buddhist practitioners observe five precepts that guide our training: practicing refraining from killing other creatures, stealing, speaking falsely or harshly, causing harm sexually, and taking intoxicants that lead to carelessness. These guidelines ground a life of spiritual cultivation; they help us realize our potential, discover peace and happiness, and fully contribute our gifts to the world.[3]

Practicing with any set of ethical commitments marshals many skills. What does it take to abstain from harsh words, harmful actions, or hateful thoughts? We must be mindful, paying careful attention to our impulses. What forces push us to violate our ethical commitments? Among them are reactivity, self-centeredness, craving, resentment, jealousy, anger, cruelty, and fear. Integrity brings mindfulness to the forces that drive harm. We learn to *feel* our reactions, letting them flow through awareness without suppressing or acting on them. In doing so, we strengthen awareness, cause less harm, and respond to life more skillfully.

Integrity includes deep inquiry into the complexities of living in an interconnected world. Sometimes answering moral questions is simple: if we listen, we know what to do. Other times, moral questions require ongoing evaluation and keen awareness. How do we respond ethically to climate change when those who have done the least to contribute to the problem are often disproportionately impacted by it? What are the ethical and environmental impacts of our own lifestyle or food choices? Are we considering future generations or robbing them of resources? If we have more than we need, how do we deploy our privilege? Are we considering how monetary choices may fund unethical labor practices or environmental destruction? In our global economy, it's nearly impossible to avoid causing harm through our use of money. But our hearts feel that tension, just as they feel the quiet satisfaction that comes from using money to plant trees, fund local services, or invest in microloans.

Integrity expresses itself in service, in solidarity with marginalized populations, and in other ways of confronting injustice. If we have advantages in status, class, wealth, or education, how do we leverage them? For those of us who are white, how willing are we to persist in learning about the realities of white privilege? Long conversations with a friend who is a social justice organizer have forced me to see how easily I fall back into the comfort of my whiteness. Becoming aware of that, I am able to ask whose voice and experience I'm centering. Am I respecting the needs of the most vulnerable that have been historically ignored, erased, or discounted?

With power comes responsibility—and sometimes remorse. As a teacher, I have unintentionally caused harm through ignorance of internalized anti-Semitism, unconscious bias, and other forms of supremacy. A student once pointed out how my joking about Jewish culture as aggressive furthered dangerous stereotypes. Looking more carefully, I realized that my attempted humor came from my discomfort and rejection of aspects of my own identity.

We have all caused harm; we learn through acknowledging this. In my personal life I've suffered most when I've hurt those

I love. This weighs so heavily, with the searing pain of wanting—but not being able—to take back our actions. Do we have the humility to admit our moral failures, to see the gap between our self-image and our actions? When we fall short of our commitments, rather than berating ourselves, can we reflect and learn? Guilt is negative self-obsession. By contrast, remorse provides an opportunity to assess our actions and respond to our ethical violations. When we allow ourselves to feel remorse, we embody integrity and recommit to aligning our actions with our convictions and our heart's beauty.

Harm at any level hurts. When we don't heal the harm we've sustained, we risk passing it on to others. In some cases, this can even lead to abuse. Abuse—especially when committed by those who are supposed to love and protect us—tears relationships apart and shakes us to the core. With great sadness, I have met countless practitioners struggling to restore their faith in spirituality after experiencing harm by a spiritual leader—verbal, emotional, financial, or sexual.

Harm calls for repair. In response, integrity holds us accountable as we take responsibility and seek to make amends, asking what others need and seeking restitution, forgiveness, and reconciliation. Integrity acts collectively just as much as interpersonally. In the United States we grapple with a history of land theft, enslavement, and racism foundational to our nation. Are we listening to the needs and requests of Indigenous-led and Black-led movements for social change? How can we repair broken relationships? Local communities are leading the way. In 2015, the Chicago City Council passed landmark legislation providing reparations to survivors of police torture.[4] In 2021, the city of Evanston, Illinois, passed the first tax-funded reparations bill in the United States for residents of African descent. In recent years, land has been returned to Indigenous peoples, including 465 acres of sacred Rappahannock land in Virginia, and 9,243 acres of ancestral land to the Colville Tribe in Washington.[5]

Living aligned with our values brings freedom from remorse, deep satisfaction, and wholeness. Refraining from harm, we nourish dignity and self-respect. When our minds are not fragmented by deceit or tormented by remorse, we settle and feel glad. If you attend to integrity, a subtle happiness is born, a quiet joy that uplifts your heart-mind and fills your body. Do you appreciate your own goodness? When was the last time you saw yourself in the mirror and smiled? To smile in this way doesn't mean ignoring your shortcomings, it means appreciating your heart and honoring your innate goodness as you negotiate the complexity of life.

Integrity also confers the strength to withstand immense pressure without being compromised. Examples of steadfast integrity—like that of the Grimké sisters—can inspire in us the courage, energy, and resolve to change our world. Nearly a century after the Civil War, Fannie Lou Hamer rose from picking cotton in poverty to advocate tirelessly for voting rights and equality throughout the southern United States. Despite monumental challenges, including being barred from the ballot and brutally beaten by Mississippi police, Hamer persisted, firmly rooted in the integrity of her efforts. In 1964, she helped organize the historic Freedom Summer and cofounded the Mississippi Freedom Democratic Party, which challenged the local Democratic Party's efforts to block Black participation. Hamer also went on to help found the National Women's Political Caucus, and she spearheaded a range of innovative economic programs including a livestock bank, land cooperatives, and low-income housing.

The Buddhist monk Maha Ghosananda was a force for peace, nonviolence, and reconciliation during and after more than twenty years of invasion, war, genocide, and bombing in his homeland of Cambodia. Amid this intense violence, he led peace walks. Speaking on International Peace Day in 1995, alluding to the horror that more than ten million land mines had been set in Cambodia, he called on his audience to recognize the inviolable connection between the inner and the outer: "We must remove the land mines in our hearts which prevent us from making peace. The land mines in the heart are greed, hatred, and delusion. We can overcome greed with the weapon of generosity; we can overcome hatred with the weapon of loving kindness; we can overcome delusion with the weapon of wisdom."[6]

When we investigate closely, doing what's ethical may not be easy, but feels better than causing harm. We experience the power of right living in our nervous systems, sensing the effects of our actions in our own hearts. Look carefully. Causing harm arises from clinging, reactivity, or self-centeredness. Integrity arises from love, asking only that we let go of what ails us. Our present world and the world we leave for our children are the result of our actions. What is our moral obligation to future generations? Our commitment to integrity forms the foundation for the transformation of our hearts and our world, for them.

REFLECTION
Getting Started

Deepen your commitment to integrity by reflecting on the results of your actions. Recall a time when your words or actions had a relatively small but negative impact on someone. (As always, start with an example that feels manageable.) Open to your feelings, from guilt to shame, anger, defensiveness, or remorse. Notice any residue your action leaves in your heart and mind. If self-judgment stimulates guilt or shame, recall that we all make mistakes. It's not about being perfect; give yourself the grace to recognize that you were doing the best you could at the time with the resources you had. Try to connect with the sincere remorse beneath your judgments, the feeling of pain rooted in care. Let your heart grieve the impact of your action. Finally, renew your commitment to living with integrity. Sense your care for your own well-being and the well-being of others. Focus on this brightness and strength. This integrity is the foundation of awakening.

MEDITATION

Going Deeper

Find a quiet place and settle your mind and body. Contemplating your good qualities enhances their presence and strengthens your integrity. Bring to mind any positive qualities that you recognize in yourself—perhaps some we've already explored in this book. Allow them to appear in your awareness: feeling, word, image, memory, or idea. Linger with and appreciate each. This positive self-reflection isn't about puffing yourself up but rather recognizing your heart's beauty. These are universal qualities, and you can celebrate their presence in your life. If the voice of doubt or self-deprecation tries to negate your goodness, acknowledge it and return your attention to the value you see right here in your heart.

Now connect with your aspiration to live in a way that respects the sovereignty and vulnerability of others. Recall the many times and many ways in which you have *not* harmed others: times when your speech was gentle, kind, or pleasing; when your actions were not abusive. Recollect the absence of hatred, cruelty, or resentment in these many moments. Receive the nourishment of your goodness.

ACTION
Embodying Integrity

Choose a specific domain to practice nonharming for one week or more: physical, verbal, or mental. Step up your commitment to not kill by taking extra care to remove bugs from your home rather than squashing them. Attend to speech, being mindful of your tone and level of honesty. Watch for a specific unskillful mental habit like jealousy, comparing, or complaining, making a firm commitment to accept but also bracket this when it arises. Be mindful of what drives this thinking, replacing it with more skillful orientations like self-compassion, generosity, or patience.

On the social level, attempt a moral inventory of your position in society and way of life. In what ways are you the beneficiary of the suffering of others, past, present, or future? For example, how is your access to resources or opportunities dependent on harm committed by ancestors? Conversely, in what ways are you denied access to resources or opportunities based on the suffering of your forebears and yourself? How do your consumption habits affect those in other parts of the world or future generations? Though uncomfortable, this kind of investigation contains tremendous power to release our hearts from fear, grief, and craving. Be patient with the process and bring an exquisite sense of compassion and understanding to the vulnerability and complexity of these questions. Talk with others about these issues and commit to educating yourself about how you can engage in repair, reparations, and ethical alignment with your values.

IF YOU HAVE DIFFICULTIES

If you have trouble recognizing your goodness, consider how a friend, teacher, or mentor regards you. Think of a younger person who looks up to you—or even a pet! See yourself through their eyes, appreciating your goodness. Can you let this in? If you feel overwhelmed by regret over past actions or by the immense historical harm and injustice woven into the global economy and climate crisis, take a step back and breathe. Recall that attending to your own heart-mind can be the first step toward serving others and transforming our world. Draw strength from what nourishes you. Reach out to those you trust to discuss issues that are larger than any of us. If you don't have relationships that can support these conversations, do your best to seek them out. Find communities having these conversations in ways that are healing and productive.

16. RESOLVE

> Recognizing the potency of a firm heart, I aspire to hold
> intentions that are enriching, and to ward off vacillation
> on one hand and forceful goal-seeking on the other.
> —Ajahn Sucitto

"Relax. There's nowhere to go, nothing to do."

Perhaps you've heard these instructions. I've spoken them myself hundreds of times. In an effort to heal our broken hearts, gather our fragmented minds, and counter the strain of over-achieving, contemporary approaches to meditation emphasize relaxation, ease, and nondoing. When we habitually override our limits and push for productivity, all the while beset with distressing news, permission to do nothing is a welcome relief.

But emphasizing relaxation to the exclusion of determination and action is a grave mistake. If we stop at relaxation, we miss the immense benefits of inner cultivation and risk abdicating our responsibilities to one another, future generations, and the planet. Relaxation and ease are essential in life and on the contemplative path, but they must be balanced with wholehearted resolve. Similarly, rest and pleasure are instrumental in social transformation but must be integrated with focused engagement.

Transformation takes dedication and persistence, committing fully without burning out. Most worthwhile projects take resolve: working through the hardships of relationship and family life; shepherding a complex project to its end; learning an instrument, language, or craft; building a social change campaign. Without resolve, we falter; we become stagnant in our growth and ineffective in our work. How many times have you let a New Year's resolution fall by the wayside?

Resolve lends firmness to the heart-mind, enabling us to follow through on aspirations, work with resistance, and stay the course through inevitable ups and downs. By directing and sustaining energy, resolve nourishes concentration, patience, integrity, and many other qualities. It provides the consistency we need to keep watering skillful seeds we wish to cultivate in consciousness, and it offers the restraint we need to withdraw energy from unskillful seeds we seek to relinquish.

Years after the wilderness canoe trip described in chapter 5, I would draw on what the portages taught me about resolve to sustain myself during all-night meditation vigils at the monasteries. The physical pain I felt during those meditations was less intense than a long portage, but the psychological torment could be worse. My mind reacted to the fatigue with whining, and I quickly came to find my complaining worse than the physical experience. Once I made a resolution to stick it out, I could surrender to the process and relax into the night, one moment at a time. This taught me a lot about the power of setting one's mind to a task completely and then letting go.

You have the ability to make up your mind and stick with it—whatever "it" might be. You can feel the difference between setting an alarm for 5:00 a.m. with a waffling "I'll see how I feel in the morning . . ." or with the resoluteness of absolutely knowing that when that alarm goes off you *will* get up. This firm intention is the solid determination of resolve: you can count on it.

Resolve swims against the current of society. In an era of instant gratification, hedonism, and individualism, resolve requires patience, restraint, and letting go. Resolve knows the value of gradual cultivation, honoring the craft of training the heart. It challenges the popular, seductive notions that freedom comes from the absence of responsibility and commitment and that happiness occurs through doing whatever you want. Is inner freedom simply getting what you want? What happens when you can't have your way? Even when you get what you want, how long are you satisfied before you want something else? Always following desire binds you to your impulses and whims and reinforces the felt need for comfort. What's more, without discernment, how do you know your desires aren't being manipulated by social conditioning? Some recognize this dilemma and rebel against societal expectations. But this too falls short of real freedom, for, even in that rejection, we are still reacting to options determined by others. Finally, how does following a freedom that consists of simply doing whatever we want affect society? Resolve helps us relinquish personal preference to protect the greater good.

For genuine inner transformation and for tackling the immense challenges we face together as a species, we need a firm and steady inner basis. Instead of catering to our preferences, we need to encounter and remain engaged with discomfort. With resolve we can create a fruitful friction between vision and habit, between preference and circumstance. For example, parenting a newborn pushes me in ways no portage or all-night meditation ever could. When I'm exhausted and sore in the middle of the night from the demands of parenting and our son won't fall asleep, the discomfort reveals where I need resolve to carry me.

Nonviolent direct action depends on a similar willingness to endure discomfort in healing oppression, injustice, and inequity.[1] Resolve works synergistically with other qualities to power social transformation. In 1955, during the Montgomery Bus Boycott, the city's African American community drew upon resolve for thirteen long months, walking and carpooling daily through rain, harassment, and hardship, before winning international attention and a US Supreme Court victory desegregating public buses.[2] Dr. King's dedication to freedom during this crucial era embodied resolve. Despite being the father of four, he said yes to campaign after distant campaign, from the 1955 bus boycott up to his assassination in Memphis, Tennessee, in 1968. The resolve of even one determined individual can make an immense difference. In the twenty-first century, through her unwavering commitment, the young Pakistani activist Malala Yousafzai has advanced the cause for women's education internationally in spite of severe repression and attempted assassination by her country's Taliban government.

So how do we cultivate resolve? While the initial stages of resolve depend on willpower, relying on such force creates tension and brittleness. Long-term transformation evolves from a resolve that is firm but not rigid, strong yet supple. Perfectionism, grasping, self-loathing, guilt, and shame erode aspiration and wither the foundation of commitment. In India as a young adult, I made unwise resolutions, rooted in idealism and striving, attempting to sit perfectly still for hours. The result: I broke down. On my teenage canoe trip, by contrast, I had recognized that persevering through pain would bring me closer to my destination. That knowledge—rooted in understanding rather than craving—had bolstered my intention and capacity.

Wisdom allows us to discern our capacity for resolve. With wisdom, we honor our limits, balance effort, and know when to surrender. The Thai forest meditation master Ajahn Chah famously chided one of his disciples: "You think you have an eighteen-wheeler but you're really pulling a child's wagon!" Within your capacity right now, what can you commit to? If you make a resolution beyond your capacity, you may grow resentful or defeated. On the other hand, if you don't challenge yourself at all, you'll never grow. Wise resolve functions within a range of strategic discomfort[3]—challenging us to mature without threatening us to collapse.

Wise resolve thus reflects on our process and adjusts appropriately. When portaging, if my pain felt too sharp, I put down the canoe to reconfigure the rig. As we practice with a particular resolution, we evaluate our inner feedback. Do we need to soften with gentleness, or firm up with recommitment? When we hold resolve with kindness, interest, and good intentions, the superficial binary of success/failure recedes: we learn and progress regardless of the outcome. We need this healthy nonattachment to results, in personal as well as social change, or we burn out.

Holding a resolve, a kind heart brings tenderness and eases unpleasant thoughts, sensations, and emotions. Without such kindness, a resolution may turn into a field day for your inner critic. Instead of going to war with yourself, meet inner struggle with a warm and encouraging inner gaze. This encouragement is not mere permissiveness; resolve also requires self-discipline. The word *discipline* derives from *disciple*; a disciple is one fully committed to humility in something valued. Cultivating resolve, ask yourself, "What do I want to be a disciple of? What do I want to study?"

Paradoxically, resolve also invites surrender, watering seeds of inner freedom. It teaches us to yield, open to discomfort, and release attachment. This process of letting go accepts the present and protects us against conceit, unhealthy comparing, and the mirage of self-improvement (the fantasy of finally becoming "good enough" or "even better"). So wisdom, kindness, and surrender—like stones creating an archway—all strengthen resolve.[4]

Resolve gives structure to our commitments. It empowers us to overcome discomfort, boredom, self-criticism, and inertia with the integrity of our promises. Stay with this process, connecting to your aspiration and intention. Can you fall in love with the vision behind your resolution? If you can endure your mind's temper tantrums and objections, something deeper emerges: the strength for anything and a peace free from habits and preferences.

Ancient Buddhist lore tells of how the Buddha was beset with doubt, lust, fear, and a host of other internal challenges the night of his great awakening. When Mara, the personification of his inner demons, challenged his right to awaken—claiming the Buddha's very seat—the Buddha is said to have resolutely reached down and touched the ground, saying, "The earth is my witness."

How often do we allow our wounds to claim our seat? To allow fear, doubt, hostility, greed, jealousy, or ignorance to eclipse our birthright to wholeness, meaning, and dignity? The Buddha drew upon all of his strengths to vanquish these obstacles—generosity, integrity, aspiration, energy, and more. Perhaps most of all he relied on resolve to respond to Mara's taunt with grace. Statues the world over celebrate this moment, depicting a seated Buddha touching the earth with his right hand, honoring the sacred feminine power of the earth. Such a gesture connects the strength of resolve with the vast, stable energy of the earth, tapping into a deep and immense ground always within.

Getting Started

Reflect on when you've committed and followed through, even to do something as simple as meet a friend for a walk or decide to cook a proper dinner rather than just eat a snack. Notice the clarity of your resolution. Consider where you'd like to apply resolve. What matters that is within your zone of strategic discomfort: neither too hard nor too easy? Reflect carefully on the values, obstacles, and supports you may encounter pursuing this resolution. Create accountability by saying it aloud, writing it down, or telling a friend. Listen to how your heart responds; attend to any waffling. Repeat your resolution until you feel a sense of alignment and firmness, knowing you are fully committed.

Going Deeper

Start small, letting wisdom and kindness inform your resolution. If you usually meditate daily, try adding an extra five minutes each day for one week. If you tend to be fidgety when you meditate, try remaining still for some minutes, as your capacity allows. (You can even use a timer to track yourself.) Try working on a more moment-to-moment level—for example, making a resolution to stay focused on one in-breath from beginning to middle to end, then doing the same for one out-breath. Alternatively, you can resolve to stop feeding a particular rumination or storyline. When it arises in your meditation, note it and firmly return attention to your anchor. Keep it simple and doable. Increase strength slowly, reflecting and building on your experiments.

ACTION
Embodying Resolve

Make a resolution to improve your mental patterns. Do you want to improve a quality or shift a habit? For example, you might want to cultivate a kinder inner voice or to complain or worry less about something. Whatever you choose, make your resolution specific. Rather than the gentle but vague "be kinder to myself," try "at least four times a day, say something encouraging to myself." Rather than "stop worrying about things I can't control," try "when I worry about things outside my control, take two breaths and focus on what I *can* do."

Make a resolution about a discrete task. Give your whole-hearted attention to folding the laundry today, instead of rushing, or make a final agreement to complete something you've been putting off. Ask yourself: How does it feel to determine something so clearly? Do you loosen or tighten? Do you rebel? How can you integrate all parts of your heart?

Next, resolve to do something for a time: rising at a certain hour, volunteering locally, learning how to contribute to an issue. Each resolve commits you. Evaluate your experience: What have you learned from each? What was useful? What was within your capacity? As always, the aim is to learn rather than get things right. Journal about any insights or challenges you encounter.

IF YOU HAVE DIFFICULTIES

If self-critical thinking besets you, step back, breathe, and bring tenderness to yourself. Reconnect with your purpose. After all, aren't you aiming to learn, contribute, develop skill, and free your heart? Your longing for such noble aims is precisely why you're frustrated. Give yourself some credit.

Consider if your resolve feels too ambitious or apathetic. Your resolve may be too lofty to marshal your resources. You might need to focus on rest and nourishment (for more on rest, see chapter 18). You might be resentful, pushing too hard, or needing to ease up. If you are confused about when to emphasize relaxation versus effort, try listening more carefully to what you need. Do the opposite of what is habitual and comfortable. Or else attend to the felt quality of your motivation. What would lead to more love and understanding inside?

If you struggle with your resolve, create more accountability. Tell a friend or connect with a group. Write your resolve where you can see it. Draw on your connection with something larger than yourself (see chapter 22, on devotion). Recall the Buddha touching the earth on the night of his awakening. Our deepest support for resolve may come from letting go and being held by something much larger than we are, something that can see us through. The earth supports us.

17. JOY

Discovering more joy does not save us from hardship and heartbreak. In fact, we may cry more easily, but we will laugh more easily too. As we discover more joy, we can face suffering in a way that ennobles rather than embitters. We have heartbreaks without being broken.
—Archbishop Desmond Tutu

I grew up on the East Coast, where forests of evergreen, oak, and maple soothed me. Some weekends, we would drive up the Hudson River Valley to my grandmother Joy's house in the countryside. I spent many hours near Nanny Joy's, finding streams and mossy clearings that still seem magical in my mind.

I loved spending time in a great old white pine. I'd climb into her arms, as high as her branches would support me. Near her crown, I would wrap one arm around her trunk and look out over the trees and the small, dark pond with cattails along its far shore. When the wind picked up, the great tree would sway gently, rocking me in her arms. Her sap stuck to my skin for days, reminding me of the vast, quiet space she gave me, near the sky.

Just as a plant withers without adequate water, our hearts lose buoyancy and brightness without joy. Doing work—especially the work of service and social change—requires both external and internal resources. We need resilience to face pain, strength to persevere through challenge, and joy to lift the heart. Joy is a feeling of great pleasure, characterized by satisfaction and deep connection to self, other, and the moment. Joy comes in many forms: from a quiet, contented happiness to a rush of warmth, to waves of pleasure. Joy may spring from personal circumstances, from the happiness of others, and even from deep presence.

We experience joy in countless ways. For example, my heart lifts seeing our son laugh; my heart warms recalling my childhood dog, furiously wagging her tail. Joy has roots deep in our biology: puppies and kittens play with infectious joy; dolphins leap with delight. To be touched by life, we must be willing to let it in—to open and receive (which we've explored in chapters on mindfulness and concentration). This receptivity emerges naturally when we slow down as I did, held in the arms of that pine: when we close our eyes, feel the sun on our face, or lean in to smell a flower.

Though joy is innate, conditions complicate our ability to access it. The author and neuroscience educator Sarah Peyton notes that our nervous system only experiences joy and play when we feel valued and safe. Trauma, violence, and structural oppression rob us of joy by depriving us of these needs. Ongoing grief or marginalization alienates us from joy. After significant loss, we may need time before feeling joy again. Mourning requires feeling grief, rather than papering over hurt with false well-being.

Train yourself to enjoy small moments of beauty and goodness in life: a flock of birds overhead, sunlight cutting through a window and shimmering on a glass of water, ordinary time with a loved one. How much joy do we miss in life because we're moving too quickly? If your life feels overwhelming—perhaps raising children or working multiple jobs to make ends meet—acknowledge that you face external challenges. In this way, you might create more internal space. By honoring the pressures you experience, you may find renewed capacity to open to joy.

When my friend Miki and I walk together, we begin by taking turns sharing things we want to appreciate or celebrate, building our capacity for joy. In his work on resilience, Rick Hanson offers a two-part process called "taking in the good." He invites us first to notice something nourishing, beautiful, or uplifting (or invoke it through memory or imagination), then to linger with that experience for at least twenty seconds. This nourishes us somatically, creating new neural pathways, etching the quality into our brains, and making joy easier to access in the future.[1]

Beware of two traps along the path to joy. One trap equates contemplative practice solely with calm, peace, or pleasure. This trap, common in secular mindfulness practice, leads us to avoid anything heavy or painful or to put a falsely positive spin on every experience. The second trap, more common in Buddhist circles, associates spirituality with seriousness and suffering. We may fear healthy pleasure, disengage from life, or avoid joy, worried it will stir cravings. In fact, contemplative practice neither cuts us off from the world nor suppresses anything. It teaches us to feel all of life, hard and joyful, suffering and celebration. The Bible teaches that there is a season for everything: sorrow is the shadow that brightens our joy.

We suffer deeply in our world. Experiences of profound isolation, news of hate crimes or police violence, the spread of war, failure to act on the climate crisis—these take a toll on our hearts. Sometimes I read the news and weep. In the face of suffering, joy nourishes the heart so we have the resilience to open to pain and anger, feeling them, rather than shutting down or turning away. Joy creates space so we may respond to difficulty with skill. Joy strengths our spirits so we can sustain courageous action. Consider again the Black civil rights movement, which resounded with uplifting songs of joy for years. In the midst of struggle, the movement for Black freedom consistently celebrated the collective joy of acting wholeheartedly in a noble cause. The sustaining power of joy rings through the life and writings of the formidable anarchist and feminist activist Emma Goldman, whose work connecting sexual liberation, creativity, and social revolution has been paraphrased in the popular slogan, "If I can't dance, I don't want to be part of your revolution."[2] Joy protects the heart and nourishes courage. The author and social justice leader adrienne maree brown argues, "Joy is important. It's not a guilty pleasure, it is a strategic move towards the future we all need to create. One in which our children are laughing, our children are free."[3]

Joy is sweeter when shared. Consider how good it feels to rejoice in a friend's unexpected good news. When the heart is open, it's natural to celebrate another's good fortune. Buddhism calls this *mudita*—empathic resonance, appreciative joy. Years ago, a friend sent me a video of their toddler in little pink boots, puddle-jumping in the rain, and I still smile, remembering it! I've been moved to tears by couples' figure skating. Envisioning the long years of training, we can join in their joy and pride as they execute an impeccable routine.

Of course, it's easier to feel happy for others when we don't covet what they have. (You're unlikely to happen across me in a televised figure-skating competition anytime soon.) Do you contract a little when others succeed? Jealousy blocks appreciative joy, inhibiting our celebration. We may compare ourselves to others, judge them, or think cynically, "I'd feel better if you weren't so darn happy!" We may think happiness is a limited resource: the happier *you* are, the less happiness for *me*. Thankfully, appreciative joy dispels such notions, recognizing envy but discovering that our hearts are big enough for it all. We can celebrate others and still pursue our goals. As the Dalai Lama has quipped, "When you count other people's happiness as your own, you have billions more chances to be happy." Cultivating appreciative joy dissolves the boundaries between self and other. Your happiness becomes mine and we enter an expansive, interconnected space.

Opening to joy, you may encounter a new challenge: feeling its fullness. Despite the collective heartache of the past few years, I've also known tremendous joy. After eight years of partnership with Evan, I felt overwhelmed by joy in the weeks leading to our wedding. The prospect of standing before our community and taking vows connected me with the depth of my love for her and devotion to my path. I worked to expand my capacity to feel that joy. I spoke with friends, explored my thoughts and feelings, and created a larger container for joy by relaxing and breathing. When I finally stood at the altar before Evan, our family, and friends, I felt solid, clear, and open. In turn, this experience prepared me to welcome our son into this world with a full, strong heart.

Connecting with life as it is—blessings and hardships, alike— brings deep joy. This joy does not depend on getting what we want. Feeling the full range of human experience—the joy and the sorrow—ennobles the heart. It's not *what* we experience but how we *relate* to it that frees us. When we engage all of our being, we encounter a holistic satisfaction (see more about this in chapter 22, on devotion). When we are open, curious, and kind toward all that arises in us, the sincerity of our presence offers its own reward: the joy of connection to truth.

Getting Started

What brings you joy in life? Start small and let your mind wander, open to memories even of little things: a good night's rest, a cup of tea or coffee, a walk outdoors, talking with a friend. Notice how your body feels as pleasurable memories arise. Linger in these moments, letting them nourish you. What do you overlook in life that could bring joy if you attended to it more carefully? Consider how you might nourish this joy.

MEDITATION

Going Deeper

Settle your mind and body in a comfortable, upright position. To practice mudita, appreciative joy, bring to mind someone who is doing well, for whom you can feel joy. Think of their fortunate condition. Visualize them smiling, or get a kinesthetic sense of being with them. Notice their happiness. Invite your heart to celebrate their joy. Try silently repeating a simple phrase: "May your joy and happiness increase" or "I'm so happy for you. I appreciate the blessings in your life." One moment at a time, aim your heart toward their happiness, cultivating your own joyful appreciation. When you're ready, allow the visualization to return to the simplicity of your breathing. What did you notice? What hinders or supports you rejoicing with them?

ACTION
Embodying Joy

Every morning for a week or more, set an intention to notice small moments that nourish you or bring you joy. Slow down. Taste your food. Notice the flowers or trees. Look at the sky. Call a friend. Spend time in nature and allow your heart to be touched. Begin by noticing what is uplifting, letting it register in your heart. Then let your attention linger there. How does this experience feel in your body? Soak in any sensations of happiness or pleasure, however subtle.

IF YOU HAVE DIFFICULTIES

You can't force joy or control its presence. In the face of grief or stress, joy may not be appropriate. Honor your feelings, inviting tenderness toward your experience. Explore the difference between resisting your feelings—fighting, fearing, or avoiding them—and allowing yourself to open to them. How does it feel to accept an emotion even a little? Notice any movement from contraction toward well-being or ease. Relax into that shift; savor it, though it may be small. Consider that this could be a kind of bittersweet joy, the joy of knowing the truth.

If you feel stuck or low, engage your imagination. Not as an attempt to escape the present, but as a way to nourish your heart and bring more inner resources to what you are facing. Recall a time you felt well. Imagine a person or place that brings you joy. Let this become clear in your mind's eye, noticing as many details as you can. Absorb the goodness of this memory. When you're ready, let this image fade, but retain its nourishment. Bring this back into your present circumstance: the seed of joy is already within you.

18. REST

If the great ocean herself needs replenishment, what could make you think you don't? —Salma Farook

An old story tells of a burly woodcutter. One day, he noticed he'd cut fewer trees than the day before. The trend continued—each day taking longer than the last. He worked harder and longer to feed his family, from dusk until dawn, but couldn't keep up. Exhausted, he finally stopped to rest and realized—he hadn't sharpened his axe in ages.

Many people I meet are exhausted. With all that we're living through, it's natural to feel worn out and *bone tired*. Recognizing a deep need for healing and renewal, it can be a kind of koan to inquire, "What do I need to resharpen my axe? How often do I need that?"

Given the state of the world, it makes sense that resilience—the ability to respond to stress adaptively, to bounce back from adversity and grow from challenges—has become a buzzword. Yet I've seen how otherwise nourishing activities aimed at resilience—like meditation or exercise—can become another nagging item on the to-do list. If we're unable to maintain these healthy routines, they can fuel our inner critic's narrative of failure, becoming another piece of evidence that we don't measure up. Even if we manage to fit in healthy activities, they can inadvertently feed the harmful habit of pushing ourselves past our limits.

When exhaustion is deep and stress is chronic, sometimes the wisest thing to do is nothing. When we're tired—physically, intellectually, or emotionally—the most natural thing is to rest. Rest rejuvenates body, mind, and spirit. Learning when and how to rest is as essential for spiritual practice as it is for navigating our lives and creating social transformation.

Tricia Hersey, founder of the Nap Ministry, defines rest as anything that connects our mind and body.[1] Notice how this broadens your sense of what might be restful. Art, music, time in nature, a craft—all can be forms of rest. Evolutionary biologists believe our ancestors engaged in regular periods of rhythmic activity like walking, grooming, weaving, shelling, grinding, and so forth. These activities create downtime for the nervous system. Easy chitchat and social interaction can serve the same function.

In today's world it's become hard to rest. Since the Industrial Revolution, economic and social pressures never cease pushing us. There's a coffee shop on nearly every corner of every city in the global North. As a society, we're overcaffeinated and underresourced. Technologies addict and distract us. How often do you find yourself looking at a device, exhausted, instead of shutting your eyes to rest? Whether raising a family, working two jobs, or struggling for social change, being busy has become the norm. Capitalizing upon this, the wellness industry co-opts our innate capacity for rest and sells it back to us.

Additionally, in the United States, where much of the social safety net has been stripped away, individuals face tremendous economic pressure to meet basic needs like housing and healthcare. Can we envision economic and social structures that honor our need for rest? Imagine the far-reaching social effects of all new parents receiving extended paid family leave. How might something as radical as universal basic income affect our quality of life? What renaissance in creativity might occur from eliminating the violence, stress, and hardship of hunger and poverty?

Internal factors can also interfere with our capacity to rest. The media teaches us to seek relief through distraction. We may have swallowed the lie that our value is measured by worldly success, or we may have become entranced by the illusory promise of fulfillment after completing a to-do list. When our sense of self-worth and belonging is tied to how much we accomplish or how well we perform, how do we give ourselves permission to rest? We may even feel proud of our busyness, wearing it as badge indicating how important we are or how valuable our time is.

In a world on fire, taking time to rest is radical. I've been meditating since I was nineteen and have experienced much transformation. Still, I periodically slide back into the old habit of busyness. If I'm not attentive, I can end up packing my days, driven by a kind of restless, agitated energy churning just below the surface.

Some of us have the opposite challenge, struggling with apathy or listlessness. We may have downtime, yet still feel exhausted—equally unable to find nourishing rest. These patterns of over- and underexertion become embedded in our lives. We can track them in everything from daily chores to work to spiritual practice. Do you push hard, only to burn out and collapse at the end of the day? Do you drag your feet and procrastinate, avoiding what you know is most important? How do you transform a dysfunctional relationship with *doing*—be it the frenzy of activity or sinking into immobility—and begin to reclaim your right to *resting*? On the other hand, how can we justify taking a break when there's so much urgent work to be done in our world?

First, rest is not self-indulgent or lazy. It's not collapsing under the weight of things or always choosing what's easiest. It's not burying our head in the sand or ignoring challenges personally or collectively. Rest brings balance and honors limits. If we don't balance the energy we put into *doing* with time and space to relish *being*, we burn out. Over fifty years ago, the Trappist monk Thomas Merton wrote about the violence of being too busy: "To allow oneself to be carried away by a multitude of conflicting concerns, to surrender to too many demands, to commit oneself to too many projects, to want to help everyone in everything is to succumb to violence."[2]

Many activists and those in helping professions are so focused on giving they barely take care of themselves. Yet *there is no action without rest*, no healing or renewal without stopping. Mushim Patricia Ikeda, a teacher of Engaged Buddhism in the San Francisco Bay Area, offers a modern bodhisattva vow: "I vow to not burn out."[3] In her book *Rest Is Resistance: A Manifesto*, Tricia Hersey writes: "Productivity should not look like exhaustion. The concept of laziness is a tool of the oppressor. A large part of your unraveling from capitalism will include becoming less attached to the idea of productivity and more committed to the idea of rest as a portal to just be."[4]

Nature teaches us to rest: the sun rises and sets; the tides advance and recede as the moon waxes and wanes. Life itself expands and contracts as the seasons turn. In winter, the earth grows quiet and still. In spring, new life emerges from the soil. As all farmers and gardeners know, a field needs fallow time to regenerate its soil for the next season's harvest.

Rest begins with respecting our body, taking breaks, and getting enough sleep. It extends to slowing down, receiving nourishment, and appreciating when a task is complete. Ultimately, rest invites us to touch our own innate value and dignity as creatures on this planet. More than replenishment, rest opens into creativity, joy, and the mystical.

In musical notation, a "rest" is a pause between notes. This is a lovely metaphor for accessing rest through periods of silence and nondoing. As we explored in chapter 3 on energy, honoring cycles of activity and rest has been enshrined in the Abrahamic religions' Sabbath for over five thousand years. Rabbi Abraham Joshua Heschel writes:

> Six days a week we live under the tyranny of things of space; on the Sabbath we . . . attune to holiness in time . . . to turn from the results of creation to the mystery of creation; from the world of creation to the creation of the world. On Shabbat we stop and turn to care for the seed of eternity planted in the soul.[5]

In contemplative practice, cultivating rest lays the foundation for deeper stages of concentration and insight. We unlearn habits of striving and nurture stillness for its own sake.

Recognizing the value of rest—physiologically, emotionally, and spiritually—we can reclaim our right to it and nurture it in our lives. Initially, this may involve dismantling the ways we ignore our need for rest: our unnatural pace, the blue light of screens that disrupt our circadian rhythms, or simply pushing through tiredness. Reawakening sensitivity to our need for rest takes time. The signals our bodies and hearts send for rest may feel faint at first—muffled by our anxiety or the sheer force of our habits. Learning to honor those signals and rediscover what rest really entails may take experimentation and resolve. We can support this process by cultivating self-compassion, which counteracts the tendency to override limits. We can practice saying "no" more, and ask how much of our busyness is necessary and how much is merely self-imposed.

The to-do list never ends. The idea that you will rest when you finish everything is an illusion. As soon as you think you've arrived, your goal recedes. The more efficient you get at doing something, the more people will ask you to do it. A pithy Tibetan teaching states, "Activities do not cease by completing them. They cease when you stop." To rest, you must be willing to reevaluate your priorities and question your relationship with keeping busy. What can you let go of? Can you relinquish pleasing others to care for yourself? Can you lower any standards of perfectionism to recover more downtime? What would it be like to not have to be productive every single moment? To not always need a purpose or be working on something?

The more whole we feel inside, the less our service and work come from codependency or needing validation and the more they come from generosity, compassion, and a natural desire to contribute. There is a Zen saying: "When I'm hungry I eat, when I'm tired I sleep." When we heed the signals of our body, trusting that we are enough just as we are, rest is the most natural thing in the world.

REFLECTION

Getting Started

Investigate how your conditioning (personal and social) influences your relationship with rest, with doing and being. What did others model early in life? What messages did you internalize from society? What interferes with prioritizing rest and receiving nourishment? What would it be like to let yourself stop and rest? To *surrender*—even for a little—to your tiredness?

MEDITATION

Going Deeper

Experiment with doing nothing. Sit comfortably and, if you like, take in your surroundings—sights, sounds, smells. Notice any physical safety in your immediate environment. Now recline, resting your body on the earth. Feel how you are held and supported by this vast, generous, breathing planet. Lightly rest your attention on something simple like breathing, the ground beneath you, or the sounds around you. Notice any tendency to want to get somewhere, accomplish something, become concentrated, or do it "right." Observe mental habits of planning, worrying, or fantasizing. Can you settle into a relaxed and easy state of rest in the present moment? What's it like to allow your body to receive the nourishment of each in-breath, to savor the release of each out-breath?

ACTION

Embodying Rest

Find new ways to integrate rest into your life. Begin with prioritizing the physiological foundation of rest: are there ways you can eat more nourishing food, move or exercise more, and create sufficient time to sleep? Practice good sleep hygiene, aiming for an hour to wind down without screens before bed.

From this, build toward integrating cycles of rest into your day. Instead of rushing on to the next thing, tumbling forward, see if you can allow your nervous system to feel the satisfaction of completing one activity. Pause for a moment or two after finishing simple things like eating a meal, washing the dishes, or cleaning your teeth. Rest for a breath after sending an important email or text. Just for a moment, can you touch the stillness of being?

IF YOU HAVE DIFFICULTIES

Insomnia is rampant in the modern world. If you have trouble *literally* getting enough rest, be sure you're attending to all possible factors. Seek medical advice to address physiological causes. Explore supports such as hypnosis or guided relaxation.[6] Pay attention to how you use your mind during the day, and see if you can soften rushed and anxious energies that can carry over into the night.

If chronic pain interferes with your ability to rest, try using light stimulation of the senses to provide more comfort and ease. Pleasing music, gentle movement, or aromatherapy may provide enough sensory stimulation to interrupt neural habits. Try to dwell in these subtle, pleasant sensory experiences, rather than in the discomfort or frustration of pain.

Burnout is a state of exhaustion so deep it can prevent rest and replenishment. With burnout, you may need more time or additional support to rest naturally. Seek simple activities that bring you pleasure, and allow yourself to enjoy this relief. You may need to reintroduce rest slowly, like a gentle rain softening parched desert soil. Experiment by alternating between short cycles of light activity and rest as a way to reregulate your nervous system. With burnout, as with insomnia, if these suggestions don't help, seek additional support. Offer yourself simple, heartfelt reassurance— it's okay.

19. WONDER

Those who contemplate the beauty of the earth find re-
serves of strength that will endure as long as life lasts.
—Rachel Carson

One spring, my seventh-grade science teacher, Mrs. Cecelia, gave
us the curious homework assignment of drawing a tree branch
every other day for a month. Though I assumed this would be
a waste of time, I dutifully found a young maple and began to
sketch. The first week, I drew the same dead brown stick, day after
day. Then something happened. Out of the dry, stubby end of that
twig emerged the tiniest bud. I *knew* deciduous trees grew new
leaves, but I'd never looked closely enough to *see* it. Each day I
watched in amazement as the most delicate, translucent green leaf
unfurled from the bud.

We need wonder to nourish the heart, to live well, and to work
for change in our complex world. Without wonder, life appears
empty, lonely, and mechanical. Wonder uplifts us and guides us
toward insight and connection. It fortifies our hearts and builds
our capacity to strive for inner and outer transformation.

Wonder is a state of openness and awe we experience by perceiving the world afresh. Characterized by amazement and deep connection to the present, it cleanses the dullness and familiarity of habit. Encountering the world, children naturally embody wonder and awe. As adults, we can rekindle our wonder.

There is enough wonder in this world to fall down in awe every day, if we only had eyes to see and ears to hear. Pause for a moment to consider that water falls from the sky; some trees live over a thousand years; plants the world over create delicious edible fruit, from raspberries to dragon fruit; bees pollinate flowers, producing honey that will last thousands of years without spoiling. Look deeply enough into anything, from a grain of sand to the vast night sky, and you will be amazed. Look deeply enough into yourself, and you will discover that you are a walking miracle. This discovery is available to each of us, yet we rarely live with this awareness.

Nature opens a doorway to the belonging and mystery systematically erased by the distactions of modern life. Monocultural food production, reliance on screens, obsession with clock time, ignorance of natural rhythms, manicured lawns, high-speed travel—these all disconnect us from the basic wonder of life. Opening to the mystery and beauty of nature, something profound stirs within us. In the city, wildflowers bloom, leaves shimmer in the wind, and birds still fly. In the wild, the dusty, sweet smell of pine needles rises from the forest floor; streams overflow in spring; the ancient faces of the mountains endure. Nature calls us back to embodied, wakeful awareness. To connect with the wonder of the natural world brings joy, reminding us that we too are alive and that our very existence is a blessing.

Wonder opens the door to new experiences. It invites us to reclaim our bodies' deep knowing, integrating emotional and somatic intelligences with our mental knowledge. We sense how the vitality flowing through us—the energy that animates our body, heart, and mind—connects to all life. We remember in our bones that we are not separate from this world but are nature made conscious and self-aware.

In the Buddhist tradition, human birth is considered precious for the unique opportunity it offers to do good in the world and to spiritually awaken. A human life balances pleasure and pain, giving us the chance to aspire, learn, and grow. We are here long enough to do things of value, but short enough to remain cognizant of our mortality.

Wonder and awe beget reverence, which we then express through action. Recognizing the preciousness of life, we honor and protect all beings. In this way, wonder provides a base for action, fuels our work for transformation, and urges us to act on behalf of future generations.

If the fabric of our society continues to fray—if political differences cause further polarization and if, as is nearly certain, the climate emergency intensifies—we will need wonder and awe to sustain ourselves and forge new connections. With wonder, we marry inner and outer, the spiritual and the material. Wonder opens the door to the power within all of us to become active change agents in our world. The Chicana poet, writer, and feminist Gloria E. Anzaldúa writes: "With awe and wonder you look around, recognizing the preciousness of the earth, the sanctity of every human being on the planet, the ultimate unity and interdependence of all beings—*somos todos un país*."[1] This awe reminds us of our true kinship with all of life, joining us in a beautiful mosaic that honors our diversity even as it connects us. It enters our hearts, gathers force, and fills us, calling us to the greatest task of our times: to participate in the healing and transformation of our world.

As we open more fully to wonder, we also open to the profound grief connected to climate chaos. Perhaps one of the reasons we are reluctant to slow down enough to experience wonder is because we know that, if we let ourselves open to the beauty of being alive, if we truly feel how much we love this planet, our home, we will be overcome with sorrow for the devastating harm we have wrought—harm that will continue to befall generations to come. This grief is so immense we need help to process it. We need inner resources like compassion, courage, and forgiveness; we need each other; and we need the support of our ancestors and future generations who depend on us becoming fully alive to the power within us. Only then will we have the strength to do what is needed today.

Embracing wonder does not depend on having novel or exciting experiences (though of course they can help) but instead depends on the quality of our attention. Wonder can grow with age and wisdom. Anything might be a doorway to wonder, but we rarely encounter awe when our senses have become dulled, our attention fragmented, and our hearts numbed with grief and overwhelm. How can we return to feeling openness, awe, and interconnection?

My science project of drawing a tree branch highlights the privileges of my childhood: access to nature and education that inspired me, physical and emotional safety, and leisure time to devote to my schoolwork. These privileges illustrate how meeting our basic needs for safety and sustenance support the arising of wonder. Poignantly, though deprivation challenges our capacity for wonder, it cannot destroy it: the misery of our childhood can also point us to wonder, even when all we have is the blue sky. Our human spirit can find wonder even in horrific circumstances. As Etty Hillesum, a young Jewish woman writing from the Westerbork transit camp a few months before her death at Auschwitz reflects, "Despite everything, life is full of beauty and meaning."[2]

To access wonder, find ways to be naturally mindful and curious. Pay complete attention, like a child observing a butterfly for the first time. This requires humility. You must be willing to become fully absorbed in the present, setting aside ideas about what you know and what will come. Intellectual analysis, comparison, and craving corrode wonder. They block your capacity for connecting with the raw experience of the moment—be it marveling at the morning light glinting off tile, the aroma of a cup of hot coffee, the voice of an old friend, or the hummingbird sipping from a summer flower.

As with other qualities, we can cultivate wonder. A schoolteacher once told me about an emergent-curriculum activity she enjoys doing with kindergarteners. To water the seeds of wonder, she invites her students to share something they wonder about—a question or curiosity. They begin sentences with the phrase "I wonder..."

- "I wonder why butterflies fly?"
- "I wonder where the light goes when it's dark?"
- "I wonder how the heart gets feelings?"

When any children who wish to have spoken, everyone gathers the questions and considers which one they most want to pursue—their teacher calls this "the most beautiful question." They sit together in a circle, only one person speaking at a time, without raising hands, often having remarkable conversations. A beautiful question can pique our curiosity, invite us into deeper intimacy, and reconnect us with the wonder and mystery of life.

REFLECTION
Getting Started

Recall a time when you were filled with wonder: listening to music that moved you deeply, watching the sunset, contemplating the galaxy, gazing into the eyes of a toddler. Immerse yourself in the memory, recalling as many details as you can—where you were, the quality of the light, the temperature of the air, the sounds, smells, and sensations around and within you. Now ponder: How did this experience arise? What factors helped to sustain it? How did it feel? What can this teach you about wonder?

MEDITATION
Going Deeper

Formal meditation offers many ways to connect with wonder. Begin this meditation gently, allowing your mind and body to settle. As things come into balance, focus your attention on any of your senses with a fresh and open attitude. Imagine that you had never heard sounds before, never felt a sensation, never seen color or light. Receive the sensory impressions as they come and go. Open to the vividness of having a body with senses to perceive the world and organs to draw nourishment from the earth. Touch the wonder of being alive.

ACTION
Embodying Wonder

Give your full attention to any daily activity, aiming to experience it afresh. For example, take one sip of water as slowly and mindfully as you can. Close your eyes, hold the glass with two hands, and feel the weight of this clear, precious liquid. Bring the glass to your mouth, allowing the cool, yielding water to touch the skin of your lips. Imagine all that this water has ever been: a cloud in the sky, rain falling to the earth, a stream washing over pebbles, a river running to the sea, a wave breaking on the shore. Touch the water's vitality and beauty with awareness. Slowly open your mouth, allowing the water to enter your body. Feel this soft, jeweled liquid flow into you, bringing moisture and life. Have you ever known this moment before?

Bring a slow, caring attention to another activity: showering, washing a dish, holding hands. When we are truly present, we can imbue simply walking on the earth with profound reverence. Alternatively, do something comforting or pleasing, like enjoying a special food, singing, or listening to your favorite music. Light a candle at night and enjoy the beauty of its light. Bring your full attention to the experience, putting aside any thoughts of the past or future. For this one moment, let this present experience be all that exists. Notice how it feels to live mindfully, awake to wonder.

Investigating further, allow yourself a period of unstructured time to wander outdoors, open to wonder. Explore your environment like a child, as if it were entirely new. Walk barefoot and feel the textures and temperature of the ground. Look quietly at something small, like a pine cone or a leaf, for a long, long time, until you begin to see it anew.

IF YOU HAVE DIFFICULTIES

Recall that wonder, like all experience, arises due to certain conditions. If you are having trouble connecting to wonder, attend to your mind, body, and environment. Are you too tired, stressed, or otherwise distracted to open to wonder? Would more downtime and rest be helpful? Another common obstacle is trying too hard. Are you forcing yourself to feel wonder or trying to create a special experience? Recall that wonder is completely ordinary, and it arises naturally from relaxed and open attention rather than from trying to control your mind or produce a feeling. Let go a little. Do nothing. Let your eyes and ears wander until they happen upon something that catches your interest.

PART FOUR

In the short introductions to the previous sections, we've explored the foundational qualities that undergird our practice, their energetic dimensions, and the role of friendship in their cultivation. As we begin this fourth leg of our journey, we attend to the relationship between the qualities and the earth, our home.

Home evokes many things: ideally it is a place of shelter and safety, an abode of rest, and a space we care for which in turn cares for us. I am grateful to my parents for providing the home I grew up in, and feel deeply fortunate to have a physical home today in which to raise a family. I also wish to provide our son a secure home base from which he can explore and contribute to the world. *That* home lies in the heart. Cultivating the qualities explored in this book builds an inner refuge that can equip you to meet the world with poise, approach others with curiosity, and greet the unknown with strength and humility.

In my community, an ongoing housing crisis is forcing more and more people into the streets. At the same time, I see more of what we might call "inner homelessness" all around me. We can lose our inner home when domestic violence or abuse robs us of safety or when the trauma of oppression steals our sense of belonging. We grow emotionally homeless when we forget—or perhaps never learn—our true connection with the land that sustains us.

In 1968, when NASA released the first photograph of earth from space, many believed it would spark a leap in human consciousness and herald a new era of stewarding the planet as our shared home beyond the imaginary borders of nation-states. Instead, we've continued down a path of self-destruction. As Naomi Klein highlights in *This Changes Everything,* we are not parents charged with the care and protection of the earth, but rather we are one of the many fragile, vulnerable children that depend on the earth for our survival. As the Gaia theory suggests, the earth herself is a complex, self-sustaining organism that will endure long after we are gone. What does our contemplative practice have to offer us as we face mounting climate disruption? How can it support us in responding?

While the image of earth as our collective home may inspire many of us and broaden our views, it is usually our relationships with *specific* places and creatures that move us. For example, my time in the great white pine at Nanny Joy's seeded an intimate relationship with trees that sustains and motivates me to this day. In the beginning of part 3, we noted how willingness to engage in high-risk, high-cost activism often depends on strong ties with others. Perhaps the same is true here: strong ties to specific places might open us to a larger sense of home. Could our cultivation of these qualities highlight not only the home within but also the home without: the miracle of our sojourn on this precious planet?

As the qualities mature, they take us beyond the self. Released from the illusion of separation, we feel less inhibited in our courageous, compassionate action. In this final section, consider how the earth teaches us to embody and nourish the qualities we discuss. Is your connection to nature calling you to greater action in service of life?

20. GRATITUDE

Gratitude for the gift of life is the primary wellspring of all religions, the hallmark of the mystic, the source of all true art. —Joanna Macy

When I was training as a Buddhist monastic, we rose at 4:00 a.m. for chanting and meditation. I generally enjoy waking up early, but 4:00 is a stretch. The first weeks I felt groggy and irritable, and I found it difficult to meditate. At my teacher's suggestion, I began reflecting on gratitude for the first ten minutes of the early morning meditation. I directed my attention to any circumstances or events for which I felt grateful, lingering with the feeling they gave me.

After running through the obvious conditions—food, shelter, my health, this opportunity to study and practice—I was stumped. Nonetheless, I continued contemplating gratitude each morning, and, interestingly, long-forgotten memories began to appear: eating a snow cone at a Little League game; gleefully chasing our dog in the park; my mother buying me clothes for school. My heart lifted, my mind brightened, and energy returned.

Equally fascinating, I began to notice small moments of goodness outside of meditation: a kind remark from a monk, a lay visitor asking after my well-being, the beauty of the monastery's masonry, the cozy warmth of my bed. Those ten minutes' reflection each morning set a tone for the whole day, as if I had tuned my heart to the frequency of gratitude. Indeed, if we look closely, we find countless inspirations for gratitude daily.

Gratitude is being thankful for what one has received, for the blessings in one's life. Gratitude teaches us to appreciate goodness. It nurtures presence, creates energy, and opens the heart. Gratitude has many flavors, from gentle happiness to pervasive joy, from sincere humility to deep fulfillment. Feeling gratitude, I often experience an inner gesture of bowing my head in appreciation, my hands raised in honor and celebration.

As I experienced at the monastery, cultivating gratitude brings happiness. It transforms our inner life, improving our well-being. A growing body of research shows that "gratitude is strongly and consistently associated with greater happiness. [It] helps people feel more positive emotions, relish good experiences, improve their health, deal with adversity, and build strong relationships."[1]

Gratitude also counteracts our negativity bias—the pervasive habit of noticing what's missing, what's gone wrong, what could be better. When the brain veers off into negativity, rather than objecting, gratitude turns toward it with appreciation and understands its adaptive function. Meeting our negativity bias with gratitude quiets it, allowing our hearts to rest. Gratitude, which wants nothing, subverts the culture of consumption, competition, and achievement. A mindset of gratitude opens the door to contentment and feeds generosity: the more aware we are of what we have received, the more we long to give back.[2] This cycle of giving and receiving has kept Buddhism alive for more than two millennia, as monastics minister to laypersons who in turn donate food, shelter, clothing, and medicine to monastics.

When we face how quickly the years pass and how radically everything can change at any moment, we appreciate the immense gift of being alive. The Talmud instructs Jews to recite one hundred blessings every day (opening the eyes upon waking, seeing something beautiful, eating, drinking, and eliminating, washing one's hands, doing anything for the first time, and so on). Similarly, Thich Nhat Hanh taught short verses, which he called mindfulness *gathas*, to cultivate awareness all day long.[3] Such practices nourish gratitude for the uniqueness of each moment. When we leave a loved one, gratitude reminds us of impermanence: this could be our last goodbye.

During a time of successive mass shootings in the United States and a grinding war in Ukraine, a student asked me, "How do we hold the dissonance between our gratitude for the blessings in life and our grief over the pain and suffering in our world?" Gratitude and grief may seem to be in tension with one another. Looking more closely, we see that gratitude and loss are inseparable. Awareness of what is present calls forth what is absent. On this paradoxical nature of gratitude, the writer and philosopher Báyò Akómoláfé reflects:

> Ultimately, gratitude is not just sharing one's appreciation, it is the vocation of touching the conditions of our passing away. To put gratitude to work in ways that are politically generative, one must consider it alongside grief, loss, and the pain of being carried away from home. When gratitude is reconsidered in the context of loss, we come to grace.[4]

In this way, grief embodies our humanity even as gratitude allows us to embrace pain and hardship. Far from imagining some rosy alternate reality, or suggesting that those who are structurally disadvantaged should be "grateful" for what they have, genuine gratitude opens the heart to all of life—the hurt and grief alongside the blessings. It broadens our view so that we don't overlook goodness in the face of suffering. It supports us in opposing injustice and oppression while also affirming, "This too is true."

Making space for all of our feelings keeps the heart healthy and supports wise responses within a complex world. Lulled to sleep by comfort and convenience, we don't act. Overwhelmed with grief, we can't engage. We must widen to include all of our emotions, lest we enter what Kahlil Gibran called "the season-less world where you shall laugh, but not all of your laughter, and weep, but not all of your tears."[5] Sharon Salzberg shares the story of divulging to her Burmese meditation teacher, Sayadaw U Pandita, that she had been crying in meditation. As he was known for being austere, she expected to be chastised, but he replied, "When you cry, cry your heart out. Then you'll get the best release."

Gratitude supports social change in important ways, simultaneously strengthening us and urging us to respond to social hardships. In turn, awareness of suffering can enrich our appreciation for simple things, like a glass of clean water. When I appreciate the beauty and love in my life, I am more available to connect with the suffering in our world. Acknowledging how aspects of my gratitude are connected to my privilege invigorates my commitment to use those advantages to combat injustice.

Collectively, gratitude flows into celebration. We need celebration to sustain us on the long road to freedom. The climate and racial justice activist Daniel Hunter sees celebrating our victories, even minor and mixed ones, as an antidote to the cynicism that saps our energy for the difficult, constructive work of social change. A small Quaker group in Philadelphia that practices direct action worked for four years to convince PNC Bank to partially divest from mountaintop-removal coal mining, eventually succeeding. After encouraging the group to celebrate, Hunter reflected, "We cheered amidst tears and relief. We weren't cheering PNC, or even the policy change, but the web of communities and practices of resistance that were building a better world, inch by inch."[6] As Hunter argues, since injustices may never end, we must stop, now and then, to celebrate—to renew ourselves, connect with one another, and keep going. Gratitude forms the foundation of this renewal.

REFLECTION

Getting Started

How do you relate to gratitude? Do you feel cautious, concerned you'll be disappointed in the end? Do you focus on gratitude to avoid difficult emotions? How can you find the middle path between these two extremes and cultivate a more balanced, integrated relationship with gratitude? Reflect on any time in your life when you've been grateful. How did that feel? What conditions supported it? Now recall a time when you found it difficult to feel grateful. What was happening within and around you? Contemplate the relationship between the grief and losses you've sustained in life and your experience of gratitude. How do these inform each other?

MEDITATION
Going Deeper

Settle the mind and body in a still, comfortable position. Rest quietly with the sensations of breathing or any other grounding experience—your hands in your lap, the weight of your body, the sounds around you. Now turn your attention to gratitude. Recollect specific moments, people, events, or conditions for which you feel grateful—a kind remark, a generous act, a fortunate circumstance, a moment of beauty. Allow the event, person, or condition for which you feel grateful to come to mind as clearly as possible. Linger with any pleasant feelings or sensations of gratitude that occur. You might feel a sense of warmth or openness in your heart, a subtle lightness, or an overall pleasant quality. Notice where you feel this in your body or heart. When the feeling fades, bring to mind another moment, event, or circumstance for which you feel grateful, and repeat the process.

You can think of this two-step process as striking a bell and listening to it ring. Clearly recalling the source of gratitude is like ringing a bell; lingering with and feeling its effects are like listening to the bell resonate. (You can use this process to deepen any of the qualities in this book: noticing or evoking its presence, then lingering on its effects.)[7]

ACTION
Embodying Gratitude

Gratitude can be sweeter when shared. Take time to consider someone whom you appreciate. This could be someone who did something for you recently or someone who has been there for you over time. Identify one or two specific things you appreciate about them, your relationship, or what they've done or said. How do you feel when you think of this? Why did it matter to you? How did it help you? How might you express it to this person, including all these elements of what they did, how it made you feel, and why? Last, find a time to open your heart and share your appreciation directly with this person—face-to-face if possible. If it's not possible to speak in real time, consider sending a letter or email.

You may feel vulnerable about sharing your true feelings and appreciation with others. Remember to start small and gradually stretch beyond your comfort level in ways that feel manageable. Work up to more challenging conversations in time. As an additional practice, whenever you appreciate someone, tell them. When you express your gratitude directly, the bond between you deepens. If you like, pair any of these activities with journaling. Each day, write down what you feel grateful for and why. What needs of yours were met by the things you feel grateful for? Why did they matter to you? How does it feel to acknowledge this?

IF YOU HAVE DIFFICULTIES

Sometimes all we can think of are our hardships, losses, or grief. If right now you are suffering with some intensity, gratitude may not be the right medicine. Consider if something else would be more appropriate and helpful: reaching out to someone who cares, cultivating self-compassion, or engaging in healthy comforts or self-soothing to create some internal space and ease.

Guilt is another common obstacle to gratitude. When we feel connected to others' pain, it can be challenging to appreciate goodness in our own lives. You may feel that allowing yourself to relish good things somehow invalidates others' suffering, or that you don't deserve to feel good when so many are struggling. If you find yourself stuck here, a few things can help. First, try to differentiate between genuine grief and mourning on the one hand and the self-centered movement into guilt on the other. Recall that feeling guilty doesn't help anyone—least of all you—as it focuses judgmentally on the self, rather than on responding compassionately to others. Second, remember that life is rich and different things can be true simultaneously: exquisite blessings and horrific tragedy. Gently explore your heart's capacity to hold the joy and gratitude you feel alongside the mourning and compassion. Notice what happens. Finally, you can't help anyone if you are overwhelmed. Gratitude feeds the heart. When you allow yourself to be nourished by life, you have more to offer others.

21. GENEROSITY

The best thing to do with the best things in life is to give them away. —Dorothy Day

My good friend Amita recently moved to a small community where people kept to themselves. A longtime meditator and spiritual seeker, Amita undertook an experiment in generosity. She began leaving anonymous gifts on neighbors' doorsteps: a loaf of bread here, some flowers there, a candle, a couple pieces of fruit. The first thing she noticed was how this practice affected her own mind: it uplifted her. She paid more attention to her neighbors, seeing what she could learn about them in order to find things they would appreciate. Instead of being preoccupied with her own issues, she kept her eye out for small gifts. The culminating act of surreptitiously placing the gift on their doorstep took on a delightful, mischievous quality. Over time, her neighbors began chatting about these gifts. They became more friendly, curious, and even started leaving other gifts for each other. Her generosity spread to the whole community.

All cultures and religions extol generosity and charity. Generosity uplifts the heart and brightens the world. Groups of species as diverse as bees, birds, bats, and primates act from generosity, suggesting a biological basis for this trait.[1] We can learn from our fellow beings. Rather than teaching newcomers meditation, wisdom, or ethics, the Buddha encouraged would-be disciples to begin by giving from their hearts. He understood the power of generosity to nourish well-being, heal our brokenness, and reveal the joy of letting go.

To give, we must first trust that we have something worthwhile to offer: our time, our attention, our energy, our love. Every time we slow down enough to truly see another, we give with our presence. One kind word, or even a genuine smile, can make a difference in another's life. Generosity illuminates our goodness and reminds us that we can make the world better. This instills dignity, wholeness, and self-respect, each of which helps us regard ourselves with love and accept our shortcomings.

True giving exists beyond obligation, performance, or exchange. It comes without strings attached, without any script saying "please" or "thank you." It is not about the gift itself, nor is it meant to deplete us so much that we are left without enough for ourselves or our family. It arises spontaneously from a natural impulse to share. We give not because we have to, because we think we should, because someone is watching, or because we want something in return. *We give because we can.*

Marshall B. Rosenberg, in his book *Nonviolent Communication: A Language of Compassion*, remarked: "When we give from the heart, we do so out of a joy that springs forth whenever we willingly enrich another person's life."[2] Rosenberg's reflection brings to mind Sam, a janitor at our local children's hospital who cleans the floors and empties the trash bins and who, for the last twenty years, has also given every patient he meets a crisp new two-dollar bill.[3] He says—with a big grin—that this is his way of bringing a little joy to the children.

When we give as Sam does, the roles of giver and receiver dissolve, for contributing is one of our deepest needs. Indeed, the Buddha taught, "If people only knew, as I do, the benefits of giving and sharing, they would not eat without first giving, and the stain of stinginess would not occupy their minds. They would not eat without sharing even their last mouthful, their last morsel, so long as there was someone to receive it."[4] When you connect with the joy of giving, more and more of your actions will flow from generosity. Becoming aware of why you do what you do, you may notice that even mundane acts connect you to yourself, to others, or to things you value. With this awareness, you can touch the joy of giving even when doing laundry, washing dishes, grocery shopping, or answering emails.

Generosity protects the heart from being judgmental. Just after winning the 1968 Houston Open, the Argentine golfer Robert De Vicenzo gave several hundred dollars to a woman who shared a wrenching tale about her daughter's battle with leukemia. When later he was told he'd been scammed, he is said to have joyfully replied, "Her daughter's not dying? My friend, that's the best news I ever heard!"

How could De Vicenzo say that? Because generosity carries us beyond the narrow purview of self-interest. We often burden the beauty of generosity with the specter of obligation, the fear of debt, or the ghost of insecurity. To truly give, we must see beyond our desires and preoccupations long enough to notice the human being in front of us and recognize that they too have needs. In giving, we relinquish grasping. The Dalai Lama calls giving "enlightened self-interest," as helping others contributes to our own well-being. The eighth-century Buddhist monk and philosopher Shantideva wrote, "All the joy the world contains has come through wishing happiness for others. All the suffering this world contains has come through wanting pleasure for oneself."[5] Twenty-first-century research confirms Shantideva's view: generosity makes us feel good.[6]

Liberating us from self-centeredness, generosity can heal the disease of craving that is destroying our biosphere. In forging bonds of relationship and belonging, it also assuages the isolation, fear, and lack that plague our hearts. If I give you a gift, we share a connection. Giving in any way—helping a neighbor, breaking bread together—creates relationship and builds community.

While Western culture idealizes the "self-made" person, many cultures are guided by a different understanding—individuals are intrinsic members of the collective. Rather than being a form of charity, giving expresses natural care for the community, much as the left hand cares for the right. For example, many Australian Aboriginal communities equate wealth with having enough to *share* with others rather than accumulating goods or resources to *consume*.[7]

While the modern era has improved many aspects of life—on the whole, better sanitation, lengthened life spans, and so forth—it has also produced unconscionable wealth inequality. The top 10 percent of humanity holds 85 percent of human wealth.[8] In the United States in 2017, the three richest individuals held combined financial wealth worth more than the total wealth of the poorest half of the entire US population.[9] In *Winners Take All*, Anand Giridharadas critiques the relationship between capitalism and modern philanthropy, calling out "a set of social arrangements that allow [wealthy elites] to monopolize progress and then give symbolic scraps to the forsaken—many of whom wouldn't need the scraps if the society were working right."[10] Giridharadas highlights how individuals who have accumulated massive wealth through destructive and exploitative means attempt to create positive legacies through spectacular donations that inscribe their names onto elite institutions.

Given these complexities, how might we collectively reclaim the beauty and power of generosity, harnessing it to move us toward a more just and equitable society? What would generosity look like beyond individual acts of sharing? Societies founded on generosity do not allow members to go hungry or unhoused. Communities practicing generosity respond to all members' needs. Around the world, intentional communities, religious orders, and other forms of communal settlements explore this collective generosity.

How might generosity function if we took this further and questioned the very concept of ownership? Look deeply: What actually belongs to you? Is not everything borrowed in the end? Even your very body is a gift you never could have created. Recognizing that our brief sojourn on the planet requires that we return everything, we begin to see that we own nothing. We are simply caretakers. Can we share accordingly?

Many Indigenous traditions recognize that our physical resources—land, soil, air, and water—are shared. Economists, ecologists, and others have used the phrase "the tragedy of the commons" to describe the modern collective negligence of stewarding community resources. This implies more than we realize. Humans have shared resources with one another and other living beings for the vast majority of our history. It took massive force and violence to destroy that sharing. For example, from 1600 to 1900, over one-fifth of the land in England was privatized by law and force in a process known as "enclosure," effectively transferring ancestral common land to the rich and powerful. The real tragedy of the commons is that many of us have forgotten our capacity for shared power through cooperation.

Nevertheless, we can still find inspiring examples of generosity on a collective level. Vinoba Bhave, a disciple of Gandhi, led a movement known as the Bloodless Revolution over twenty years, walking thousands of miles from village to village in rural India. Through this work, known formally as the Bhoodan (land gift) Movement, he convinced landowners to gift over four million acres to the poor. In 1953 *Time* magazine observed, "To those who have land he says: 'I have come to loot you with love. If you have four sons, consider me as the fifth, and accordingly give me my share.' To impoverished tenants and landless laborers he says: 'We are all members of a single human family.'"[11] Inspired by Vinoba, the Buddhist leader A. T. Ariyaratne began organizing camps in Sri Lanka to donate labor to impoverished villages. The camps grew, built local infrastructure, empowered villagers, and, through these communal gifts of labor, Ariyaratne's Sarvodaya movement became the largest grassroots development network in Sri Lanka.[12]

Public libraries are perhaps the most common example of collective, structural generosity. Community-run tool-lending libraries, seed repositories, community gardens, and land trusts all offer hopeful models for reweaving the fabric of interdependent generosity at the social level. Organizations and local groups around the world are taking generosity even further, experimenting with alternative economic structures and replacing the transactional model of capitalism with the relational model of gift-giving. In *The Gandhian Iceberg*, Chris Moore-Backman explains, "Instead of relying on fees and price tags, the gift economy is anchored by a trust that the bearer of gifts . . . will be cared for in return."[13]

In a world beset by insecurity and income inequality, mutual aid networks offer an alternative to wealth accumulation, sharing resources based on need. This aid both *relies upon* and *forges* strong communal bonds. The basic premise? If you want to experience more security, build community. Connection protects against emotional, physical, *and* financial hardship.

To facilitate generosity, we must also be willing to share our own needs and allow ourselves to receive support. It's not always easy to let others know we need help. We may have been taught that we should be able to make it on our own, that asking for help is selfish, or that we should put ourselves last. Consider though: when we hide our needs, we deprive others of the opportunity to be generous. When we open up, there is no telling how far one gift can reach.

The insight meditation teacher Steven Smith spent several years training as a monk in Myanmar (then Burma), a nation with a rich and ancient tradition of Buddhist monastics walking on alms round through the villages each morning and receiving food. Even children participate in this giving. A young girl, inspired by Steven having traveled so far to practice the Buddha's teachings, wanted to offer him something special. She saved for weeks until she could at last buy him a can of Coca-Cola. Steven recalls how she beamed as she offered it to him. Knowing the village's extreme poverty, moved by her generosity, Steven formed an aspiration to give back to this culture that had offered him so much wisdom and kindness. Steven and the girl formed a friendship that eventually helped her build a house, and they have remained close. But the ripples of that one can of soda have spread even further: Steven cites her generosity as a catalyst for his cofounding the MettaDana project, which has built hospitals and schools, provided humanitarian aid after natural disasters, and supported Burmese refugees.

To this day, the project continues to provide relief to Burmese communities in need.[14]

When our newborn son arrived, I was struck by his complete dependence on us. The rawness of his needs was staggering but was also a gift. His tiny vulnerable body called forth in us profound generosity, love, and compassion. When we reveal our needs, allow ourselves to receive generosity, or give from the heart, we become part of the cycle of giving and receiving that sustains all life. We discover within ourselves an abundance of spirit and energy.

REFLECTION

Getting Started

Think of a time you gave someone a gift, lent a hand, or helped out—not because you had to or thought you should, but simply because you wanted to. Recall the situation: where you were and what you offered. How did it feel then? How does it feel now?

Now contemplate how it feels for you to *receive* generosity. Are you able to let in the goodwill of others, or do you resist? What ideas or beliefs get in the way? Can you shift your attention to focus on the joy others feel when giving? What would it be like to experience your own needs as a gift to others? Can you allow yourself to fully receive?

MEDITATION

Going Deeper

Sit or stand in a comfortable position. Let your body be at ease yet upright, so you feel stable, steady, and alert. If it's helpful, take a few slow, deep breaths, letting your mind and body settle. Consider this meditation a gift of time and space to yourself, to simply be here with nowhere to go and nothing to accomplish, achieve, or untangle. Can you receive this gift of time?

Let your attention settle with the sensations of breathing in and breathing out. (If breathing is stressful or activating for any reason, try paying attention to the sounds around you.) Attend to each moment as an act of generosity, offering the gift of conscious attention to your inner life. How does it change your experience of *paying* attention if you think about it as *giving* attention? Allow yourself to experience breathing or hearing as a gift. Receive each in-breath as a gift from life, from the trees, plants, and clouds. Offer each out-breath as a gift to life, to all of the green, rooted beings with whom we share our air. Bring this meditation into your day. As you walk, open your senses to the world. Allow yourself to receive sights, sounds, smells, and the feeling of the air. Can you receive these as a gift?

ACTION
Embodying Generosity

At the beginning of each day, set an intention to notice and act upon any opportunities to give, share, or be generous. Look for small ways to give: smiling, holding the door, really meaning it when you say, "Good morning." In conversation, practice generosity by listening with full attention, offering your wholehearted presence. If you have access to material resources, share them. Give spontaneously. Explore giving in a more considered way through aid organizations or research-based initiatives. Stretch beyond your comfort zone, while taking care not to give in ways that harm yourself or your family. Give with your heart, connecting to the innate goodness of sharing. Whenever you give, pay attention to three things: first, the impulse to give; next, how it feels during the act of giving; and finally, how it feels to reflect back on the experience. Attune to any joy or happiness you feel.

IF YOU HAVE DIFFICULTIES

It's common for doubt, fear, shame, worry, or anxiety to complicate our natural impulse to give. Look gently at your experience and identify what's blocking you from generosity. Question any fears or worries: Do you really know they are true? Offer your compassionate, curious attention to such beliefs, giving yourself time to discover more about your fears. What would you need to feel secure enough to give freely?

Alternatively, try focusing your attention on the benefits of giving or on a time when you were able to give freely, without hesitation. Try to let this in. If you still find giving challenging, take more time practicing gratitude, focusing your attention on the gifts you've received in life. When your heart feels full, it's easier to share that fullness with others.

22. DEVOTION

Any aspiration can be accomplished, if you are whole-hearted and know the way.
—Acharya Anagarika Munindra-ji

I was drawn to Buddhism because of its commonsense approach to life and its empirical method for transformation. I didn't have to sign up for or believe anything. Buddhism outlined concrete steps to follow, and my teachers encouraged me to verify them through my own experience. On first listening to the teachings, I felt like I'd come home. Yet I had trouble trusting my heart; my thinking mind still needed convincing. I stayed up late, considering everything our meditation teachers had shared—the preciousness of human life, our inevitable hardships and pain, how we might free ourselves from unnecessary suffering—until my mind finally aligned with my heart.

One of the many effects of patriarchy has been the elevation of the intellect as the highest form of knowledge and the devaluation (in fact, active suppression) of traditional ways of knowing like intuition, emotion, and embodiment.[1] Acknowledging the Western split between the emotional heart and intellectual mind, the renowned Buddhist nun and teacher Ayya Khema urged us to integrate our entire being on the spiritual path: we can't travel this path as half of a person.

Devotion is the willingness to give our heart to something completely. It is a way of relating to anything in life with deep love, loyalty, and generosity of spirit. In wholeheartedly engaging with life, devotion helps us realize our aspirations and brings satisfaction and fulfillment. Devotion heals us, feeds our heart, and sustains us with well-being during our challenges. Devotion provides a foundation for long-term engagement and plays a crucial role in transforming our inner and outer worlds.

Like many secular Jews, whose history of persecution and pressure to assimilate have led to an overemphasis on rationality, I used to bristle at what I stereotyped as devotion. For me, the word conjured images of irrational behavior and blind faith. When I was a child, images of people praying to Jesus or the Virgin Mary seemed like idolatry to my narrow sensibilities. Since then, I've come to understand devotion entirely differently. Notice your own associations with the following words, each of which expresses a different aspect of devotion: *sincerity, reverence, respect, wholeheartedness, enthusiasm, love.* Devotion can be sensible and grounded, and yet it can open us to the mysteries of faith.

The words *devotion* and *vote* both come from the Latin *vovere*, to vow, promise, or dedicate. To be devoted means that we commit fully. When we are devoted, we give tremendously of our time, energy, and attention—to a spouse, an instrument, a practice, a garden, a quality, or the sacred. This kind of wholehearted offering can include our rational intelligence, but it needn't depend on it. Yes, devotion without reason can be dangerous, as history tragically demonstrates. But when our devotion leads to good and benefits others, we can feel confident that the object of our devotion is worthy, whether or not it makes sense rationally.

It took a long time for me to appreciate the value and beauty of Buddhist devotional practices like bowing, chanting, and offering incense. Learning more about their historical context gave me a new perspective on these practices. The Buddha radically challenged traditional views that holiness was about one's birth (caste) and that spiritual purity or attainment could be found through rituals like bathing in the Ganges. He asserted that true righteousness lies in the heart, and that the primary value of ritual is *symbolic*. In ritual, intention matters more than action. Thus to offer incense to a Buddha statue is to offer gratitude for the Buddha's teachings and respect for our own capacity for awakening.

Devotion expresses humility, gratitude, and appreciation; we may literally lower ourselves to honor another. In this way, bowing is a whole-body mudra (symbolic gesture) signifying deep respect. Devotion to the sacred, one's ancestors, or a teacher uplifts the heart and calls forth our potential. Their goodness elicits the best in us.

We see the potency of devotion in a curious passage from the Buddhist Pali canon where the Buddha, just days after being enlightened, reflects, "It is painful to dwell without reverence. . . . Now what ascetic or brahmin can I honor, respect, and dwell in dependence on?"[2] Realizing that his insight had surpassed that of everyone he knew, the Buddha decides to honor and respect the truth that set him free. This floored me when I first read it. One of the few records of the Buddha's thoughts after his awakening is essentially, "How can I still show devotion?" This sentiment embodies a fundamental human longing to be in relationship with something sacred or worthy of our respect.

Without devotion we suffer from spiritual hunger; we sense something missing, perhaps without even knowing what it is. Without the opportunity to give ourselves to something worthwhile, our need for devotion may become displaced onto addictions to accumulation, substances, or appearances; onto entertainments and pleasures; or onto feelings of self-judgment, inadequacy, and self-loathing. In effect, we become what Buddhists call "hungry ghosts," endlessly consuming, never fulfilled.[3]

When we feel an absence of the sacred, we experience a void in our hearts, a pervasive emptiness. Materialism, hedonism, and hyperindividualism dislocate our need for devotion to something larger than ourselves, whether through religious observance, spiritual practice, or a transcendent experience of love. We may be devoted to art, to love or family, to the sacred, to social justice, or to all of these and more. Our devotion is not defined by its object but by the quality of attention and love we bring to it. When we act with full sincerity, connecting our heart with our purpose, even washing the dishes can be an act of devotion.

Neglecting the heart and failing to integrate devotion into our lives inevitably erode our capacity for fulfillment in some way. If we don't engage our hearts, life becomes dry and automatic. Relying exclusively on the logical and analytical part of our minds, we approach life mechanistically and lose touch with creativity and freshness. Caring for children, spearheading a new project or campaign, even meditating become obligations rather than empowering vocations, and we lose the deep joy of acting with sincerity.

Devotion expresses itself in a diverse mosaic beyond traditional ways of relating to the sacred. As the poet Rumi wrote, "There are a thousand ways to kneel and kiss the ground."[4] In 1965, when Rabbi Abraham Joshua Heschel marched for voting rights with Dr. King, he famously said, "I felt like my legs were praying."[5] Activism, caregiving, service, singing, growing vegetables, planting a tree—all can be meaningful acts of devotion that connect us to something larger than ourselves.

We don't practice devotion to get something in return. We practice it for its own sake, as a complete offering of our heart. Singing my son to sleep in my arms, lowering him gently into a warm bath, even wiping his bottom—done wholeheartedly these acts express full devotion. Shunryu Suzuki Roshi recounts how Dōgen, the founder of the Soto school of Zen Buddhism, made a devotional act of fetching water from the river, taking only half a dipper and returning the rest "without throwing it away.... When we feel the beauty of the river, we intuitively do it in Dōgen's way."[6]

In deep devotion the quality of our presence transcends our actions. What we do with wholehearted devotion becomes a holistic expression of our being, an act of beauty and selflessness beyond the everyday realm of time, roles, and duties. Released from such daily pressures, we open to the transpersonal realm of the mythopoetic, the archetypal, and the sacred. A single moment of generosity, offered with complete devotion, connects us with all acts of generosity. Planting one tree with devotion connects us with the limitless capacity of life. Devotion thus reaches beyond discrete acts. Vows of love, aspiration, and justice require devotion. Long-term commitments like marriage, child-rearing, and ordination all call forth enduring devotion, as we show up again and again each day. Such devotional commitments, combined with resolve and awareness, power social change in the face of obstacles and repression.

In northwestern India a hundred years ago, Badshah Khan's devotion to nonviolence and education as forms of rebellion sparked a peaceful revolution that challenged at once British colonialism, the authority of local mullahs, and an ancient culture of violence. Advocating for a united, independent, secular India,

Khan founded the world's first nonviolent "army of peace," which grew to one hundred thousand members in spite of brutal British repression. His visionary devotion drew global attention to the power of nonviolence and was vital to India's liberation.[7]

Devotion can transform protests into pilgrimage and demonstrations into ceremony. In 1978, advocating for tribal sovereignty and protesting threats to treaties and water rights, several hundred American Indian activists and supporters marched for five months across the United States, from San Francisco to Washington, DC.[8] Known as the Longest Walk, this pilgrimage secured several legislative victories, including the American Indian Religious Freedom Act. More recently, in 2016, opposing the construction of the Dakota Access Pipeline (an oil conduit that passes through ancestral burial grounds and under tribal water sources), Lakota elders at Standing Rock frequently reminded demonstrators that their actions were a form of ceremony.[9]

In such efforts, we can glimpse devotion's capacity to extend even beyond our lifetimes. Held strongly enough, and by enough people, devotion bridges generations in liberating visions—from emancipation, women's suffrage, and marriage equality to ongoing movements for nuclear disarmament and for racial and climate justice. When we give our whole being to anything skillful—be it for one moment of complete presence or a lifetime of tireless work—our being itself becomes a blessing, and we drink from a source of strength and goodness beyond our personal history or identity.

REFLECTION
Getting Started

Take time to examine what you habitually devote yourself to. To what activities, persons, values, or habits do you unthinkingly give yourself? Is part of you devoted to time, money, efficiency, or control? Consider how this serves and how it limits you. Now reflect on who or what is *worthy* of your devotion. Is there a person, activity, or value to which you would like to be more devoted? Perhaps your family, a craft or project, a social movement, or even a quality like generosity or gratitude? What would that look like for you?

MEDITATION

Going Deeper

Sit, stand, or recline and settle your mind and body in any way that feels supportive. Let yourself be completely natural, without trying to control your thoughts or focus in any special way. In your own time, when you're ready, pose one of these questions to your heart:

· What is sacred to me?
· What do I hold dear in life?
· What upholds and supports me?
· What is the deepest truth I know?
· What is too important to forget?

Simply ask the question and listen to whatever arises. Make space for anything and everything—memories, images, sensations, and emotions, as well as discursive thought. Give more attention to the depth and quality of your question and your sincere listening than to finding an answer. Whenever your mind wanders, return to something simple and grounding in the present moment, such as your breath. Continue your inquiry by asking the question again or posing one of the others. Keep listening, honoring whatever arises, not needing to figure things out. If something clear emerges, shift your focus to appreciating your connection with whatever feels sacred, worthy, or true to you. When you feel ready, let go of the question and return to being present. Make a mental note of anything significant you want to remember.

ACTION

Engaging Devotion

Choose an activity to take on as a devotional practice for the next two weeks. This could be praying, bowing, chanting, or any other spiritual observance. It could equally be walking in the garden for ten minutes every morning, mindfully drinking a cup of tea, reading your child a bedtime story, or even cleaning your teeth! The quality of presence and intention you bring to the activity is what matters. If the activity you choose seems to lack meaning, *create* that meaning. For example, if you choose drinking water as your devotional act, when you drink you might focus on the wish that all creatures have access to clean water. If it's cleaning your teeth, you might connect with the heartfelt wish that all creatures have the means necessary to care for their bodies.[10]

Each day, before doing the activity, pause, gathering all of your attention. Set a clear and firm intention to give this activity your full attention. When you do it, do it wholeheartedly, connecting with the meaning this activity, person, or task has (or that you've created). As you act, stay attuned: Are you aware? Is your heart engaged? Are you rushing ahead or settling into the moment? Return to the aim of offering your entire being. As the days unfold, notice whether any resistance, impatience, or control comes up. If so, recall that meeting these habitual challenges is also a practice. What happens if you let go of having things the way you want and surrender to the process?

Alternatively, choose an ongoing commitment in your life that you'd like to reinvigorate with devotion. Can you notice ways devotion and other qualities we've examined imbue not only this commitment but all great actions, such as parenting, intimate partnership, lifelong friendship, and following one's vocation?

IF YOU HAVE DIFFICULTIES

If terms like *the sacred* don't speak to you, find ones that do. What connects you with something larger than yourself or your lifetime? What lights you up inside? If the word *devotion* turns you off, try using a synonym like *commitment* or *wholeheartedness*. Practice doing something with complete and total sincerity; put your whole heart into it. If you struggle to do this, use that as an opportunity to practice patience, forgiveness, and mindfulness and try again. If you find yourself growing tight, straining to do it "correctly," pause in that very moment. Try relaxing your face and jaw. Exhale. Come back to the spirit of devotion: offering your heart to that which is worthy. Consider your time, energy, and presence a gift you can offer. To whom or what shall you offer it? Return to the practice of devotion with this new orientation.

23. PLAY

We don't stop playing because we grow old; we grow old
because we stop playing. —George Bernard Shaw

All mammals play. Pets romp, dolphins leap, cubs and pups tus-
sle. Play unlocks a storehouse of joy and vitality in us, supporting
healthy social, emotional, and neurological development.[1] As they
explore their bodies and emotions through play, children learn to
engage, cooperate, set limits, and build relationships. Play encourages imagination, creativity, and endurance. In humans, playfulness is even tied to flexibility, empathy, altruism, problem-solving,
and resilience.[2]

Geez—play's beneficial. Better get on that!

With so much to be serious about in life, from the climate crisis to our own mortality, it may feel surprising to associate weighty
endeavors like spiritual practice or social justice with play. But the
laughter and lightness of play are essential to keeping the heart
nimble, accessing creativity, and maintaining healthy perspective.
Rather than distracting us from the work at hand, play infuses our
being with vital energy and protects our hearts from stagnation
and hopelessness.

~

Play lets us enjoy this moment and laugh at what happens next. It's fun, alive, and frees us from flat, boring stuff like social roles and linear time.[3] Play is recreation: games and sports. Play is creativity: dance, art, music. And play is more: socializing, debate, cooking, yes, even meditation.

Keeping a spirit of play alive is essential. Our four-month-old son delights at my slightest invitation—sticking out my tongue, speaking in gibberish. Being with him refreshes me, counteracting my adult conditioning to suppress play and conform to expectations. Without the vitality of play, life can become dull and rote. As we age, the world of schedules, efficiency, and accomplishment may colonize our minds. When it does, our capacity for play withers and we fall into the trap of thinking that life is work. We succumb to busyness and productivity and become prisoners of the clock. We may even approach family life or spiritual practice with the mentality of a project manager: focused on tasks, subtasks, and deadlines, all the while missing the mystery, messiness, and spontaneity of life. We lope along like a flat tire with zero bounce, forgetting to engage with the world.

When was the last time you did something goofy? When was the last time you made a fart noise, told a riotous joke, or put on a silly face? The musician Jacob Collier says, "The creative adult is the child who survived."[4] Trauma, oppression, and the sheer force of socialization kill play. We may have learned that play has harsh consequences. We may have been taught—based on gender, class, and other factors—that only certain kinds of play are acceptable. We may have been ridiculed or punished for having fun, taught to "grow up" and stop horsing around. There's even a term for this:

play deprivation, with research behind its serious consequences.[5] When our natural, playful impulse has been injured, play can feel off-limits or even threatening. We may need a lot of safety, reassurance, and encouragement to reawaken it.

Play offers much to the spiritual journey, helping us let go of control and find beauty in the raggedness of life. It's taken a long time for me to lighten up and reclaim my own playfulness—and I've still got a way to go. (Case in point: this chapter was hard to write!) As a child focused on the script of achievement, I felt impatient. I wanted to grow up, find a job, and get on with life. In the early years of my meditation practice, friends noticed I had a "controlled peacefulness," rigidity rather than ease. Somehow, I thought that spirituality mandated restraining my expressive nature. To shake things up, a few years ago I took a clowning class. I couldn't handle it and dropped out, even though clowning is in my lineage: my grandma Nanny Joy was a clown! But I have lost my red nose. I used to keep it in my desk drawer in case things got too serious, but I literally can't find it. Still, as my understanding deepens, I discover that the loud Jewish kid from Jersey still has something to teach the quiet mystic: lighten up, and I may still get to be a clown someday. Embracing all of my personality gives me more space to appreciate the chaos in life. When I'm not trying to control myself, there's more room to play.

You can learn to play again by exploring when and how play shows up in your life. Crucially, play is free: no one can force you to play. As we've explored, we always have some measure of choice, even if only an inner choice. The more we feel our capacity for choice, the more playful we can be, undercutting engrained attitudes of obligation. Folding laundry can become a farcical opera; putting away the dishes, interpretative dance instead of drudgery. I wrote a playful song about changing my son's diapers and even added baby sign language. We bond gleefully many times a day, singing it.

Play draws us in and gives us pleasure, but dominant cultural forces in Western society have a conflicted relationship with pleasure. The media sells the pleasure of entertainment as synthetic play, offering distraction and a false promise of happiness—a far cry from the satisfaction of true play. The media associates fun with adrenaline (video games, extreme sports) and play with the limited domain of sexual expression. Meanwhile, an echo of the United States' Puritan religious past suggests that pleasure is itself somehow sinful. Poorly understood notions of renunciation can compound this confusion, casting our natural enjoyment of sensory pleasure in a negative light (see chapter 9, on renunciation).

In reality, healthy pleasure is an essential ingredient in everyday life, in spirituality, and in social change. Nonaddictive, wholesome pleasure nourishes the heart and strengthens resilience. As we've explored, there is an art to pleasure: from pausing for small moments of gratitude to noticing the richness of our sensual experience. What's more, the enduring hard work of transformation depends on the nourishment of pleasure. In her book *Pleasure Activism*, adrienne maree brown notes, "There is no way to repress pleasure and expect liberation, satisfaction, or joy."[6]

In fact, play can occupy an instrumental and sometimes unexpected role in transformative activism. In *Blueprint for Revolution*, Srdja Popovic describes how humor can effectively and playfully resist even dictatorship by eroding one its most essential tools: fear.[7] In Syria, nonviolent activists protesting President Bashar al-Assad began releasing hundreds of ping-pong balls in the steep streets of Damascus with slogans like *Enough* and *Freedom* written on them. Each time, Assad's security forces were sent—fully armed—to chase and capture tiny balls bouncing down the streets. In 2012, denied a permit to protest Russian president Vladimir Putin's rigged re-election, a group of nonviolent activists in Siberia held a stuffed animal rally in the town center, the animals holding tiny protest signs. Soon, toys and stuffed animals across the country mobilized and took to the streets to protest! Even engaging fearsome security forces, humor can undermine the credibility of brutal regimes—and make us smile.

The joy of play is also a worthy, beautiful end unto itself. As adults, this aspect of play can present a radical challenge to our goal-oriented conditioning. The global economy is designed to focus on efficiency and productivity. This influences our personal lives when our sense of value and self-worth becomes tied to external validation through success or status. Chasing after the promise of happiness through material gain, comfort, and accumulation, our whole being can become organized around accomplishment. Pause to consider: does the promised goal ever arrive? And even if it does, how long does the satisfaction last? Even after accomplishments, do you find yourself feeling empty and exhausted? Tragically, this goal-oriented attitude infects our relationship with well-being. Does your effort toward personal growth involve rejecting who you are in the present for an imagined version of yourself in the future—one that is finally attractive, acceptable, and lovable? Does it provide a date when you will be good enough?

This driven quality often shows up for meditators as striving, sometimes making so much effort that we become entangled in knots of tension, frustration, or exhaustion. On a long and intensive meditation retreat, the insight teacher Kamala Masters told me, "Take a walk. Look at the trees. Backing off is part of diligent practice." What a revelation! How much time do you allow yourself each day simply to do nothing? ("Nothing" might be looking at the sky, listening to the wind, or taking a walk without a destination.) With every minute of the day scheduled, there's no time for play. Play's destination is here and now. It topples the hierarchy of achievement, accumulation, and self-improvement in favor of presence, exploration, discovery, and fun.

Some of the most exciting, enjoyable play emerges spontaneously. Open structure allows for creative exploration. This contrasts starkly with the rigid values of order and predictability engrained through compulsory education and social norms. The linear mind wants an answer, an endpoint. Play, like life itself, is nonlinear, open-ended, unscripted—a complete and total engagement with the present that meets reality with spontaneity. Life is uncertain; we make it up as we go. Play brings this profound awareness to the lightest and heaviest moments alike.

All of these attributes of play—its voluntary, attractive nature, its spontaneity and inherent worth—give rise to two more defining qualities. First, play draws our focus into the present so deeply that we lose track of time. Second, it allows us to forget our habitual self-consciousness. Release from the boundaries and pressures of time nourishes us deeply. When we truly play, we don't watch the clock, anxious to get to the next thing or make time go more quickly. We become fully absorbed in its unfolding. Engaged with others, our environment, and the activity itself, we release our preoccupation with appearances, comparing, and performing. As we center the dynamic interplay of life, our idiosyncratic thoughts and worries fade into the background.

All of these qualities of play are keenly relevant for meditation and contemplative practice. Just like play, meditation is voluntary. We *choose* to meditate, and recalling our aspiration brings energy. Meditation frustrates our addiction to achievement, teaching us to appreciate the process of life on its own terms. It is spontaneous, exploring experience in a dynamic, creative way.[8]

Meditation reveals the timelessness of the moment and invites us to release self-centeredness.

Just like play, meditation can be enjoyable, but we may need to develop a taste for it. The pleasure of meditation is subtler than a good game of tennis or an amazing jam session with other musicians. Rather than being found in excitement, the pleasure of meditation arrives in the simplicity of doing less, learning to appreciate the absence of pressure, stimulation, and activity. It arrives in the restful quality of being still, even when the mind is busy. It teaches us to appreciate the soothing, flowing quality of the breath or the openness of space.

Going a step further, we discover that, with some patience and creativity, playfulness can actually infuse our meditation. Thay was fond of instructing practitioners to meditate with a subtle smile at the corners of the mouth, changing their physiology and brightening their spirits. This suggests one pathway to meditation itself as play. Reorienting our expectations, we can extend this spirit to a wide range of ordinary, daily activities. And remember: the more we play, the more juice we have for the inevitable difficult patches of the journey.

REFLECTION
Getting Started

Reflect on the messages you received about play growing up. What kind of play did your upbringing encourage? What kind of play did it discourage? Are there ways you were unable to play due to your identity or circumstances? How does it feel to bring awareness to these conditions?

Now turn your attention to the present. Do you have ideas about who you "should" be or how to behave? Do external circumstances and perceived obligations limit your time and energy for play? Investigate what you "have to do." What needs does this activity meet? (Don't start with the most difficult thing on your list!) Imagine completing this "have to." What would it give you? Imagine not completing it. What would happen? Be sure to frame the "have to" in the positive. For example, you can reframe "I have to do this so they'll stop bugging me" as "I *want* to do this so I'll feel at ease and have more peace of mind." Notice if awareness of your needs affects your experience of willingness, and if that frees up any energy to invite more play into your daily life.

MEDITATION

Going Deeper

Bring a spirit of play to your meditation. Settle mind and body in a comfortable posture, and invite a slight smile at the corners of your mouth. Recall that you are choosing to meditate, that nothing is "supposed" to happen, and that you're here to explore. Whatever technique you use (mindfulness of breathing, a body scan, loving-kindness), aim to relate playfully to your experience. Like a child discovering a new toy, turn things over, poke around, get curious. Eventually let your attention settle into a more and more spacious, open awareness. Without focusing on anything in particular, allow the interplay of thoughts, sounds, and sensations to flow through you. Watch how everything comes and goes by itself, a dance of life.

ACTION

Embodying Play

Write yourself a prescription to have fun! If you have trouble finding time to play, schedule an open block of fallow time—unstructured downtime where your priority is doing nothing save following your organic impulses. You may to need rest before the energy for play arises. See if you can take at least a few minutes every day to do something playful—from making goofy faces with a friend or partner, to shaking your body and dancing, to tussling with your pet or neighbor's dog. Allow yourself to be silly and unscripted. If you have trouble relaxing into it, get creative. Spend time with a toddler. Find your clown nose and don it. Try some laughter yoga on YouTube. In your journal, make a list of all the things you enjoy doing that *could be* play, even if they aren't yet. If you're stumped, think about what brought you joy or what you liked doing as a child. Appreciate any areas where you are already playful, relishing the vitality and fun of those experiences.

IF YOU HAVE DIFFICULTIES

One common obstacle to play is lack of energy. Energy declines naturally with age, overwork, and illness, but play can be small and easy: drawing or painting, telling a story, listening to music and tapping your foot, reading poetry aloud. Remember that play is not about the activity itself—it's about the spirit of exploration, creativity, and spontaneity you bring to it.

If you are struggling with painful emotions or grappling with challenges in your life, here are two ways you can move forward. One: take a conscious break from your feelings and do something entirely different that fully occupies your attention. Listen to live music, go to a dance class, do some gardening—dive into an activity that you find delightfully absorbing. Two: turn toward the feeling and engage with it playfully. Can you *play* with anger, fear, or sadness? Give the emotion a name. Dress it up in a costume or represent it as a cartoon character: Oscar the Grouch from *Sesame Street*, Eeyore from *Winnie-the-Pooh*, or your own unique creation. Alternatively, inquire, "How am I with this? Can I find some balance?" Imagine wrestling with the emotion, dancing with it, or playing tag with it. Feel its energy, its strength. If the emotion were an image, what color would it be? If the emotion were a song, what would it sing? If it were an odor, how would it smell? Explore it with imagination. Let your primary aim be to learn rather than to get anywhere or make the feeling go away. Making your emotion concrete helps you grapple with it. And as we know, grappling can become play.

24. COMPASSION

True compassion is more than flinging a coin to a beggar.
It comes to see that an edifice which produces beggars
needs restructuring. —Dr. Martin Luther King Jr.

Our nervous systems were not designed to process the vast amount of information with which so many of us are flooded on a daily basis: a war ten thousand miles away, mass shootings at home, hunger near and far. How do we stay engaged and connected in a world with so much heartache? How do we avoid shutting down, panicking with overwhelm, burning up in anger, or burning out with frenzied activity?

We need many skills to process and respond to the immense pain in our world. As we've explored, we need discernment to know when and how much to take in; we need courage to face pain and allow our hearts to grieve, mourn, or be angry; we need joy and gratitude to keep sight of the goodness in the world. But perhaps above all else we need compassion for those beset by pain and injustice, including ourselves.

Compassion allows us to receive pain and respond skillfully. It is a strong, balanced tenderness that helps us stay steady in the face of hurt, instead of turning away, lashing back, seeking someone to blame, or numbing out.

What's your habitual response to pain? Do you distance yourself or pretend it's not happening? Do you feel anxious, rush in, and try to fix it? As we've explored, resisting pain compounds it and produces suffering. Compulsively taking care of others, we may disempower them or make things worse due to a lack of understanding. Alternatively, we may pity others for their pain. Pity differs from compassion; it acknowledges pain but recoils with fear, internally distancing ourselves from others.

Compassion instead touches pain with mercy. It's engaged, strong, and available. Rooted in tenderness, it embraces hurt with love. Compassion, like aspiration, includes a twofold process: its *receptive* component feels, trembling with care, while its *active* component responds, asking, "How can I help?" With compassion, we stand securely on dry land, offering an outstretched hand to another who is drowning in the water.

Evan and I have lived through a number of losses in our community—including my own father, and two friends losing children. These losses are even more poignant for us as new parents. To respond appropriately, we need both receptive and active compassion. Receptively, we stay present and offer caring companionship *with the pain*. We sit, mourn, cry together, and hold one another. Actively, we ask, "What do you need?" Active compassion guides us to bring a home-cooked meal, leave a bag of groceries, or pick up the phone just to say, "I'm here if you need me."

One gateway to compassion is building tenderness for ourselves. How do you respond when *you* are suffering or in pain? Do you blame yourself, sinking in the hurt? Do you push it away, pretend all is well, or tough it out? Self-compassion recognizes when we're struggling and calls out, "Can I get a hand here?"

I had a powerful lesson in self-compassion in my twenties. I'd been trying to treat my colitis with diet and alternative methods. I was traveling and my health was deteriorating—pain, bleeding, urgent bowel movements—but I was in denial. One day, in the aisle of a grocery store, I didn't make it to the bathroom in time. Mortified, with poop dripping down my leg, I limped to the restroom to clean up. That was a turning point. I felt how lonely, exhausted, and scared I was, and realized I needed help. Acknowledging all of this, I let go of my rigid views about the evils of the pharmaceutical industry and the innate healing capacity of the body, and I accepted that my body needed more support. I saw that innate healing and Western medicine weren't mutually exclusive: I could continue seeking alternative treatments *and* take anti-inflammatories to ensure I wasn't in danger. In an act of self-compassion, I made an appointment with a gastroenterologist.

Compassion turns pain into medicine.[1] After her five-year-old son died in a car accident, Susan Burton turned to drugs to numb her pain, became addicted, and was incarcerated for nearly twenty years. When she finally received the support she needed to heal, she turned self-compassion into action and founded a nonprofit that provides robust reentry resources for formerly incarcerated women. "When you get locked up, you get locked out . . . of housing, you get locked out of jobs," she reflects. "Cycling in and out of prisons, I couldn't take back the years I'd put in, but I could stop others like me from putting in more years. . . . If I could help other women receive what I had received, then it could make a difference."[2]

Compassion can be fierce, helping us relinquish codependence and cut through the entanglements that entrench our suffering. Clearly perceiving the causes of suffering, compassion urges us to act. With fierce compassion, we rush to grab a child's hand as she reaches for the stove; we shout "*Stop!*" as she runs into the street. Filled with protective love, we may be sharp, decisive, even caustic. Acting from fierce compassion, we rip the bandage off all at once, sparing unneeded pain. Compassion gives us the courage to finally say no to someone we love rather than enable self-destructive behavior.

At the collective level, compassion can tip the scales in the struggle for justice and even save lives. The labor struggle that became known as the Bread and Roses Strike of 1912, in Lawrence, Massachusetts, brought together mill workers of broadly varied ethnic loyalties, many of whom were women and children, in protest against inhumane working conditions. Local authorities responded with brutal repression, but the organizers maintained the strike by tapping into the collective heart of community compassion, arranging childcare for families and meals and supplies to support the basic needs of the strikers. With bold, strategic, passionate action, rooted in dignity and shared humanity, the strike gained national attention and resulted in a decisive victory.[3]

The horror of the Holocaust also called forth remarkable compassion, courage, and integrity in individuals who risked their lives to save Jews. After Germany invaded the Soviet Union in June 1941, three brothers retreated to the woods near their home village in Belarus and set up a camp of partisans. Tuvia, Zus, and Asael Bielski created a refuge in the forest for Jews—young and old, healthy and sick. Continually moving to evade the Nazis, they sent letters to the nearby ghettos encouraging others to come and live freely. By the end of the war, the Bielski Brigade had saved some twelve hundred Jews. Today, their legacy of fierce compassionate protection is represented in the number of their approximately twenty thousand descendants.

Inevitably, we encounter pitfalls as we develop both the receptive and active dimensions of compassion. How do we stay connected to compassion when bombarded with more daily suffering than we can ever respond to? How do we stay afloat if our job puts us on the front lines of hardship? When receiving more pain and suffering than we can manage, we slide into depression and overwhelm if compassion becomes unbalanced. On the active side, if we reach out to help but lose our center, we may topple over and fall *into* the suffering. Caregiving professionals sometimes call this "compassion fatigue"—exhaustion and burnout from repeated exposure to an unmanageable amount of pain and suffering.

Both Buddhist traditions and social sciences assert that true compassion doesn't fatigue us. The social neuroscientist Tania Singer suggests that compassion fatigue is in fact a form of empathic distress.[4] Losing perspective, we become preoccupied with another's pain, identify with it as our own, and may withdraw out of self-protection. Empathic distress distorts our vision and can sink us into helplessness, compelling us to believe we can't improve things. Instead of taking action, we become paralyzed and end up doing nothing.

To stay engaged and heal our relationships, communities, and world, we must learn to distinguish compassion from its decoys that sap our strength and leave us stranded. Singer notes that true compassion is "characterized by feelings of warmth, concern and care for the other, as well as a strong motivation to improve the other's wellbeing."[5] By focusing on what we can do to help, compassion empowers us to assuage pain, rather than getting lost in it.

Wisdom complements compassion, allowing us to distinguish what's helpful from what's futile. Wisdom guides us to understand that if we jump into the water with our friend, we may both drown. With wisdom, we recognize self-care as the necessary companion of compassion. To sustain compassion, you need the clarity and confidence to honor your limits: to sometimes say no or prioritize your needs. You can't pour from an empty cup. This doesn't mean that you need to be completely healed or balanced to help others but rather that self-care is an inseparable aspect of compassion and a key resource for helping others.

Equanimity also supports compassion, giving us the big picture. As the inner balance that comes from understanding that loss, pain, and hardship are a natural part of life, equanimity helps us recognize that, while we have some influence over our immediate surroundings, we ultimately can't control the outcome of events. We can offer an outstretched hand to a friend, but it's up to them to reach for it. If they take our hand, we may be able to pull them safely ashore, but we cannot control their choices.

Unsurprisingly, having compassion for others also depends on having compassion for ourselves. If we can't make space for what's present in our own hearts, how can we be truly available to the pain of others? Developing compassion for the world includes turning our attention inward with a tender gaze and making space for all that we feel. The more tenderness we have for our pain, the stronger our resilience and the more compassion we have for others' pain. The heartbreak that occurs daily on our planet, both human and nonhuman, is greater than we can comprehend: too vast to hold and too deep to fathom. Yet with compassion, we can navigate our challenges with balance together, healing our nervous systems, relationships, and communities.

To be in right relationship with all that is happening—a relationship honoring the interconnectedness of life, the complexity of who we are, and the context of our times—we must find a way to move beyond our self-limitations and tap into a greater source of strength. Chinese Buddhism offers the example of Guan Yin (sometimes written as "Kuan Yin," Avalokiteshvara in Sanskrit), the bodhisattva of great compassion. Guan Yin hears the cries of the world and responds with compassion. Often depicted as gender-fluid, Guan Yin has a thousand arms with an eye in each palm to see suffering. When we embody compassion, our hands become Guan Yin's hands, our ears and eyes Guan Yin's ears and eyes. Embodying compassion collectively, we can heal the pain and transform the suffering of our world.

Awakening to our true nature offers another path to respond skillfully to collective pain. This awakened awareness, called the Great Heart in some traditions, is known by many names and can be different for each of us. Some find the Great Heart through devotion to the sacred. Some find it through connection with ancestors or the unborn generations to come, expanding our sense of self beyond this lifetime. Others enter the Great Heart through the gate of love and service, touching universal metta or agape. Others enter through loss and sorrow, allowing the heart to break open completely into a vastness that sees that nothing is truly separate. However we arrive, it is this opening of the self beyond our boundaries that allows the heart to quiver with such pain without being crushed.

Like all of the heart qualities we are exploring in our journey together, compassion is innate. It is indigenous to the human heart, but we must actively cultivate it for it to support us in these times.

REFLECTION

Getting Started

Reflect on the relationship between compassion for others and for yourself. Consider how you would respond to a friend who had just suffered a great loss. Imagine both the quality of tenderness you would feel (the receptive, empathic component) and your willingness to help (the active, responsive component). When you sense a state of strong, caring compassion for this friend, turn your attention to yourself and consider how you relate to your own troubles. What would it be like to offer more compassion to yourself? How would this inform your life, your choices? Imagine feeling grounded and confident enough to lovingly say no to a request when you know you need self-care. Finally, consider how having more compassion for yourself would affect the energy you have available to help others.

MEDITATION

Going Deeper

Settle your mind and body in a way that feels natural and supportive. When you feel present and steady enough inside, bring to mind a situation, image, or phrase that evokes compassion—a stable, caring attitude oriented toward alleviating suffering. You might think of stroking a distressed pet, comforting a lost child—or whatever moves you.

From this compassionate place, bring to mind the image or sense of a friend who is struggling a little bit. See their vulnerability and imagine them experiencing more ease and peace. Say silently to yourself something simple that expresses your genuine wish for their relief, such as "May your pain be eased," "May your heart be released from this suffering," or "May you find freedom within this hardship." Repeat this phrase at an easy pace. As you do so, notice any impulse to pull away or disconnect from their suffering, on the one hand, or to fall into it, on the other hand. Keep returning to the stable, balanced orientation of compassion, neither disengaged nor enmeshed.

ACTION
Embodying Compassion

Choose a situation where you'd like to contribute: a friend or neighbor going through a hard time; a local or broad issue, campaign, or project. Recall that wisdom informs compassionate action. If you're helping someone you know, make sure you determine both what they need and what you can offer. If engaging in social issues, set aside time to learn about the work that's already being done and what's most needed. Join a call or speak to someone already involved to learn how you can best apply your time, energy, skills, or resources. Describe in your journal what it's like for you to engage in this compassionate service.

IF YOU HAVE DIFFICULTIES

Several obstacles may arise when cultivating compassion. As you practice, you may not experience a clear emotional response. If that's the case, focus more on the sincerity of your intention to assuage pain than on the presence or absence of any particular feeling.

On the other hand, you may find yourself flooded with grief or sadness, consumed by another's suffering. In this case, try backing off and starting small. Choose a situation where it's easier to stay balanced or a friend whose suffering isn't currently so intense. Recollect equanimity to balance compassion. Bear in mind the limits of your control, your respect for others' autonomy, and your own boundaries. Expand your access to this kind of balanced compassion before you move to harder situations.

25. CONTENTMENT

Just to live is holy. Just to be is a blessing.
—Abraham Joshua Heschel

Autumn has always been a special time for me. The cool air, the fading light, and the golden, rust-colored leaves of the Northeast reliably evoke stillness. I fondly recall the peace I felt walking to school on fall mornings. The crisp beauty of the season revealed an internal capacity for contentment.

Contentment teaches us to feel at peace with things just as they are. It is a state of well-being, satisfaction, and ease that arises when craving is absent. To feel content, we must be released (if only temporarily) from wanting something other than what is right here, right now. A first kind of contentment comes when our needs are met; a second and deeper contentment arises as the heart discovers its fullness in renunciation.

Earlier we looked at the quality of gratitude, which is closely related to contentment. Feeling gratitude, we actively appreciate what we have received—a particular condition, experience, or blessing. Gratitude can give rise to contentment, but contentment is a quieter happiness, a stillness in which the heart rests with what is, finding satisfaction in the here and now.

A superficial contentment arises when the world aligns with our preferences. When we *like* external conditions, craving ceases, and the heart grows happy. Yet this contentment is unsteady and fickle, vanishing as soon as conditions shift. How long after a delightful meal or thrilling purchase until we resume hankering for something to occupy our attention? Lasting contentment comes neither from getting what we want nor from avoiding discomfort.

We touch a truer contentment by being mindful of when our needs are sufficiently met. How often do you eat beyond your hunger and end up feeling bloated? Or binge-watch TV, bleary-eyed and drained at the end of a series? With attention, you can learn to recognize when you've had enough and appreciate the understated pleasure of contentment. After a simple meal, a workout, or a good night's rest, we can abide contentedly. For a blessed interlude, our hearts are still. This pleasant stillness is perhaps the most common form of contentment: a quality of temporary fulfillment due to satisfaction of basic needs that breaks the trance of craving.

In our commodified world, this capacity to recognize what is enough is radical. Contentment challenges a global economy that feeds desires and destroys habitats and ecosystems. Distinguishing fundamental needs from superfluous wants, contentment frees us from longing for something different or better. It asks, "What would it be like to live with less?"—a powerful question for those of us who have more than we need.

The next stage of contentment comes from developing a taste for subtlety, a more refined happiness than the pleasure of sensory stimulation. Consider the difference between the richness of (insert your favorite food here) and the satisfaction of a sip of clean water or a breath of fresh, mountain air. The first stage of contentment arises from pleasant things and the fulfillment of needs; the next stage emerges through the peace of simplicity.

Initially this may occur by noticing the absence of afflictive states. Thay taught that we can appreciate our "nontoothache." Similarly, we can enjoy a lack of anger, irritation, fear, or anxiety, though it takes practice. I vividly recall the first time I witnessed anxiety disappear. During the early days of my meditation practice, I was out running errands and my mind was busy worrying. Then I noticed my mind had wandered and I had forgotten what was troubling me. I could even feel a habitual pull of *wanting* to worry, and *trying* to remember what had been bothering me. Instead, I opened to appreciating its absence.

You can train your heart to attune to contentment by noticing two things: the underlying agitation of sensory craving, and the quiet enjoyment of its absence. A few years ago, my wife and I visited Italy. Excited by its culture and beauty, my attention rushed out insatiably through my senses. My urge to see and do everything, coupled with fear of missing anything, pushed me so hard it inhibited my ability to actually enjoy myself. (You can imagine how it annoyed Evan!) The sights and sounds weren't themselves agitating; it was my heart's *reaching* toward them that disturbed me. Feeling that discomfort, I finally settled back and we were able to have some fun.

Noticing the agitation of subtler sensory craving takes refined attention and an appreciation of stillness. The more we train ourselves to observe it, the more we appreciate its absence and the more a different quality of contentment emerges. We abandon the endless process of looking for something to fill us up and learn to notice the absence of pressure, agitation, rushing, and craving. It's like the relief we feel when a fan or the motor of an appliance cycles off in the background. When craving ceases, pressure settles. Then, instead of growing bored when nothing is happening, we can appreciate the stillness that remains.

Translating this insight from the sensory to the psychological realm, we recognize the suffering that comes from always needing to be effective, productive, attractive, unique, or intelligent. When we let go of these desires, we touch a deeper quality of contentment.

As I've shared, I struggled to find my place or feel contentment despite my many privileges and blessings. I recall carefully practicing walking meditation on retreat, striving to be as mindful as possible, slowly noticing each nuanced sensation as it arose and changed. Using the technique of mental noting, I softly narrated the movements of each step: "lifting, moving, placing . . . lifting, moving, placing." After nearly an hour, I began to notice another voice, a whisper at the back of my mind, critiquing each step: "Not good enough . . . Nope . . . Try harder." When at last I recognized how hard I was driving myself, a flood of grief broke open. In this instant of recognizing the pain of my self-judgment, I saw it was invalid. I suddenly felt the weight of years of pushing myself to be someone else, to escape who I was. With this mourning, a tremendous tenderness arose within me. I felt held within a loving acceptance so complete it included everything: the pain, the anger and fear, even the regret of having been so unkind to myself for so long. In that moment, I discovered a quality of contentment that comes from facing the truth and embracing the totality of an experience, even when it hurts.

Fortunately, you don't need to torture yourself with slow walking meditation to realize this. Look for moments of struggle and notice what happens when you can embrace them. Stuck in traffic? Accept it. How do you feel when you relinquish rushing and resistance? Perhaps you feel your body sitting, notice the sun shining, or see a bird flying. Contentment can arise simply because you are here and alive.

My walking insight grew while training at the monastery in Canada. The abbot, Ajahn Viradhammo, asked, "Why is it so hard to be at peace? Just sitting quietly, breathing in and out, no one is bothering you. How do we keep generating suffering?" His question shifted my focus. I saw my *dis*content: always planning, worrying, finding a problem to fix, an irritation or desire to pursue. Observing this pattern, something else became apparent: the still, quiet space of awareness within which all of this was happening. In that space I could sit quietly, at peace with things as they were. I didn't need to feel great, figure anything out, or even make my thoughts stop. It was enough to simply be aware.

This was a different quality of contentment than I had ever experienced, as it didn't depend on the content of my experience but arose from appreciating awareness. This contentment shifts our vision from a narrow focus to a wider field, from the *objects* of awareness (the sights, sounds, thoughts, and feelings that fill our lives) to the space of *awareness itself.* As a musician or poet values the space between sounds, we can value the space between things.

The deepest contentment is not based on external conditions but on being with things just as they are. Relinquishing preferences, abandoning resistances, we access the peace of unconditional contentment. Rather than spiritually bypassing the pain in our hearts and the world, the contemplative's contentment arises from a radical acceptance of the truth. The road to contentment includes our discontent; it welcomes all that we feel.

This acceptance may make contentment seem antithetical to social change. After all, it is our *dis*content with injustice that moves us to work for collective healing and transformation. But contentment is not the same as approval of the status quo, complicity with harm, or acceptance of oppression. It is a deeper capacity to be at peace with the unresolved tensions of life, the vulnerability of not knowing, and the weight of suffering. Supported by equanimity, it dawns when the heart expands widely enough to include it all—the loss and grief, the rage and devastation, the urgency and exquisite beauty of being alive.

Rather than discouraging us from action, contentment fuels our work toward a better world. While the human spirit is capable of profound contentment, insight, and freedom in any circumstance, it is of course most accessible when our basic needs are met. The more we discover the space to feel all that is true, the more confidence we have to handle what life brings. Having touched profound contentment, we are more able to open to the immense weight of collective grief required for transformation—whether receiving difficult feedback, confronting privilege, or turning toward the realities of climate disruption. Transcendent contentment dissolves the boundaries of the self and reveals our interconnectedness. In that peace we realize the interdependence of liberation: none are free until all are free. True contentment urges us to create the conditions where everyone has the opportunity to find their calling, discover their true nature, and feel content.

Moments of contentment, whether mundane or transcendent, protect us against burnout and self-defeating cynicism. Many changemakers cite the strengths of community and meaning found in the struggle for justice as sources of abiding contentment. This naturally follows from our fundamental human needs for belonging and purpose. Lean Alejandro, a beloved leader and martyr in the student movement against martial law in the Philippines in the 1980s, must have been referring to this sense of contentment when he said, "The struggle for freedom is the next best thing to actually being free."[1] His companions consistently described Alejandro—though he lived in mortal repression and danger—as joyful, hopeful, and playful. Even in such dire circumstances, he was held within a committed community and thus nourished by the fruit of contentment.

Getting Started

Reflect on the last time you got something that you really wanted (whether an object or an experience). Review the thoughts and feelings leading up to getting it. Did you feel satisfied afterward? Was there any amount of contentment, and if so, how long did it last?

What is your experience of the cessation of craving, whether you've experienced that cessation through fulfilling a desire or letting it go? How do you feel it in your body? Take time to notice this. Where in your life do you feel a sense of contentment? In friendship, in work or contribution, in joy or peace? Explore the possibility that *you* are enough, just as you are.

MEDITATION

Going Deeper

Sit, stand, or recline in a comfortable posture. Allow yourself to do nothing for a while. Notice the space around your body—how it is open, nonintrusive. Attune to the absence of pressure around you: right now, in this moment, no one is glaring at you, bearing down, or demanding anything. How is it to notice the absence of that pressure? In your own time, become aware of the sounds, sensations, and thoughts passing through your awareness. Consider how everything unfolds by itself, due to causes and conditions. These thoughts, feelings, impulses, and experiences arise and pass in their own time. Notice how all of this is happening within awareness. See if you can shift the focus of your awareness from the objects within it—what you are *experiencing*—to the field within which it is all occurring—the wakeful *knowing* of it. Hold that wakefulness carefully, freely allowing things to come and go. What if there were nothing you needed to do right now, in the present moment, other than rest content in wakeful knowing?

ACTION
Embodying Contentment

Pay attention to the possibility of experiencing contentment when craving ends. Notice moments when your needs are fulfilled: after a meal, a shower, a meaningful conversation, or even a good cup of tea or coffee. Instead of rushing on to the next thing, let your attention linger. Can you soak in the ease of even a brief feeling of satisfaction? Can you allow yourself to feel content?

Once you've completed this investigation, begin to pay attention to the presence and absence of agitation during the day. Notice this as you leave the house, wait in traffic, or sit in a meeting. If you find yourself feeling rushed or impatient, pay careful attention to the moment that feeling ends—whether due to external conditions (shutting the door, traffic clearing up, the meeting ending) or internal conditions (relaxation, interest, relief). How do you experience agitation ending? How do you feel this in your body? Begin to notice the relative absence of agitation in ordinary, passing moments during your day. What happens when you bring your attention to these periods of normal, neutral experience? Is there any amount of contentment that arises? See if you can allow it to expand.

IF YOU HAVE DIFFICULTIES

We can't force ourselves to feel content any more than we can force ourselves to fall asleep. If you're struggling, notice what's driving it: Do you feel restless or anxious? Are you eager, seeking to "get" contentment? *You can't.* Contentment won't arrive through grasping, only through letting go. Instead, try bringing a kind and patient awareness to the very movement within your heart that reaches for contentment. Feel it. See what happens as you maintain awareness.

If your experience of contentment feels heavy or lethargic, look closely to see if it isn't tinged with disengagement or apathy. Attend carefully to the underlying tone in your heart. Is there any part of you that's avoiding feeling something? Can you begin to make space for more of your experience? How can you offer tenderness to yourself if you feel like contentment eludes you? What happens as you accept the absence of contentment?

26. FORGIVENESS

We have repeatedly observed that those who forgive the
most profoundly seem to heal the deepest. Love is a gate-
keeper that, unlike most, struggles to keep the gates open.
—Stephen and Ondrea Levine

In 1962, Nelson Mandela was sentenced to life imprisonment in
South Africa for his work with the African National Congress to
dismantle apartheid and overthrow the government. He spent
twenty-seven years in prison, including nearly six years in soli-
tary confinement. His mother passed away while he was serving
time, and a year later his eldest son died in a car accident. He was
unable to attend either funeral. Reflecting on his time in prison,
Mandela spoke of the inner transformation that occurred during
those years and of the profound understanding of forgiveness that
was born in him before his release in 1990. He said, "As I walked
out the door toward the gate that would lead to my freedom, I
knew if I didn't leave my bitterness and hatred behind, I'd still be
in prison."[1]

Forgiveness is a universal, timeless balm. But in cultures that
indulge in resentment and glamorize revenge, forgiveness may be
rare and radical. Still, as Mandela showed, it is possible to cultivate

forgiveness, to cease resenting harm and make peace with things we wish were otherwise. We practice forgiveness individually, offering it to others and ourselves. We share forgiveness interpersonally, rebuilding relationships. We engage it communally, healing collective pain and trauma.

Cultivating forgiveness can be hard for anyone, and it can be especially complex for those who have suffered trauma. Trauma-informed perspectives therefore encourage starting small. Try building capacity in less-threatening contexts. Look for daily annoyances: a driver who cuts you off; the gruff, unhelpful clerk; a telemarketer who won't let you go gracefully. As you gain confidence in your own strength, incrementally introduce greater challenges.

Real forgiveness includes kindness and compassion, but without bypassing anger or pain. Anger is often a protective response to threats against what we hold dear. *Feeling* anger is natural, but *holding on* to it or compulsively *acting it out* causes harm. It can make us feel temporarily strong or appear to empower us, but it ultimately traps us. Over time, anger, bitterness, and resentment destroy us from within. The Buddha likened resentment to picking up a burning coal to hurl it at someone else, or walking into the wind with a grass torch. We suffer first. Forgiveness, on the other hand, frees us. It even reduces blood pressure, stress, anxiety, and depression, improving both our sleep and our outlook.[2]

To forgive does not mean to forget, to pretend, or to condone harm, overlooking grievous acts or erasing our memory. Whoever first said "forgiveness is giving up all hope of a better past" put it well. Forgiveness releases us from suffering through fully accepting it. Forgiveness honors the past by engaging with it honestly.

Practicing forgiveness does not require befriending those who have harmed us. It does not preclude taking action, setting limits, pursuing justice, or engaging in reconciliation. We can forgive and also say, "Never again!" As the nonviolence trainer Kazu Haga explains, forgiveness is one step in a broader process of accountability that includes remorse, insight, and, often, making amends. In reconciliation, we rebuild relationships through empathy, trust, and community support.[3]

It takes strength and courage to forgive. First we must interrupt harm and reestablish safety. While there are examples of radical forgiveness—prisoners actively forgiving those who torture them—we must be careful: *forgiveness never justifies what it forgives.*

Acknowledging a harmful event and its impact, opening the heart to all it encompasses, we find forgiveness. This process may require inner patience and tenderness, as well as support from others in creating conditions in which we can feel the full impact of loss, trauma, or betrayal. We may feel numb or experience waves of intense emotion. It took me many years to acknowledge the great pain and anger of my childhood. For over a decade, I had a recurring dream in which I screamed through tears of rage at my family, desperate to be seen and heard. Having accepted that anger, my underlying grief has emerged and I have been able to forgive.

Beware of two common pitfalls when practicing forgiveness: getting stuck in pain, and trying to evade it. Recall the distinction between the first arrow of pain and the second arrow of suffering. *Feel* the pain. Open your heart to mourning without wallowing. Alternatively, don't forgive prematurely out of conflict avoidance, hunger for connection, or longing for harmony. During one romantic breakup, I wanted to stay connected so badly that before

I processed what had happened—much less mourned the loss of relationship—I blurted out, "It's okay, I forgive you."

The pain we feel contains the seed of its own healing. When we realize the weight of the burden we carry, the intention to forgive can arise out of wisdom and compassion. When we eventually grow weary of holding on to resentment, we aim toward freedom. In an interview in a documentary on the power of forgiveness, the Lakota elder Albert White Hat shared his own profound opening to forgiveness for his personal experience in Indian boarding schools and for the countless atrocities his people sustained at the hands of white settlers and the United States government. Although he had been consumed with anger and desire for revenge, he reached a tipping point where he touched a deep yearning to be happy. "I want to live. I want to be happy. I feel I deserve that. But the only way that I was going to do that was if I forgive. And I cried that morning, because I had to forgive. Since then, every day I work on that commitment [to forgive]."[4]

Forgiveness is a journey. It takes time, energy, and effort to release our hearts from pain and resentment. We can cultivate the *intention* to forgive. The dharma teacher Winnie Nazarko reminds us that, when the intention to forgive feels unavailable, we can consider the possibility of someday *wanting* to forgive. Even this sets the process in motion. Though forgiveness begins with an intention, it rarely concludes in an act of will. We can't demand or force ourselves to forgive. As adrienne maree brown notes about building relationship, we "move at the speed of trust."[5] The heart forgives when it is ready.

The author and dharma teacher Larry Yang invites us to think of forgiveness as spanning four domains: forgiving others, asking forgiveness from others, forgiving ourselves, and forgiving life.[6] We forgive others for our own sake, even if they may be unable to receive or acknowledge our forgiveness. Seeking forgiveness can be a powerful gesture of remorse, especially if accompanied by a commitment to accountability. This accountability includes being willing to hear the effects of our actions on others, offering empathy (if and when it is welcomed), and sharing insight into the causes of our actions. If your counterpart is open to reconciliation, you may inquire what might repair things and restore trust.

Forgiving ourselves can be challenging. We may have let ourselves down, hurt those we love, done unskillful things, or been cruel in ways that seem impossible to forgive. Other times, it is life we must forgive—life that wears us down, breaks our heart, dashes our dreams, or takes from us what is most precious. As I write, I try to forgive myself for being less present than I could have been with my father the last time we spoke. He called me the day before he died to confirm some logistics for his coming visit to meet his only grandchild. It was a brief, warm conversation that ended with expressing our love for one another. Yet I wish I had lingered more, asked him about his day, and told him how much we were looking forward to seeing him. In working through his loss, I find forgiveness for myself through his enduring love.

Many doors can open our hearts to forgiveness; empathy perhaps most widely. In his sermon "Loving Your Enemies," Dr. King reminded, "The evil deed of the enemy-neighbor, the thing that hurts, never quite expresses all that he is. An element of goodness may be found in even our worst enemy."[7] With empathy, we witness one another's humanity and accept that we all make mistakes. We forget what's most important to us and act unknowingly out of ignorance; we act knowingly out of fear, greed, or hatred. With empathy, we can also acknowledge that people can change. Archbishop Desmond Tutu, chair of the Truth and Reconciliation Commission assembled in postapartheid South Africa in 1996, said, "To forgive is to say: 'I give you another chance to make a new beginning.'"[8]

Becoming aware of the cycles of violence in our lives, we can also catalyze forgiveness by healing ourselves of intergenerational and historical trauma. Instead of burdening future generations with our unresolved hurt and anger, we can transmute "dirty pain" into "clean pain," to use Resmaa Menakem's terms. Adults who were abused as children break the generational cycle of violence when they process their pain and renounce "toughening up" their own kids with beatings. Though we lack the power to end all violence or heal all hatred, forgiveness gives us the power to release *ourselves* from hatred. And that can begin to shape a new future.

Expanding our view to include the vast web of conditions creating our lives, we recognize things just as they are. This doesn't mean we *approve* of all of those conditions, only that we acknowledge what exists, even as it may break our hearts. If we find a way to broaden our scope in this fashion, we may begin to understand that things in this moment could not be other than they are. We do not choose the unfolding of our lives or our times, only how we respond.

This brings us to the prospect of death, the final doorway to forgiveness. Everyone dies. *You* will die. This powerful tonic can free your heart. In seeking to forgive, ask yourself, "Do I want to bring this to my grave?" In the end, what really matters? In death, the promise of tomorrow dissolves. When the time comes to let go of everything, how do you want to cross into the unknown? Do you want to be filled with bitterness and regret, or with gratitude and love? Thankfully, we need not wait until our last day to let go and forgive. Not knowing how much time we are granted, we can practice forgiveness every day, as a way of life, cleaning the slate instead of carrying a burden. When we forgive, we discover freedom here and now. Recall Thay's instruction to his students: "Walk as a free person: free from the past, free from the future."

I feel tremendous appreciation for both the blessings and challenges in my life. The hardships I've faced, from growing up with a mentally ill family member to the trials of chronic illness, have humbled me, opened my heart, and deepened my compassion. They've taught me that we are connected through our vulnerability, not our triumph. That facing hurt and loss, we discover what endures beyond those experiences. That meeting pain with love brings healing, peace, and wholeness to the heart and mind. And that a whole heart can embrace the entire world with compassion.

REFLECTION

Getting Started

As you go to bed, cast your mind over the past day. Attend to gratitude, appreciating anything that uplifts you. Now notice any lingering pain: any worry, fear, anger, or hurt. Step back and reflect on what's needed. Do you feel called to act or respond? Differentiate between needing to respond skillfully and clinging to events in a way that produces suffering. Consider whether forgiveness could offer relief. What really matters in the end? When death comes and it is time to let go, will this matter?

Expand your reflection beyond today. Open to the possibility of making peace, allowing everything to be as it is. (Importantly, this "allowing" includes empowerment to rise up.) Invite gratitude for the gift of life; for all you've experienced; for having a heart, mind, and body. Dwell in this. Now review what is unfinished. What are you holding tightly? What can support you to let go and be at peace? Suppose this is your last night on earth: what do you still need to forgive? Breathing quietly, feeling reassured by the steady presence of awareness, let these questions move through your heart. Recall that forgiveness is a journey; accept wherever you are in that process.

MEDITATION

Going Deeper

Settle your mind and body in a comfortable, upright position. Invite tenderness into your heart, recollecting the shared vulnerability of being alive. Breathe quietly as you connect with the rawness of living in a world of change so often beyond our control. In your own time, bring to mind someone you'd like to forgive (this could be yourself). Remember to start small. Choose a specific situation or incident and carefully attend to any thoughts, feelings, or reactions. Make space for all of it. Notice any contraction in the heart, bringing compassion to the hurt. What helps you to see a broader picture, recall shared humanity, or understand that we are each doing the best we can with the resources we have at any given moment? Silently explore expressing your intention to forgive. Modify or rephrase the following suggestions to fit your own voice and circumstances:

Forgiveness for others:

- "For whatever harm you have caused me, intentionally or unintentionally, I freely forgive you—as much as is possible in this moment."
- "Just as I, at times, have acted out of ignorance and caused harm to those around me, so too have you acted out of ignorance and caused harm. I forgive you."
- "Someday, I want to be able to forgive you."

Forgiveness from others:

- "For whatever harm I have caused you, intentionally or unintentionally, I humbly ask for forgiveness."

Forgiveness for yourself:

- "I forgive myself for being imperfect. I allow myself to make mistakes, to be a student still learning life's lessons."[9]

Forgiveness for life:

- "For any way that life has caused harm to me or other beings, directly or indirectly, in thought, word, or deed, may I have forgiveness as my intention."[10]
- "Thank you for teaching me to love. May I forgive you for breaking my heart."

Continue making space for thoughts, feelings, and reactions, holding it all with tenderness. When you're ready, allow the situation or person in your contemplation to fade, and return to the simplicity of feeling your body, your breathing, and the sights and sounds around you.

ACTION
Embodying Forgiveness

As you move through your day, notice when things don't go as planned or when your wishes aren't met. To whatever degree possible, slow down and give yourself time to feel these feelings, great or small. What would it be like to cultivate forgiveness as a way of life? To meet disappointments and hardships with tender, loving acceptance? To respond from wisdom and love, rather than reactivity? Pause and consider the possibility of forgiving yourself, others, and life when things don't go your way. Journal about your process of forgiveness—the obstacles, inspirations, or insights you encounter.

IF YOU HAVE DIFFICULTIES

If you find yourself in grief or anger, do something to take your mind off the pain. Spend time with good people, engage in a hobby, or connect with healthy sense pleasures—nourishing food, fine art, good music. Feel the joy of life. Wait until you feel more nourished and balanced to return to the practice of forgiveness.

If you are stuck in resentment, make space for it. Notice if it feels empowering or protective; if so, receive that. Now compassionately notice any tension, hurt, or pain associated with it. Consider what it would be like to be free from resentment. What part of you is holding on to it? What does that give you? Do you want to hold another accountable? To protect yourself from future harm? To be understood for your experience? What if it were possible to fulfill those needs without the resentment? What resources can you draw on to find more creative ways to meet your needs?

If you have experienced serious harm, such as trauma or abuse, you may need to focus on healing before contemplating forgiveness. Attend first to your safety—physically, psychologically, and emotionally. Seek support from those who can honor the intensity of what you've lived through. Consider working with a trained professional such as a trauma therapist or grief counselor to reclaim your agency and power. Give yourself *as much time as you need* to process the events before considering forgiveness. Allow that seed—perhaps the mere hope of your transcendent power to forgive—to be sufficient until your heart is ready.

Acknowledgments

If you've read this far, I celebrate your skillful qualities—particularly energy, patience, and resolve. Completing anything these days seems like a feat—how much more an entire book! If it's supportive, I invite you to take a moment to appreciate the time and effort you've offered to your heart, and so to our world.

Though I'd long considered writing on the gradual cultivation of wholesome qualities, the inspiration for this particular book came in response to the events of 2020. In the early days of the COVID-19 pandemic, before a vaccine was available, frontline workers (including my wife) lived in great uncertainty and enormous risk. Then came the spiritual and cultural upheaval of George Floyd's public murder and, on its heels, a very different kind of upheaval in the form of historically devastating wildfires in the western United States. Most folks I knew were scared, overwhelmed, numb, or struggling. As a dharma teacher, I thought to make the small contribution of writing about the qualities essential for moving beyond simply surviving to thriving and becoming a force for positive change.

I wrote the first draft of this book during the spring and summer of 2022, as Evan and I were expecting the birth of our first child. I completed it after he was born, during a dark, cold, and wet California winter: between diaper changes and lulla-bies, sleep-deprived and lovestruck, as we navigated the colossal changes of becoming new parents and getting to know our son.

In a very real way, you would not be holding this book with-out Evan's generosity. She pulled extra weight taking care of our son during the final weeks of editing, and she bore my underslept grouchiness with the patience and love of a bodhisattva. Evan's mom, Alicen Wong, provided further joyful support to our fam-ily during those long winter months—affording me more time to write and edit. Alongside their support, our son has shown me how each of us enters this world with remarkable, pure inner beauty. Being with him has intensified my love for our world and consolidated the deep care I feel about so much that is hurting and uncertain today.

This book also would not exist without the love and gen-erosity of countless other beings. I am indebted to my spiritual teachers Anagarika Munindra-ji and Godwin Samararatne for in-spiring me by embodying what is possible in a human life. Joseph Goldstein, Michele McDonald, Kamala Masters, and Steve Arm-strong have, in their turns, guided my spiritual practice over the decades. In particular, I owe immense gratitude to my monastic teacher, Ajahn Sucitto, who, through his own example and gener-ous friendship, has affected me profoundly. His teachings appear throughout this book. I also offer gratitude to my friend and men-tor Sharon Salzberg, whose guidance teaching metta retreats over the years has deepened my understanding and embodiment of the brahma viharas. Her wisdom, love, and accessibility have shaped these pages as well.

Finally, I owe an immense debt of gratitude to both Chris Moore-Backman and Franz Metcalf, each of whom came through in tremendous ways when I needed support with the second draft. Chris stepped in with invaluable consultation, wisdom, and feedback on the social change dimensions of the book. A scholar of Gandhian nonviolence, a longtime activist, an author, and a dad, Chris helped me make more concrete connections between the qualities and social change. Many of the social change examples and stories that grace these pages entered the book via Chris's deep knowledge and heartfelt embodiment of principled nonviolence. Meanwhile Franz, an author, Buddhist scholar, and father as well, tirelessly edited every chapter, teaching me how to write better sentences while vastly improving (and shortening) the text.

A host of other friends and colleagues graciously offered their input on portions of the text. Thank you Amita Schmidt, Carol Melkonian, Derek Haswell, Donald Rothberg, Douglas Kennedy, Emily Horn, James Baraz, Jesse Maceo Vega-Frey, JoAnna Hardy, Kathy Simon, Kristin Masters, Lily Huang, Matthew Brensilver, Rae Houseman, Roxy Manning, Sumi Loundon Kim, Stephanie Bachmann Mattei, and Kaira Jewel Lingo. Special thanks to Jay Michaelson and Sean Feit Oakes, who, in addition to reading several chapters, pushed me to think more carefully about the role of individual action in social change. Similarly, in addition to her input, Kaira Jewel generously offered her blessing on the title in spite of its striking similarity to the title of her excellent book, *We Were Made for These Times*.

Joe Reiffer and Jennifer English diligently researched references, tracking down the source and exact wording of quotes and reformatting citations. Many practitioners from my email list offered their thoughts on excerpts during the early stages of writing. Finally, several volunteers transcribed talks and collated reader feedback; thank you Lily Huang, Deborah Carlon, Michelle Cordon, and Nancy Ney-Colby.

Notes

Introduction

1. Fred Pearce, "Global Extinction Rates: Why Do Estimates Vary So Wildly?" YaleEnvironment360, August 17, 2015, https://e360.yale .edu/features/global_extinction_rates_why_do_estimates_vary _so_wildly.

2. Karan Deep Singh and Bhadra Sharma, "How Nepal Grew Back Its Forests," *New York Times*, November 11, 2022, https://www .nytimes.com/2022/11/11/world/asia/nepal-reforestration-climate. html; Erik Eckholm, "Seedlings Dot Nepal's Once-Barren Slopes as Country Battles Forest Crisis," *New York Times*, February 21, 1984, section C, page 2, https://www.nytimes.com/1984/02/21/science /seedlings-dot-nepal-s-once-barren-slopes-as-country-battles-forest -crisis.html.

3. Some of the theory and aspiration that animate Engaged Buddhism also draw from Mahayana Buddhism, which introduced the concept of the bodhisattva—one who works for the spiritual awakening and freedom of all beings, vowing to forego their own enlightenment until all beings are free. This emphasis on the interconnection of our suffering and our liberation resonates with contemporary anti-oppression and liberation movements that teach that we all suffer from oppressive systems (though not equally) and that none of us are free until all of us are free.

4. Thich Nhat Hanh, *Peace Is Every Step* (New York: Bantam Books, 1991), 91.

5. David Wallace-Wells, "Greta Thunberg: 'The World Is Getting More Grim by the Day,'" *New York Times,* February 8, 2023, https://www.nytimes.com/2023/02/08/opinion/greta-thunberg-climate-change.html.

6. Thich Nhat Hanh, *Love in Action* (Berkeley, CA: Parallax Press, 1993), 47.

Chapter 1. Attention

1. "The Seeds of Vandana Shiva Trailer | 2022," The Seeds of Vandana Shiva, May 20, 2021, YouTube video, 2:39, https://www.youtube.com/watch?v=YEqTo8lDivs.

2. This definition of *citta* comes from the teachings of the Theravada forest monk Ajahn Sucitto. Throughout the book, I will use the words *heart*, *mind*, and *heart-mind* interchangeably to refer to this domain of sensitive, responsive awareness.

3. This was not merely a haphazard event that went viral. Dr. King and the Southern Christian Leadership Conference carefully and strategically planned the demonstrations in Birmingham. Charlie LeDuff, "A Black Teen, a White Cop, and a Photo That Changed the Civil Rights Movement," Vice, March 2, 2015, https://www.vice.com/en/article/mbw843/a-black-teen-a-white-cop-and-a-photo-that-changed-the-civil-rights-movement.

4. Vandana Shiva, "See Freedom Is Earth Rights," Global Alliance for the Rights of Nature, July 9, 2012, https://www.garn.org/vandana-shiva-seed-freedom/.

Chapter 2. Aspiration

1. The Pali Buddhist word for this quality is *saddha*, often translated as "faith." *Saddha* is the first of the five spiritual faculties (*indriya*) and encompasses a range of nuance: conviction, trust, aspiration. Here I use the translation "aspiration," which carries fewer religious connotations and emphasizes an active, empowered relationship with the quality.

2. Throughout the chapter, I refer to aspiration in both the singular and plural, since there can be one or many.

3. Ed Yong, "Our Pandemic Summer," *Atlantic,* April 14, 2020, https://www.theatlantic.com/health/archive/2020/04/pandemic-summer-coronavirus-reopening-back-normal/609940/.

4. See the Movement for Black Lives policy platform at https://m4bl.org/policy-platforms/.

5. Sharon Salzberg, *Faith: Trusting Your Own Deepest Experience* (New York: Riverhead, 2002), xiv.

6. Patrick Overton, "Faith." Originally published in *The Leaning Tree* (Bloomington, MN: Bethany Press, 1975), 91. Also available at https://patrickoverton.com/faith-poster/.

Chapter 3. Energy

1. Effort and energy are related but distinct factors. Energy is our capacity to do something or exert a force, while effort is the application of that energy—where and how we use it.

2. For more on rest, see chapter 18.

3. "Radical Self Care: Angela Davis," Afropunk, December 17, 2018, YouTube video, 4:27, https://www.youtube.com/watch?v=Q1cHoL4vaBs.

Chapter 4. Mindfulness

1. I believe that Godwin was paraphrasing the opening lines of the Satipatthana Sutta, in which the Buddha states, "This is the direct path for the purification of beings, for the surmounting of sorrow and lamentation, for the disappearance of suffering and discontent, for acquiring the true method, for the attainment of Nibbana, namely, the four establishments of mindfulness." Analayo Bhikkhu, *Satipaṭṭhāna: The Direct Path to Realization* (Cambridge, UK: Windhorse Publications, 2003), 3.

2. I first learned this exercise from the Thai monk Ajahn Jumnien. The insight meditation teacher Pascal Auclair offers a similar exercise with the thought "I place my hand on the floor."

3. This insight is found in many holistic traditions, from spiritual practices like insight meditation to a range of humanist psychology modalities like Somatic Experiencing, Internal Family Systems, or the Hakomi method.

4. An example here in the United States of structural inequity was the administration of progressive legislation after World War II like the GI Bill, which granted mortgages and other benefits to many white veterans but denied them to Black veterans. For specifics, see Erin Blakemore, "How the GI Bill's Promise Was Denied to a Million Black WWII Veterans," History (website), April 20, 2021, https://www.history.com/news/gi-bill-black-wwii-veterans-benefits.

5. A "microaggression" is a term coined by Harvard psychiatrist Dr. Chester Pierce and later defined by Dr. Derald Wing Sue and colleagues as "brief and commonplace daily verbal, behavioral, or environmental indignities, whether intentional or unintentional, that communicate hostile, derogatory, or negative racial slights and insults toward people of color." Derald Wing Sue et al., "Racial microaggressions in everyday life: Implications for clinical practice," *American Psychologist* 62 no. 4 (2007): 271–86. For more on microaggressions, see Jenée Desmond-Harris, "What Exactly Is Microaggression?" Vox, February 16, 2015, https://www.vox.com/2015/2/16/8031073/what-are-microaggressions. On white supremacy culture, see Tema Okun's website White Supremacy Culture, https://www.whitesupremacyculture.info.

6. For examples of white privilege, see Peggy McIntosh's seminal 1989 essay, "White Privilege: Unpacking the Invisible Knapsack," reprinted at SEED, https://nationalseedproject.org/Key-SEED-Texts/white-privilege-unpacking-the-invisible-knapsack.

7. It is less that mindfulness "creates space" and more that it reveals the space that is already present in awareness.

8. If you have difficulty walking, pay attention to the sensations in your body as you move from one place to another.

Chapter 5. Concentration

1. In Buddhism, the word for concentration is *samadhi*, which literally means "gathered together." From this point forward, I use the term *concentration* to refer to this skill of natural, holistic inner stability.

2. Julia Butterfly Hill, *The Legacy of Luna: The Story of a Tree, a Woman, and the Struggle to Save the Redwoods* (New York: HarperOne, 2000), 246.

Chapter 6. Wisdom

1. Being both white and Jewish in the United States entails a complex tension. For an exploration of these dynamics, see Paul Kivel's excellent article, "I'm Not White, I'm Jewish: Standing as Jews in the Fight for Racial Justice," first delivered as a talk during the "What Is White?" conference at the University of California, Riverside, Spring 1998, reprinted at http://paulkivel.com/wp-content/uploads/2015/07/imnotwhiteimjewish.pdf.

2. This interaction is a classic example of a microaggression (see above, note 5 of Chapter 4). For more on navigating microaggressions skillfully see: Roxy Manning, *How to Have Antiracist Conversations* (Oakland, CA: Berrett-Koehler, 2023).

3. Resmaa Menakem, *My Grandmother's Hands* (Las Vegas, NV: Central Recovery Press, 2017), 20.

4. Martin Luther King Jr. Research and Education Institute, "Beyond Vietnam," Stanford University, accessed March 19, 2023, https://kinginstitute.stanford.edu/encyclopedia/beyond-vietnam.

Chapter 7. Curiosity

1. Curiosity, interest, and investigation are translations of the Buddhist term *dhammavicaya*, one of the "seven factors of awakening." While some distinguish between *interest* and *curiosity*, defining the former as a more primary movement of attention and the latter as more intellectual, in this book I use the terms interchangeably as synonyms.

2. I tell part of Davis's story in my first book, *Say What You Mean*, to illustrate the power of curiosity and care to build meaningful relationship through genuine conversation. *Say What You Mean* (Boulder, CO: Shambhala, 2018), 74–75.

3. David Cook, "How Do We Erase the Swastikas of the Heart?" *Chattanooga Times Free Press*, September 19, 2020, https://www.timesfreepress.com/news/2020/sep/19/cook-erase-swastikas/.

4. Nandini Rathi, "Gandhi Jayanti 2018 Special: When Mahatma Gandhi Was Welcomed by Textile Mill Workers of Lancashire," *Indian Express*, October 2, 2018, https://www.mkgandhi.org

/newannou/When-Mahatma-Gandhi-was-welcomed-by-textile-mill-workers-of-Lancashire.html.

5. BBC, "When Gandhi Met Darwen's Mill Workers," September 23, 2011, https://www.bbc.com/news/uk-england-lancashire-15020097. In this example, the "adversary" shifted their position. A nonviolent approach requires the openness to also shifting one's own position when exposed to new information or perspectives of the other party.

Chapter 8. Courage

1. Kazu Haga, *Healing Resistance* (Berkeley, CA: Parallax Press, 2020), 100–101.

Chapter 9. Renunciation

1. Rebecca Solnit, "Big Oil Coined 'Carbon Footprints' to Blame Us for Their Greed: Keep Them on the Hook," *Guardian,* August 23, 2021, https://www.theguardian.com/commentisfree/2021/aug/23/big-oil-coined-carbon-footprints-to-blame-us-for-their-greed-keep-them-on-the-hook.

2. Michelle Martin, "The Possibility Alliance: Ethan Hughes' Educational Homestead," *Mother Earth News,* April 25, 2011, https://www.motherearthnews.com/sustainable-living/nature-and-environment/possibility-alliance-zeoz11zmar/.

3. See Jia Tolentino, "The Pitfalls and Potential of the New Minimalism," *New Yorker*, January 27, 2020, https://www.newyorker.com/magazine/2020/02/03/the-pitfalls-and-the-potential-of-the-new-minimalism.

4. Audre Lorde, "Age, Race, Class, and Sex: Women Redefining Difference," in *Sister Outsider: Essays and Speeches* (New York: Penguin, 2020), 105.

5. The events and aims of Bacon's Rebellion are complex. Those rebelling in part sought to annex additional Native land, while the ruling elites aimed to employ Native Americans to return escaped servants and slaves. See Jacqueline Battalora's excellent account for a more nuanced treatment of the rebellion in her book, *The Birth of a White Nation: The Invention of White People and Its Relevance Today* (Houston: Strategic Book Publishing and Rights Co., 2013), 16–24.

6. The Virginia Slave Codes of 1705 are one example of such legislation.
7. Andrea Miller, "Zen Is All of Life: Remembering Roshi Bernie Glassman," *Lion's Roar*, November 4, 2022, https://www.lionsroar .com/zen-is-all-of-life-remembering-roshi-bernie-glassman/.

Chapter 10. Kindness

1. B. L. Fredrickson et al., "Open Hearts Build Lives: Positive Emotions, Induced through Loving-Kindness Meditation, Build Consequential Personal Resources," *Journal of Personality and Social Psychology* 95, no. 5 (2008): 1045.
2. Kristen Weir, "The Lasting Impact of Neglect," American Psychological Association (blog), vol. 45, no. 6, June 2014, https://www .apa.org/monitor/2014/06/neglect.
3. Stefan G. Hoffman, Paul Grossman, and Devon E. Hinton, "Loving-kindness and Compassion Meditation: Potential for Psychological Interventions," *Clinical Psychology Review* 31 (7) (July 2011): 1126–32.
4. Mark Lindley, "Gandhi's Challenge Now," Bombay Sarvodaya Mandal and Gandhi Research Foundation, Mkgandhi.org. Reprinted from *Sarvodaya* 1, no. 5 (January–February 2004), https://www .mkgandhi.org/articles/Mark%20Lindley.htm.
5. Martin Luther King Jr., *Strength to Love* (Minneapolis: Fortress Press, 2010), 51.
6. Dhammapada verse 5. Based on a translation by Gil Fronsdal, *The Dhammapada* (Boston: Shambhala, 2008), 2.
7. Martin Luther King Jr., "A Christmas Sermon on Peace," *The Trumpet of Conscience* (San Francisco: Harper, 1967), 69.
8. "Do Small Things with Great Love: Mother Teresa Graces Diocese," *Catholic Light*. The University of Scranton Digital Collections, The University of Scranton, 27 August 1987, https://digitalservices .scranton.edu/digital/collection/clippings/id/16278.

Chapter 11. Ease

1. In this chapter, I speak of a range of calming qualities on the Buddhist path: *passadi*, one of the seven factors of awakening, is often translated as "tranquility"; *shamata* means "calm abiding."

2. Renee D. Goodwin et al., "Trends in Anxiety among Young Adults in the United States, 2008–2018: Rapid Increases among Young Adults," *Journal of Psychiatric Research* 130 (November 2020): 441–46, https://www.ncbi.nlm.nih.gov/pmc/articles/PMC7441973/.

3. "Racism and Health: Racism is a Serious Threat to the Public's Health," Minority Health, Centers for Disease Control and Prevention, last reviewed November 24, 2021, https://www.cdc.gov/minorityhealth/racism-disparities/index.html. According to the World Health Organization, numerous studies suggest that social determinants of health account for 30–55% of health outcomes. Social determinants of health include conditions such as income, job security, housing, access to food, clean water and air, and social inclusion and non-discrimination. See: "Social determinants of health," Health Topics, World Health Organization, accessed March 28, 2023, https://www.who.int/health-topics/social-determinants-of-health#tab=tab_1.

4. We touched on orienting in chapter 1, when we introduced some of the guiding principles for trauma-informed mindfulness. This practice is based on Peter Levine's Somatic Experiencing and Stephen Porges's work on polyvagal theory. Levine noted that prey in the wild, such as deer, periodically orient to assess for safety. Porges points out that the structures that innervate the movement of the head, eyes, and neck are connected to the ventral vagus nerve, which down-regulates the nervous system.

5. Shunryu Suzuki, *Zen Mind, Beginners Mind* (New York: Weatherhill, 1993), 46.

6. Nicole Karlis, "Why Doing Good Is Good for the Do-Gooder," *New York Times*, October 26, 2017, https://www.nytimes.com/2017/10/26/well/mind/why-doing-good-is-good-for-the-do-gooder.html.

7. Thich Nhat Hanh, *Being Peace* (Berkeley, CA: Parallax Press, 1987), 11–12.

Chapter 12. Patience

1. I've heard this metaphor many times in different places, including Eve Decker's song "Gardener": "Every little seed in time will flower . . . I am the garden but I'm also the gardener." Lyrics available on Eve's website: https://evedecker.com/gardener/.

2. Martin Luther King Jr., *Why We Can't Wait* (New York: Penguin Publishing Group, 2000), 69.

3. Donald Rothberg and Alan Senauke, "Four Movements in the History of Socially Engaged Buddhism and Their Central Contributions," Clear View Project, May 31, 2008, https://www.clearviewproject .org/2008/05/four-movements-in-the-history-of-socially-engaged -buddhism-and-their-central-contributions/.

4. Sid Naidu, "Nelson Mandela on Developing Patience That Can Change the World," Medium.com, July 18, 2018, https://medium .com/sncd/nelson-mandela-on-developing-patience-that-can -change-the-world-44025a6e224d.

5. Thanissarro Bhikkhu, "Patience," in *Meditations: Forty Dhamma Talks* (Valley Center, CA: Metta Forest Monastery, 2003), 72. Also available online at: https://www.accesstoinsight.org/lib/authors /thanissaro/meditations.html or as a PDF at https://www.dhamma talks.org/Archive/Writings/Ebooks/Meditations1_181215.pdf.

6. Martin Luther King Jr., *Where Do We Go from Here* (Boston: Beacon Press, 1968), 181–82, 191.

Chapter 13. Equanimity

1. I am indebted to my friend and colleague Greg Scharf for this beautiful analogy.

2. Kazu Haga, *Healing Resistance* (Berkeley, CA: Parallax Press, 2020), 75.

3. The Buddha's teaching is in fact broader and subtler than what I present here. While he likens painful sensations to arrows, he applies the same logic to pleasant and neutral sensations as well, pointing out how our untrained minds react to those experiences in a similar way—with clinging or delusion, respectively. For the original text, see the Sallasutta, Samyutta Nikaya 36.6. Several translations can be found for free online at https://suttacentral.net /sn36-sagathavagga?view=normal.

4. Viktor Frankl, *Man's Search for Meaning* (Boston: Beacon Press, 2006), 66

5. The widely known "Serenity Prayer" captures this well: "God grant me the serenity to accept the things I cannot change, courage to change the things I can, and the wisdom to know the difference."

6. Sarah Van Gelder and Vandana Shiva, "Earth Democracy: An Interview with Vandana Shiva," *Yes Magazine*, January 1, 2003, https://www.yesmagazine.org/issue/democracy/2003/01/01/earth-democracy-an-interview-with-vandana-shiva.

7. ICNC: International Center on Nonviolent Conflict, *A Force More Powerful: A Century of Nonviolent Conflict*, produced and directed by Steve York, 1999, YouTube video, 47:00, https://www.youtube.com/watch?v=O4dDVeAU3u4 (posted Nov 22, 2019).

8. The author, teacher, and deep ecologist Joanna Macy has devoted the latter part of her career to an initiative called the Work That Reconnects, which offers a robust tool kit of practices to grieve, vision, and rebuild as we move into this unknown period of transition that she calls the Great Turning. For more, see https://workthatreconnects.org.

9. I was introduced to this exercise by the vipassana teacher Gil Fronsdal.

10. This reflection is based on an equanimity exercise from Ajahn Sucitto, *Pāramī: Ways to Cross Life's Floods* (Hemel Hempstead, UK: Amaravati Publications, 2012).

Part Three. Introduction

1. Bhikkhu Bodhi, trans., "Upaddha Sutta (Half of the Holy Life)," in *The Connected Discourses of the Buddha: A Translation of the Samyutta Nikaya* (Boston: Wisdom Publications, 2000), 1524. Also available online at: https://suttacentral.net/sn45.2/en/bodhi?reference=none&highlight=false.

2. See, for example, Anguttara Nikaya 10.61 in Bhikkhu Bodhi, trans., *The Numerical Discourses of the Buddha: A Translation of the Anguttara Nikaya* (Boston: Wisdom Publications, 2012), 1415–18.

3. Doug McAdam, "Recruitment to High-Risk Activism: The Case of Freedom Summer," *American Journal of Sociology* 92, no. 1 (July 1986), 64–90.

4. For more on exploring relationship with ancestors, see Sandhya Rani Jha, *Rebels, Despots, and Saints: The Ancestors Who Free Us and the Ancestors We Need to Free* (Des Peres, MO: Chalice Press, 2023).

Chapter 14. Empathy

1. In the definitions I am using here, empathy is the broadest capacity of the heart that attunes to the full range of human emotion and experience, while compassion is tenderness in the face of suffering accompanied by the impulse to alleviate pain. See chapter 24 for more on compassion.

2. The psychoanalyst John Bowlby's formative theory defines healthy attachment as "lasting psychological connectedness between human beings," suggesting that factors like emotional attunement, sufficient safety balanced with freedom to explore, appropriate comfort and soothing for distress, and inspiring healthy self-esteem all contribute to a child's capacity for healthy relationship and empathy. The psychoanalytic work of D. W. Winnicott suggests that the "good enough" parent meets a threshold of responsiveness and sensitivity and yet allows their child the freedom to fail and grow.

3. Adam O. Horvath and Lester Luborsky, "The Role of the Therapeutic Alliance in Psychotherapy," *Journal of Consulting and Clinical Psychology* 61, no. 4 (1993), 561–74.

4. For more on balancing empathic distress, see chapter 9 of my book *Say What You Mean* (Boulder, CO: Shambhala, 2018), 74–75.

5. See the work of David Blankenhorn's Braver Angels (https://braverangels.org) and Joan Blades' Living Room Conversations (https://livingroomconversations.org), as well as "Deep Canvassing" (https://deepcanvass.org) for more on empathy, dialogue, and political change.

6. For more on the power of empathy to connect with people of divergent views or harmful action, see Marshall B. Rosenberg, *Nonviolent Communication: A Language of Compassion* (Encinitas, CA: 2002) or visit www.cnvc.org.

7. Margaret Cullen and Ronna Kabatznick, "Interview with Marshall Rosenberg: The Traveling Peacemaker," *Inquiring Mind* 21, no. 1 (Fall 2004), https://www.inquiringmind.com/article/2101_4w _rosenberg-interview-with-marshall-rosenberg-the-traveling-peace-maker/.

8. Quote from email conversation used anonymously with permission.

Chapter 15. Integrity

1. For a powerful historical fiction account of the Grimké sisters' story, see Sue Monk's excellent novel *The Invention of Wings* (New York: Viking, 2014).

2. Known in Buddhism as the "guardians of the world," these two qualities are *hiri* and *ottappa* in Pali.

3. In Pali, the word translated as *precept* is *sikkhapaddaṃ, which* literally means a "step of learning" or "training." The root of *paddam* is the same as the Latin *pod*—meaning "foot" or "step" (as in *podiatry* or *pedestrian*).

4. Amnesty International, "Chicago City Council Passes Landmark Police Torture Reparations Ordinance," press release, May 6, 2015, https://www.amnestyusa.org/press-releases/chicago-city-council -passes-landmark-police-torture-reparations-ordinance/.

5. Ivana Saric, "Sacred Land Returned to Native American Tribe in Virginia," Axios, April 3, 2022, https://www.axios.com/2022/04/03 /native-land-return-virginia; Owen L. Oliver, "Significant Washington Land Returned to the Colville Tribe, Its Original Stewards," Nature Conservancy, May 3, 2022, https://www.nature .org/en-us/about-us/where-we-work/united-states/washington /stories-in-washington/land-back-figlenski-ranch-colville-tribe/.

6. Interfaith Peacemakers, "Maha Ghosananda (1929–2007)," September 19, 1995, https://readthespirit.com/interfaith-peacemakers/maha -ghosananda/; Heng Sok Chheng, "Maha Ghosananda leads prayers on Day of Peace," *The Phnom Penh Post,* https://www.phnompenhpost .com/national/maha-ghosananda-leads-prayers-day-peace/.

Chapter 16. Resolve

1. Nonviolent direct action is termed *satyagraha* in Gandhi's model. The nonviolence scholar, author, and activist Chris Moore-Backman points out, "I think more than anything else, it is aversion to discomfort that keeps such a large majority of justice-concerned folks focused on personal transformation and constructive program areas of nonviolence, and not venturing into satyagraha" (personal communication).

2. Martin Luther King Jr. Research and Education Institute, "Montgomery Bus Boycott," Stanford University, accessed March 10, 2023, https://kinginstitute.stanford.edu/encyclopedia/montgomery-bus-boycott.

3. I was introduced to the term *strategic discomfort* by Miki Kashtan. The concept appears in many fields under various labels: for instance, in trauma healing as the *window of tolerance* and in education through Karl Rohnke's *comfort, stretch,* and *panic zones* (which itself was based on a theory from 1908 known as the Yerkes-Dodson law, describing the relationship between pressure and performance).

4. I could add that courage helps our resolve when we feel small, ease provides relief if resolution flags, humor and play lighten the load when self-judgment arises, and so on, but we engage these qualities in other chapters.

Chapter 17. Joy

1. Hanson's method for "taking in the good," described in his book *Resilient* (New York: Harmony Books, 2018) and on his website at www.rickhanson.net/take-in-the-good/, mirrors a basic structure in mindfulness practice, which includes a proactive and a receptive element. The proactive aspect of mindfulness (*vitaka*) directs our attention to connect with the object of our meditation. (Thus Hanson's *noticing* a resource.) The receptive aspect of mindfulness practice (*vicara*) lingers with and tastes the flavor of that experience. (Thus Hanson's savoring the resource for twenty seconds.)

2. Emma Goldman, *Living My Life* (New York: Knopf, 1934), lvii.

3. Truth Be Told Team, with radio host Tonya Mosley, "Holding on to Joy," KQED, July 2, 2020, https://www.kqed.org/podcasts/521/holding-on-to-joy. For more of adrienne maree brown's work, see her books *Pleasure Activism* (Chico, CA: AK Press, 2019) and *Emergent Strategy* (Chico, CA: AK Press, 2017), or visit https://adriennemareebrown.net.

Chapter 18. Rest

1. For much more on her teaching, see Tricia Hersey, *Rest Is Resistance: A Manifesto* (New York: Little, Brown Spark, 2022).

2. Thomas Merton, *Conjectures of a Guilty Bystander* (Garden City, NY: Doubleday, 1966), 86.

3. Mushim Patricia Ikeda, "I Vow to Not Burn Out," *Lion's Roar*, August 11, 2022, https://www.lionsroar.com/i-vow-not-to-burn-out/.

4. Hersey, *Rest Is Resistance*, 150.

5. Abraham Joshua Heschel, *The Sabbath* (New York: Farrar, Straus and Giroux, 1979), 10.

6. Having had insomnia on and off for years, I have found great benefit from Michael Krugman's Rest Assured audio program based on his Sounder Sleep system. Many people also find a yoga nidra practice to be helpful for sleep. Additionally, I have created many guided audio exercises for sleep, which you can find on the Ten Percent Happier app.

Chapter 19. Wonder

1. AnaLouise Keating, "'I'm a Citizen of the Universe': Gloria Anzaldua's Spiritual Activism as Catalyst for Social Change," *Feminist Studies* 34, nos. 1–2 (Spring–Summer 2008), 53.

2. Etty Hillesum, *Letters from Westerbork*, trans. Arnold J. Pomerans (New York: Pantheon Books, 1986), xi.

Chapter 20. Gratitude

1. Harvard Health Publishing, "Giving Thanks Can Make You Happier," Harvard University Medical School, August 14, 2021, https://www.health.harvard.edu/healthbeat/giving-thanks-can-make-you-happier.

2. This mindset is known as *katanu-katavedi* in Buddhism.

3. See Thich Nhat Hanh, *Present Moment Wonderful Moment* (Berkeley, CA: Parallax Press, 1990).

4. Báyò Akómoláfé, LinkedIn post, accessed March 29, 2023, https://www.linkedin.com/posts/bayoakomolafe_for-the-yoruba-of-west-africa-every-seemingly-activity-6983769192927834112-GipT/.

5. Kahlil Gibran, *The Prophet* (New York: Knopf, 1923), 17.

6. Daniel Hunter, "Why Climate Activists Need to Celebrate—Even If We're Not Feeling Like It," *Waging Nonviolence*, August 8, 2022, https://wagingnonviolence.org/2022/08/why-climate-activists-need-to-celebrate-inflation-reduction-act/.

7. This two-part process is based on mental factors identified in Buddhist meditation as *vitaka* and *vicara* (as mentioned above in note 1 of chapter 17), alternately translated as "aiming" and "sustaining" attention, or "directed" and "evaluative" attention. It is the process of connecting with an object of attention and then sustaining that connection as you feel its qualities.

Chapter 21. Generosity

1. Summer Allen, "The Science of Generosity," Greater Good Science Center, May 2018, https://ggsc.berkeley.edu/images/uploads /GGSC-JTF_White_Paper-Generosity-FINAL.pdf.
2. Marshall B. Rosenberg, *Nonviolent Communication: A Language of Compassion* (Encintas, CA: 2002), 5.
3. Name changed for privacy.
4. John D. Ireland, trans, "Dāna Sutta," in *The Udāna & The Itivuttaka* (Kandy, Sri Lanka: Buddhist Publication Society, 1997), 168. Also available online at https://suttacentral.net/iti26/en/ireland?refer ence=none&highlight=false.
5. Shantideva, *A Guide to the Bodhisattva's Way of Life* (Boston: Shambhala, 2006), 214.
6. Studies show that people are happier when spending money on others rather than on themselves. Young children consistently engage in generous acts, further supporting the argument that we are biologically inclined for generosity. See Allen, "The Science of Generosity."
7. Jessica Irvine, "Wealth Is a Thing You Share: An Indigenous View to Make Us All Richer," *Sydney Morning Herald*, May 30, 2019, https://www.smh.com.au/business/banking-and-finance/wealth -is-a-thing-you-share-an-indigenous-view-to-make-us-all-richer -20190529-p51sho.html.
8. "2018 Global Wealth Report," Credit Suisse AG, Zurich, 2018, https:// www.credit-suisse.com/media/assets/corporate/docs/about-us/re search/publications/global-wealth-report-2018-en.pdf/.
9. Chuck Collins and Josh Hoxie, "Billionaire Bonanza: The Forbes 400 and the Rest of Us," Institute for Policy Studies, Nov. 2017, https:// inequality.org/wp-content/uploads/2017/11/BILLIONAIRE -BONANZA-2017-Embargoed.pdf/.

10. Anand Giridharadas, *Winners Take All: The Elite Charade of Changing the World* (New York: Knopf, 2018), 7.

11. Acharya Vinoba Bhave (website), "India: A Man on Foot," reprint of article in *Time* magazine, May 11, 1953, https://www.vinobabhave .org/index.php/9-articles/177-timemagazine. Though the movement faced challenges in following through with all of the gifted land, something profound still occurred. Generosity became contagious. Arguably some of the benefactors may have been driven by the lure of prestige (attempting to give more than their neighbor), but for many others the generosity was sincerely connected to a longing for justice and equity.

12. Donald Rothberg and Alan Senauke, "Four Movements in the History of Socially Engaged Buddhism and Their Central Contributions," Clear View Project, May 31, 2008, https://www .clearviewproject.org/2008/05/four-movements-in-the-history-of-socially-engaged-buddhism-and-their-central-contributions/.

13. Chris Moore-Backman, *The Gandhian Iceberg: A Nonviolence Manifesto for the Age of the Great Turning* (Reno, NV: Be the Change Project, 2016), 148.

14. To learn more about the MettaDana project or to offer support, see the Vipassana Hawai'i website, https://vipassanahawaii.org/mettadana/.

Chapter 22. Devotion

1. For example, the widespread witch hunts that began in medieval Europe and continued into the eighteenth century, and which also extended into the North American colonies, decimated the knowledge and wisdom of midwives, herbalists, and traditional healers. See Riane Eisler, *The Chalice and The Blade: Our History, Our Future* (San Francisco: Harper, 1995).

2. Bhikkhu Bodhi, trans., Anguttara Nikaya 4.21, in *The Numerical Discourse of the Buddha: A Complete Translation of the Anguttara Nikaya* (Boston: Wisdom Publications, 2012), 406.

3. In the Buddhist cosmology, hungry ghosts are beings who suffer from insatiable thirst and have throats as narrow as a needle.

4. Coleman Barks, trans., *The Essential Rumi: New Expanded Edition* (San Francisco: Harper Collins, 2004), 36.

5. Susanna Heschel, "Theological Affinities in the Writings of Abraham Joshua Heschel and Martin Luther King, Jr.," in *Black Zion*, ed. Yvonne Chireau and Nathaniel Deutsch (New York: Oxford University Press, 2000), 175.

6. Shunryi Suzuki, *Zen Mind, Beginners Mind* (New York: Weatherhill, 1993), 93.

7. Michael Nagler, "Who Was Badshah Khan?" *Waging Nonviolence*, July 17, 2013, https://wagingnonviolence.org/2013/07/who-was-badshah-khan/.

8. National Institutes of Health, National Library of Medicine, "1978: 'Longest Walk' Draws Attention to American Indian Concerns," Native Voices: Native Peoples' Concepts of Health and Illness, accessed March 28, 2023, https://www.nlm.nih.gov/nativevoices/timeline/546.html.

9. Kazu Haga (personal communication), 2023.

10. For additional ideas, see Thich Nhat Hanh's collection of mindfulness gathas, *Present Moment Wonderful Moment* (Berkeley, CA: Parallax Press, 1990).

Chapter 23. Play

1. Robin Marantz Henig, "Taking Play Seriously," *New York Times*, February 17, 2008, https://www.nytimes.com/2008/02/17/magazine/17play.html.

2. Chris Kresser, "10 Benefits of Play," ChrisKresser.com, March 27, 2019, https://chriskresser.com/10-benefits-of-play/.

3. Based on a definition from Stuart Brown, *Play: How It Shapes the Brain, Opens the Imagination, and Invigorates the Soul* (New York: Avery, 2009), 17–18.

4. Manoush Zomorodi, "Jacob Collier: The Language of Harmony," TED Radio Hour, June 17, 2022, https://www.npr.org/programs/ted-radio-hour/1105496499/jacob-collier-the-language-of-harmony.

5. Lisa M. Lauer, "Play Deprivation: Is it Happening in Your School Setting?" Institute of Education Sciences, September 12, 2011, https://files.eric.ed.gov/fulltext/ED524739.pdf.

6. adrienne maree brown, *Pleasure Activism* (Chico, CA: AK Press, 2019), 21.

7. Srdja Popovic, *Blueprint for Revolution* (New York: Spiegel & Grau, 2015), 97–123.

8. In Zen and Ch'an traditions, koan practice opens the channel for spontaneous, selfless response to life.

Chapter 24. Compassion

1. I first heard this particular turn of phrase, "turning pain into medicine," from my friend and colleague Vickie Chang. Vickie cites the Native American elder and psychologist Eduardo Duran, who teaches "the medicine is in the wound." In a similar vein, Rumi writes, "The cure for the pain is the pain." Jalāl al-Dīn Rūmī, "There's Nothing Ahead," in *The Essential Rumi*, trans. Coleman Barks (San Francisco: Harper, 1995), 205.

2. Encore.org, "Susan Burton," accessed March 19, 2023, https://encore.org/purpose-prize/susan-burton/. Learn more about Susan's story and work at https://beingsusanburton.com/about/.

3. MassHumanities, "January 12, 1912: Bread and Roses Strike Begins," MassMoments, accessed March 30, 2023, https://www.massmoments.org/moment-details/bread-and-roses-strike-begins.html.

4. See the work of Tania Singer at https://taniasinger.de/. This concept is also well summarized in Trisha Dowling, "Compassion Does Not Fatigue!" *Canadian Veterinary Journal* 59, no. 7 (July 2018): 749–50, https://www.ncbi.nlm.nih.gov/pmc/articles/PMC6005077/.

5. Tania Singer and Olga M. Klimecki, "Empathy and Compassion," *Current Biology* 24, no. 18 (September 2014): R875–78, https://www.sciencedirect.com/science/article/pii/S0960982214007702.

Chapter 25. Contentment

1. Precious Jara Prestosa, "The Quintessential Life of Lean Alejandro," Medium, June 14, 2017, https://medium.com/@lttrsnscrbbls/the-quintessential-life-of-lean-alejandro-1960-1987-ec9472eedab5.

Chapter 26. Forgiveness

1. Hillary Rodham Clinton, *Living History* (New York: Scribner, 2003), 236.

2. Fred Luskin, "The Choice to Forgive," in *Greater Good Magazine*, Sept. 1, 2004, https://greatergood.berkeley.edu/article/item/the_choice_to_forgive/.

3. Kazu Haga, *Healing Resistance* (Berkeley, CA: Parallax Press, 2020), 221.

4. Don Coyhis, "The Wellbriety Movement: Journey of Forgiveness," March 1, 2011, YouTube video, https://www.youtube.com/watch?v=vZwF9NnQbWM.

5. adrienne maree brown, *Emergent Strategy* (Chico, CA: AK Press, 2017), 42.

6. For more on Larry's work, see: Larry Yang, *Awakening Together: The Spiritual Practice of Inclusivity and Community* (Boston: Wisdom Publications, 2017).

7. Martin Luther King Jr., *Strength to Love* (Minneapolis: Fortress Press, 2010), 45.

8. Desmond Tutu, "Is Violence Ever Justified?" *The Forgiveness Project Lecture 2010*, London, May 12, 2010, https://www.theforgivenessproject.com/videos/.

9. Based on a forgiveness phrase by the author and dharma teacher Kate Lila Wheeler.

10. Larry Yang, "Four Directions of Forgiveness Practice," Love and Will (blog), https://loveandwill.files.wordpress.com/2019/05/forgiveness-phrases-by-larry-yang-awakening-together.pdf/.

About the Author

OREN JAY SOFER teaches Buddhist meditation, mindfulness, and communication internationally. He holds a degree in comparative religion from Columbia University and is a Certified Trainer of Nonviolent Communication and a Somatic Experiencing Practitioner for the healing of trauma. Born and raised in New Jersey, he is the author of several books, including the best-selling title *Say What You Mean: A Mindful Approach to Nonviolent Communication.* His teaching has reached people around the world through his online communication courses and guided meditations. Oren lives in the San Francisco Bay Area with his wife and son, where he enjoys cooking, spending time in nature, and home woodworking projects.